speaking
with skill

an introduction to
Knight–Thompson Speechwork

DUDLEY KNIGHT

B L O O M S B U R Y

Bloomsbury Publishing Plc

First published in 2012

Bloomsbury Publishing Plc
50 Bedford Square
London WC1B 3DP
www.bloomsbury.com

A CIP catalogue record for this book is available from
the British Library.

ISBN: 978 1 408 15689 6 (paperback)

Typeset by Country Setting, Kingsdown, Kent CT14 8ES
Printed and bound in UK by MPG Books Ltd, Bodmin, Cornwall

To Marta

Contents

Part 3: Phonetics

Acknowledgements

For a book whose gestation has been as long as this one, I would have to express appreciation to an unseemly number of people; so I dare not try to name all the names at the risk of leaving someone out. As a general statement, then, I am firstly indebted to everyone whom I have taught since the early 1970s. That's a lot of debt, but it's also true. As soon as I carried into the classroom my slightest suspicions about the way that speech was being taught in the United States and in English-speaking countries generally, I received fundamental guidance from the students with whom I was work- ing. They, not I, provided the environment, the keen interrogation, and the excitement for exploring sound change within which my questions could grow and answers slowly emerge. Further, every professional actor with whom I have worked along this journey has provided new impetus to me, either as a fellow actor or as a colleague in voice/text/dialect work in professional productions. But I must express my particular gratitude to all my students in the MFA acting program at the University of California, Irvine; and to all the professional colleagues who have participated in the Knight-Thompson 'Experiencing Speech' workshops. Their intelligent questions and explorations of this work – and this text – as it has developed over the past years have been the most immediate crafters of the contents of this book.

I am indebted to my colleagues Eli Simon, Richard Brestoff, Cam Harvey, Cynthia Bassham, Keith Fowler, and Annie Loui in the Department of Drama, Claire Trevor School of the Arts, at the University of California, Irvine, for their support and friendship. I am particularly indebted to Professor Robert Cohen for showing me through his own writings how well a textbook can be constructed; and for being the most tactful of goads to me to complete this work. Most of all, I thank my UCI colleague Professor Philip Thompson for his close collaboration in all aspects of this book. This text, and the work it represents, has been fundamentally shaped by his extraordinary gifts as a teacher and colleague. The approach to speech and accent training that we now call Knight-Thompson Speechwork (www.ktspeechwork.com) is as much Philip Thompson's creation as it is mine. For the errors in this book, however, I proudly claim full credit.

I am grateful to the editorial and production staff at Bloomsbury Publishing, especially Claire Cooper, Judy Tither, and Simon Trussler, for their unswerving professionalism and editorial acumen. Jenny Ridout has guided this project from the start, and I owe her special thanks. I thank Wendy Rasmussen for her excellent anatomical illustrations; and also the UCI actors who posed heroically for the muscle isolation photos: Kyra Zagorsky, Karin Jarnefeldt, Nathan Crocker, Tyler Seiple, Paul Culos and Jennice Butler.

As a student myself, I am indebted to Kristin Linklater for shaking up my ideas of what speech training should or should not be. I am most profoundly grateful to Catherine Fitzmaurice, who has been – and who remains – my teacher, friend, and mentor. I also appreciate the astute comments of my colleagues in the Voice and Speech Trainers' Association on the progress of this work. Professor Charles A. Knight has provided a lifelong model of excellence in scholarly writing.

Finally, and most of all, I am indebted to my wife, artist Marta Whistler, whose contributions to this book, and to my life, surpass enumeration.

Preface

Principles, perhaps

Whether they are called techniques, systems, approaches, methods, explorations, or any other label, and whether their practitioners admit to it or not, anything we teach in the arts is based on some set of underlying propositions. If these propositions are examined regularly, poked at occasionally to enliven them, soundly thrashed if required, rearranged when necessary, dusted off, polished, and generally looked after, the owner can offer them – all shiny and nearly new – to the partaker as principles. If they are neglected or ignored they gradually atrophy into inert assumptions. I hope that the following list will bear scrutiny as the principles on which this text is based and that the text will bear witness to the principles.

1. **This work tries to respond to the genuine needs of the actor or vocal performer as related to speech.** The text attempts to stay true to the actual, practical needs of the actor as distinct from applying a system based on the convenience of the teacher.

2. **This work is based on the observation that the vocal and speech needs of the actor within performance are constantly changing and are never fixed.** The actor, as an enactor of human behavior, is a scavenger of all behaviors and therefore of all speech actions. They are all useful to the vocal performer.

3. **This work recognizes that biases about the beauty of individual speech sounds are endemic and inevitable.** All speakers possess them, no matter how broad their linguistic experience or eclectic their approach to art – or, for that matter, how virtuous their aesthetic politics. In themselves, biases are usually innocuous as long as the possessor does not take them too seriously; however, when combined with other social influences, they can inflate themselves into

larger and always questionable judgments about the relative worth of accents or dialects. Then the actor is in dangerous territory.

4. **This work tries to place a firewall between these inevitable biases – including those of the author – and the pedagogy itself.** It does so not because of "political correctness" but because such biases – however subtle their manifestation in the teaching of speech – are always limiting to the actor if they start to set barriers against the explorations that the actor can make.

5. **The only "standard" that we can set for speech training is intelligibility.** By "standard" I mean a constant criterion that should be adhered to always. Actors must always be understood easily by their listeners. Everything else is optional: beautiful sound, interesting accents, speaking trippingly on the tongue – all are optional; highly desirable in many instances, of course, but not a constant criterion. Or, to put it in its opposite context, speech that is merely intelligible and nothing more is likely to be uninteresting, but it fulfills the most fundamental requirement of human communication and the only requirement that remains constant in all circumstances. Artful speech that is unintelligible serves no purpose at all.

6. **This work is based on the development of useful skills that the actor can own.** No training program can teach an actor all the accents she or he might need throughout a career. No set of classes can acquaint an actor with all the vocal demands that a career will elicit. But focused training can provide tools that the actor can use to shape the unique voice of every character that the actor will ever play.

7. **This work embraces complexity in its content.** Complexity nourishes art. Reduction of the complexity of speech choices reduces the art.

8. **This work embraces contradiction as an essential tool of teaching.** It is always interesting and useful to learn how to put more activity into speech actions. It is also always interesting and useful to learn how to do less. Getting stuck anywhere is never interesting.

How to use this text

Do everything.

Don't just read it – do it!

Figure 1. Mijnheer Rembrandt van Rijn explores lip corner protrusion.

Introduction

We all know how to talk. If you – as the reader of these words – are not the victim of some disorder of the nervous system or injury to the muscles that we use to speak, you can be confident that you can talk in a way that communicates clearly to those listeners with whom you converse most frequently

We use a number of different techniques to communicate our messages to others: our tone of voice, our facial expressions, our vocal inflections, our timing, our loudness or softness, even the vocal "quality" we use, such as nasality or an abrasive sound. But the actions that communicate the most basic information are the words themselves, those combinations of vocal sounds that any speaker of a particular language understands to represent very specific things. A breathed "h" followed by the "ow" sound (something that alone might express a sudden pain) followed by the hiss of an "s" sound, when combined in English, represent a place to live, a residence, a "house." Different speakers might say the word "house" with a number of different accents of English and still be sure that the people who speak the same way and who listen to them all the time would understand them, especially if they are speaking in an informal conversation.

But suppose the conditions change. Suppose that you have to communicate to people who speak our common language but do not share your particular accent, or the slang you use, or the pace at which you talk. Or suppose that your listeners not only do not themselves speak the way you do but also haven't heard many other people who speak like you.

Another set of possibilities: suppose that you need to command the attention and understanding of a group of people while other people are talking, or perhaps you need to speak unfamiliar words to a large group with a clarity that also allows your listeners to take in also your thoughts and attitudes about those words and about your listeners: in the first case, you might be a teacher or an administrator; in the second case, you might be a classical actor.

One choice that we can make when people don't understand us easily is to shut up. Many of us do just that; some people stop speaking when they are around people who talk differently from them and therefore don't understand them. Another tactic might be to fight back: people might aggressively accentuate their own speech patterns to make sure that people who are outside their familiar accent group *don't* understand them. But if we want to engage our listeners, whatever their accents might be, if we want to be able to communicate fully and effectively with other speakers of our shared language, we need to open ourselves up to speech actions that can be commonly understood by all speakers of that language, no matter what that accent might be.

The only real test for the effectiveness of our individual speech patterns is represented by the somewhat clunky term *intelligibility*. It doesn't mean that we have to produce speech sounds that impress listeners as "beautiful", or "cultured", or "cultivated." It means that we have to be able to produce verbal sound actions that everybody who speaks our language can understand easily. If they can understand us easily on this core level, they will also be free to pay attention to all those other messages of tone or gesture that we are sending woven through and around the words themselves.

As speakers in any context, we need to speak intelligibly no matter what the accent comprehension skills of our listeners might be. If we are actors on the stage or even in film or television, we need to establish that same intelligibility for all listeners *within* whatever accent or vocal characterization we might be using onstage. Obviously, with accent variability from both actor and audience, it follows that the intelligibility bar gets raised considerably for actors and that the demands on the speech skills of the actor are much greater than for most other speakers.

In the past, the increased demands for intelligibility – often termed "clarity" – onstage were met by imposing a fixed accent pattern of "good speech" for actors. Today we are beginning to recognize that such fixed accent patterns – based as they are on the theatrical conventions and aesthetic standards of a bygone era – are no longer appropriate for the speech training of the professional actor.

One reason why a fixed "good speech" pattern doesn't work very well is that the appropriate level of intelligibility from speaker to listener does not always rise in one direction toward ever more detailed speech actions. The fact that we need to *be able* to provide our listeners with a lot of detailed, sharply differentiated speech actions does not mean that it is always appropriate for us to speak this way all the time, either onstage or off. The speaker who is locked into a highly formalized pattern may find that, just because of the excessive effort being made, she or he is sending messages to the listener that were not intended.

Rather than relying on a fixed pattern of "good speech", the approach to speech and accent training that you will find in these pages is founded on the observation that actors are best served by developing a set of precise physical skills for shaping sound into articulate speech. The ways that the actor will use these skills are as unique to the particular actor and the particular role, as are the vast number of individual impulses and conscious choices that an actor makes in the course of building a performance. Because the skills are still separable from one another, they allow the actor to vary them to meet any requirement in stage, film, or voiceover work.

Part 1
Making sounds

Silence

War is diplomacy carried on by other means.

Von Clauswitz

Silence is argument carried on by other means.

Che Guevara

To understand sound we must know silence. To hear sound fully we must hear silence.

An easy aphorism to write, but silence is a difficult thing for most of us to experience these days. What passes for silence in our lives is an ongoing stew of hums, whirrs, intermittent buzzes, and occasional roars from the machines that populate our world; squeals of car tires, the blare of car horns, TVs and radios left on in an endless ambient drone as a weird substitute for the enfolding presence of human conversation, the endless fuzzy sigh of air-conditioning units spreading dehumidified air (and mold, and spores, and germs) throughout offices and homes. For many people born into industrialized societies since the early nineteenth century, silence is – well – almost unheard of.

In the last fifty or so years, the escalation of background sound has been matched by the decibel overload of foreground sound. Dire reports are published all the time about the widespread hearing impairment (particularly loss of high frequency overtones) in young people because of the excessive loudness (measured in decibels) of the sounds to which the ears are exposed; personal stereos with headphones are frequently cited as the worst culprit, but only one among many.

Contrast this trend with the writings of anthropologists who study indigenous peoples in the jungles of Amazonia or Indonesia. They report that among hunter-gatherer cultures it is still common for people to be able to hear and interpret extremely faint sounds: the rustle of animals moving through the fallen leaves on the forest floor a half-mile away, the flutter of bird wings that tell both distance and direction of flight, the change in insect sounds that warn of a change in weather several hours hence. While some observers of these skills are apt to ascribe them to some sort of extra-sensory power, it seems clear that nothing these people are doing requires any power beyond an unimpaired hearing ability combined with the skill of attentiveness and the experience to interpret very small sound differences.

These abilities are not beyond us, even if we have spent many hours connected to our iPods. But we have some work to do. Over the years we progressively hold more and more tension in our skeletal muscles – the muscles we consciously use to move our internal structure of bone and cartilage around. We do so as an unconscious way of bracing against the shock of a loud – or just a new – sound. These held or "residual" muscle tensions desensitize us, so that eventually we no longer even seem to hear the annoying ambiences that accompany us throughout the day.

It's a perfectly legitimate way of coping with contemporary life, and to some degree we all do it. But we pay a price. We are armoring ourselves against the rest of the world. Specifically, we are no longer fully available to the world of sound around us; we are less likely to really pay attention to other people speaking to us unless they are speaking loudly, or even better, are speaking loudly on television or radio or podcast.

People who enjoy classical music but are used to hearing it on the speakers or headphones of the home-entertainment centers in their living rooms often express disappointment when they actually go to a concert; the orchestra just doesn't sound as brilliant and powerful as it does on the

CD at home. People who go to films a lot often complain about difficulties in understanding the actors when they attend a live theatre performance even when the actors are speaking at a reasonable volume with full clarity of articulation. Unfortunately such complaints often lead to decisions by theatre managements to put body microphones on the actors to amplify their voices, or to engage in general "sound enhancement," so that the human voice now reaches the audience's ears from loudspeakers in a general wash rather than in specific, subtle, direct communication from the individual actors' bodies. I believe I am not too far wrong when I speculate that a growing number of audience members at live theatre events are becoming willing to sacrifice much of what makes live theatre a unique art form in order to recreate the feeling that they are really sitting in a movie theatre being bathed in the pumped-up surround sound: the Multiplex Experience.

So the ability to let go of residual tension in the skeletal muscles becomes crucial in finding our way back into a fully sensitized, available body; a body that can listen. I have to emphasize that the process of becoming sensitized, or available to stimuli, or "finding neutral", *in no way* means that as actors or people we are becoming passive or non-analytical. On the contrary, our sensory availability simply gives us more data to evaluate. Famed director Peter Brook puts it eloquently in describing this state of vibrant, alert awareness within which to find an equally vital form of silence:

In the search for the indefinable, the first condition is silence, silence as the equal opposite of activity, silence that neither opposes action nor rejects it. In the Sahara one day, I climbed over a dune to descend into a deep bowl of sand. Sitting at the bottom I encountered for the first time absolute silence, stillness that is indivisible. For there are two silences: a silence can be no more than the absence of noise, it can be inert, or at the other end of the scale, there is a nothingness that is infinitely alive, and every cell in the body can be penetrated and vivified by this second silence's activity. The body then knows the difference between two relaxations – the soft floppiness of a body weary of stress telling itself to relax, and the relaxation of an alert body when tensions have been swept away by the intensity of being. The two silences, enclosed within an even greater silence, are poles apart.

Threads of Time, pp. 106–7

The listener is fully open to the silence, and the energy of listening comes from the attentiveness of every cell of the body. But there would seem to be another crucial element. The vitality of the stillness that Brook perceives in the empty desert proceeds at least in part from the space which is always fully open to the potential for sound, an environment which expands the presence of the listener by continuously encouraging a greater and greater attentiveness. So there is a profound difference between the living silence that Peter Brook found in the vastness of the Sahara Desert and the silence that one might encounter in an anechoic chamber – a chamber in which all walls, the floor, and the ceiling are completely damped acoustically, so that no sound waves can reflect. Sounds produced in anechoic chambers are useful to acoustic engineers who wish to study only those frequencies emanating from a sound source without the complication of reflected sound from the environment. But the sound that a human voice produces in an anechoic chamber is a voice crying in a void, pure but strangely inhuman. The silence that envelops one in such a place is the silence of the dead.

In a silence alive with the potential for sound, our awareness continues to expand and our acuity of perception increases. Emerging from this attuned awareness of silence, even the tiniest sound can have texture, imagistic power, and can evoke the entire world within which the sound lives.

This is some of what Catherine Fitzmaurice, noted voice teacher and a trained and acute listener, heard during a stay in Moscow and Petersburg:

Some sounds heard in Russia

*Fricatives, deep-throat vowels; militia sirens; laboring buses; horses'
hooves at night; endless traffic; endless talk in four-hour Tolstoy dramas;
long applauses becoming unison clapping; in his house, Scriabin recorded,
playing his own piano compositions; beggar children asking, asking;*

loudspeakers in public places; pressed voices singing folk songs with a little yelp at the end of the phrase; a young woman on her cell phone giggling during a performance of Giselle at the Bolshoi Ballet; more Scriabin in the Moscow Conservatory great hall; high heels clipping on uneven pavements; a youth pissing in a bottle and laughing in the back row during a theatre performance in English; gun shots at two in the morning; someone (unanswered) banging on the door to my apartment at two in the morning; the phone (unanswered) ringing at two in the morning; metal whining during a high-speed train trip back from St. Petersburg; the urgent clatter of feet on the marble floors of the Moscow metro; loud passionate arguments between big men with love in their voices and ending with three noisy kisses, shoulder slaps, and a grunting bear hug.

If we can listen out of an alive, sensitized personal silence, there is a lot in the world worth hearing. If we then can feel our own sounds moving through our bodies with the same alert availability, we can feel subtle changes in vocal sound and action. This is where our journey from silence into vocal sound – the assertion of our humanity – needs to begin.

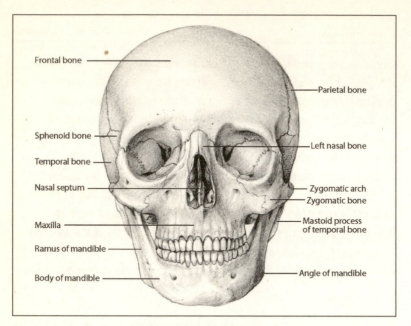

Figure 2. The human skull, front view.

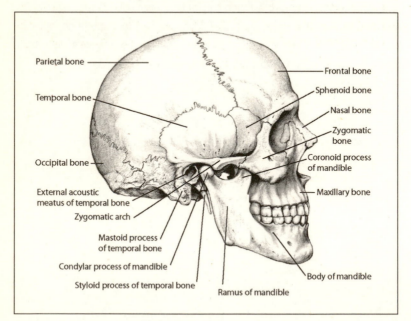

Figure 3. The human skull, lateral view.

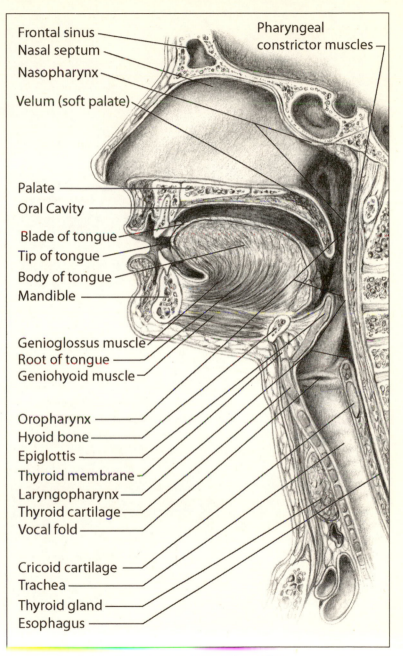

Frontal sinus

Nasal septum

Nasopharynx

Velum (soft palate)

Pharyngeal
constrictor muscles

Palate

Oral Cavity

Blade of tongue

Tip of tongue

Body of tongue

Mandible

Genioglossus muscle

Root of tongue

Geniohyoid muscle

Oropharynx

Hyoid bone

Epiglottis

Thyroid membrane

Laryngopharynx

Thyroid cartilage

Vocal fold

Cricoid cartilage

Trachea

Thyroid gland

Esophagus

Figure 4. The vocal tract: median section.

2 The space that shapes sound

On page 9 is a lateral – or side – view of a human head, seen as though the head were cut in half. (Not exactly into two equal halves, though; if it were cut exactly in half, it would be called a **sagittal** section.) This view allows us to see the structure that we call the **vocal tract**, the space that shapes sound. The vocal tract begins at the vocal folds (often misnamed

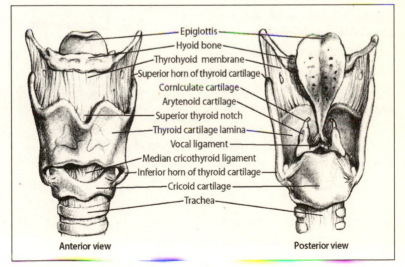

Figure 5. Larynx: anterior and posterior views.

the "**vocal cords**" or worse misnamed the "**vocal chords**") contained within the **larynx**. The larynx is a structure of cartilage and connective tissue that houses the vocal folds and hangs downward in the neck from the **hyoid bone.**

The hyoid bone is the only free-floating bone in the human body: it isn't knit to, or jointed to, any other structure of bone or cartilage. But a number of muscles and ligaments do attach to it, holding it relatively in place, even though it can move easily up and down within a limited range of motion.

When we breathe in, we inhale the air through the nose or the mouth back and downward through the larynx – past the vocal folds – and into the **trachea**, the "windpipe" that brings the air into the **bronchi** and then into the **lungs**.

The pharynx

When we breathe out, starting from the lungs a flow of breath can move up the trachea through the larynx, from the larynx past the vocal folds and into the space that we call the throat, but that more accurately is called the **pharynx**. First, the air flow moves into the **laryngopharynx**, the space immediately above the larynx, with the pharyngeal wall in back and sides, and the root of the tongue (with a few interesting attachments) in front. The air flow then moves into the **oropharynx**, the space at the back of the throat that you can see if you shine a light into your open mouth.

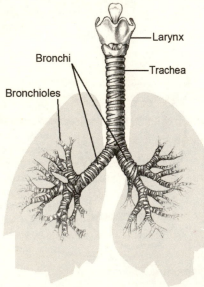

Figure 6: Larynx, trachea and bronchi.

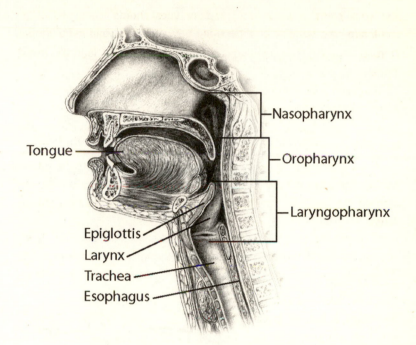

Figure 7. The vocal tract.

At this point the air can continue straight upward into the **nasopharynx,** the space that leads directly to the **nasal cavity**. We use this route when we breathe through the nose.

But it can also turn and move into the **oral cavity,** the mouth, and then out between the lips.

And obviously, the air can also move just as easily inward from the nose or mouth toward the lungs.

As the lateral view on page 8 shows us, the nasal cavity is surprisingly large. It is divided into two side-by-side spaces – two **nostrils** – by the **septum**, a thin vertical sheet of bone and cartilage.

The oral cavity can be large also. But its size can be varied by how dropped open the jaw might be. Then, too, the oral cavity is largely filled by a thick group of interrelated muscles called the **tongue**.

13

> **By the way, what's the difference between bone and cartilage?**
>
> *Bone* is rigid, self-repairing, composed largely of calcium phosphate and contains an outer structure of compact bone with an inner core of marrow.
>
> *Cartilage* is resilient, flexible, variably elastic, only minimally self-repairing (hello, arthritis!) and slippery. This last is useful in joint articulations, because most bones are capped with cartilage at the joints.

The tongue

The non-medical terminology for the surface portions of the tongue includes the **tip**, the **blade**, the **dorsum** (or **body**) of the tongue, and the **root.** The dorsum is further divided into three parts, imaginatively labeled the **front,** the **middle**, and the **back.**

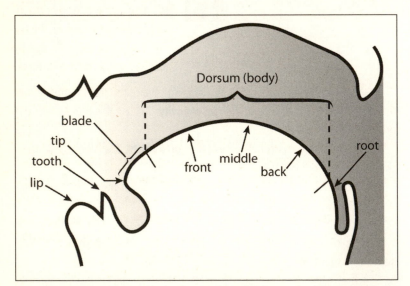

Figure 8. Left profile of oral cavity, showing the roof of the mouth and the tongue.

The tip and the blade of the tongue are the parts that we easily can stick out of our mouths. They are the extremely flexible portions of the tongue, and can engage in activity that is quite different from the activity in the dorsum of the tongue at the same time, a very useful quality in speaking.

The tip, blade and dorsum of the tongue are the parts that you can see if you open your mouth and look at your tongue in the mirror. The root of

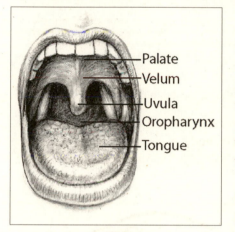

Figure 9. The oral cavity.

the tongue is the surface portion way in the back that you cannot see because it curves downward to form the front wall of your **laryngopharynx**. You can move the root of the tongue, however, pulling it back or protruding it forward to decrease or increase the size of the pharynx.

The dorsum of the tongue is less nimble than the tip or blade, partly because it is much thicker and also because it is directly attached to the base of the oral cavity. But it is still capable of a variety of actions in order to initiate swallowing and to participate in the process of shaping vocal sound through articulation.

The only tricky part about naming the parts of the tongue is to remember that the front of the tongue is *behind* the tip and the blade.

In defining the areas of the tongue surface, there are two other non-medical terms that we can employ. The **midline** of the tongue, a slight depression moving down the middle of the tongue from tip to back, is easily seen if you look at your own tongue. **The edges** of the tongue are exactly that: a continuous edge around the tongue dividing the upper (**superior**) surface of the tongue from the lower (**inferior**) surface.

At this point, it is not necessary to consider the individual muscles that enable the tongue to move in such complex ways. We will do so when we isolate the tongue actions.

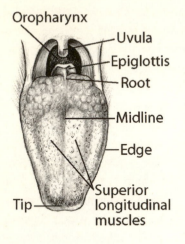

Figure 10. The tongue: superior surface.

Behind the dorsum of the tongue – in back of the back, as it were – the surface of the tongue turns downward toward the hyoid bone and the rest of the larynx. This is the root of the tongue, and it defines the anterior (or front) limit of the laryngopharynx.

The epiglottis

At the very base of the tongue root, and attached to it, is a spoon-shaped piece of cartilage covered with mucous membrane called the **epiglottis**. In its resting position it is raised up out of the way of the flow of air through the vocal tract. When a person initiates a swallowing action with the tongue, the epiglottis swings down and covers the top of the larynx, so that when we swallow food, that piece of food is safely moved back past the larynx and into the esophagus, the tube located directly behind the larynx and trachea that carries the food down to the stomach. After the swallowing action is completed, the epiglottis swings back up and out of the way. The epiglottis can contribute to a very few speech actions in some languages.

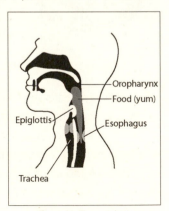

Figure 11. The epiglottis.

The roof of the mouth

In other words, the top of the oral cavity.

The gateway to the oral cavity is the lips. The muscles that control lip action are not only crucial to the act of speaking, they are also what we call

muscles of expression. While the lips are in the act of speaking, they can also send simultaneous visual messages simply by their shape, messages that may modify or even contradict the words that are spoken – as can the rest of the muscles of expression, which include all the muscles you can use to move your face around.

Behind the lips are the teeth, and right behind the upper teeth, on the roof of the mouth, is a slight thickening of the gum tissue that is termed the **alveolar ridge**. A lot of articulation targets this narrow area, so it is important to know where it is.

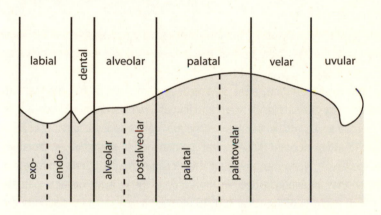

Figure 12. The roof of the mouth.

Behind that alveolar ridge is what we commonly call the "hard palate". Technically, it is simply called the **palate**. It is a bony structure that arches over the front half of the oral cavity. Obviously it does not move, but the tongue moves toward it or touches it frequently in articulation.

Behind the palate is the area we usually call the "soft palate". The correct term, however is the **velum**. Because the velum is composed of muscle covered by mucous membrane, it is capable of movement. The lower surface of the velum, the part that we see on the roof of the mouth, can lower or raise to shape the acoustics of vocal sound or to assist in the articulation of some vowels and consonants. The upper surface of the velum can raise to close off the passage of air to the nasal cavity, or it can lower to allow sound to move into the nose, as all Americans do when they say "m", "n" or "ng".

The rear portion of the velum extends back past the limit of its attachment to the sides of the skull and so becomes very flexible. Consequently it droops down at the back of the oral cavity to form the **uvula**, a conical structure hanging downward. The uvula is important in triggering the gag reflex, but even as a passive participant is also crucial in the production of certain speech sounds.

The glottis

The **glottis** is the lowest limit of the vocal tract, the opposite end of the vocal tract from the lips or the nostrils. It is defined as being the space between the vocal folds.

The vocal folds themselves are infoldings of mucous membrane that also contain tiny muscles inside them and fibrous ligament on their inside edges. They can thicken or thin themselves and they can be brought together or apart by the action of other muscles that are attached to the cartilage structures of the larynx. When they are apart, the air can move past them unimpeded. When they are brought together, the action of the air flow interacts with the unique elasticity of the vocal folds to produce a very rapid oscillation of the folds. This, in turn, chops up the flow of air into pressure waves. These pressure waves flow through the vocal tract producing more complex wave-forms. *Only when these complex pressure wave-forms reach the ears (or even more specifically, the brains) of listeners, do we interpret them as what we choose to call "sound", the sound – in this case – of the human voice.*

So "sound" is a perceptual term. While we will obtain a lot of crucial information for ourselves about speech through listening to the changes in sound that we can make, we will also learn a great deal by the tactile sensations of the pressure waves flowing through the vocal tract. We learn by listening, but we also learn by literally feeling the voice.

If this were a text about vocal production, we would explore the action of the vocal folds in much more detail. But while the vocal folds – and the

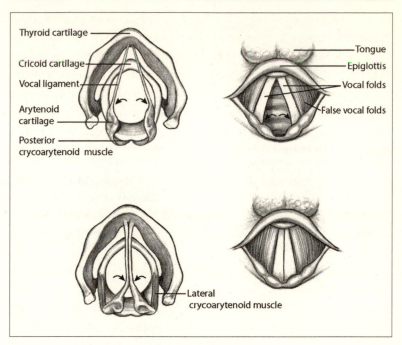

Figure 13. The vocal folds and their action.

glottis between them – do play an important part in the shaping of voice, they are limited to the shaping of only a few distinct sounds in their contri- bution to human speech action.

Now that we have defined – in a very general way – the territory through which the flow of air can pass, we can start to explore the process of moving from silence to sound.

Terms to know

Vocal tract

Vocal folds

Larynx

Hyoid bone

Trachea

Bronchi

Pharynx

Laryngopharynx

Oropharynx

Nasopharynx

Nasal cavity

Oral cavity

Nostril

Septum

Tongue

Tip

Blade

Dorsum: front, middle, back

Root

Midline

Edges

Epiglottis

Esophagus

Muscles of expression

Alveolar ridge

Palate

Velum

Uvula

Glottis

3 From silence to sound

Forget that you know how to talk.

Of course, I have just asked you to do the impossible, but give it a try anyway. The fact that we do know how to talk (and that we know we know) will come in handy along the way, but for now try to let it go.

Rediscovering the familiar

The process we will be going through in this work is to rediscover how we shape simple vocal sound into complex language. We are going to become precisely aware of some physical actions we take to shape sound that we have been doing for most of our lives with great ease but with little or no sensory awareness. So try to put yourself in the role of someone who is just starting to explore the language process – a very young child, perhaps. But as you explore like a child, feel free to bring your adult abilities to analyze and interpret information along with you.

We will start very simply, by preparing the space in which the shaping of sound will take place.

TOOLS
A hand mirror. Always hold the mirror just above mouth level. Make sure that you have plenty of light to see inside your mouth.

Exploration 1

Sit or stand. Float your head up as though a string were attached to the top of your head, gently pulling it upward toward the ceiling. Relax your shoulders and arms.

The amateur yawn. Yawn the back wall of your throat (your pharynx) as open as possible, from the back of your nasal cavity all the way down to your vocal cords. Notice, as you do this action, that you probably are pulling the root of your tongue back at the same time and opening your jaw very wide.

◀)) **Audio track 1:** *The amateur yawn.*

The professional yawn. Yawn again, but this time leave the jaw relaxed open, but not forced open, during the entire yawn. After you have yawned the pharyngeal muscles in the back and sides of your throat open, try to stretch the tongue root forward, away from the back wall of the pharynx. The tongue root is the part of your tongue that lies between the back of your tongue and your larynx. The rest of your tongue will protrude also when you stretch the tongue root forward, but the muscular work is all being done way in the back of the throat. You will feel a strong stretch along the sides of the pharynx if you are advancing the tongue root sufficiently. Relax out of the yawn, but notice that the feeling of openness in the pharynx is still there.

◀)) **Audio track 2:** *The professional yawn.*

The inevitable yawn. Inducing a yawn deliberately, as you have just done, almost always causes people to yawn for real. This is all right. But if it happens to you, stretch your tongue root forward so that it becomes an Inevitable Professional Yawn.

Exploration 2

Breathing through the nose. Leaving your jaw relaxed open, lightly close your lips so that no air can get in or out of the mouth. Breathe normally through your nose. Make no attempt to breathe more strongly. Simply note the feel of the cool air moving into and through your nasal cavity. You can also feel the cool air flowing down across the top surface of the **velum** (the soft palate) and down through the upper part of your pharynx, the **nasopharynx**. The cool air that you inhale (you sense it as cool assuming you are doing this exercise at a room temperature lower than your own normal body temperature of 98.6 degrees F!) is easier to feel than the warmed moistened body-temperature air that you breathe out through your nose.

Breathe more energetically through your nose a few times.

◀)) **Audio track 3:** *Nasal breathing.*

Notice that if you inhale very strongly it is hard to get the air in and out efficiently. Partly this happens because your nostrils may actually be pulled partially closed on the inhale because of the lower air pressure within the nostril. Another reason is that the **turbinates** (or **conchae**) in the nasal cavity (curved bony projections covered with mucous membrane that filter, moisten, and warm the air) are also obstructing any fast airflow. Thirdly, the tissues of the nasal cavity actually expand and contract to make it easier to breathe first through one nostril and then through another.

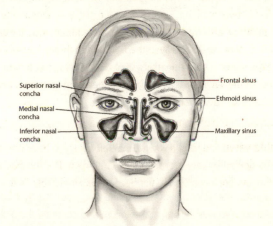

Figure 14. The nasal cavity and the sinuses.

When we are breathing easily and normally, the restricted airflow through the nose presents no problem. But if we are going to use this airflow to communicate to other human beings, the time and effort involved in inhaling through the nose while speaking would be prohibitive. So most of the time, when we are speaking several sentences in a row we inhale through the mouth even though we inhale through the nose most of the time when we listen to our conversational partner speak

Breathing through the mouth and nose. Breathe through the nose as described above with the jaw dropped open in a relaxed position but with the lips lightly sealed together. Continue breathing through your nose as you let the lips drop apart so that air can now enter and leave your body through your mouth also. Even though the mouth immediately takes over most of the airflow, you can still feel the breath flowing in and out at the nostrils. When you breathe through both the mouth and nose at the same time, you are completely relaxing the velum. Enjoy this, because the velum is about to go to work.

Breathing through the mouth. In order to go from breathing through the mouth and nose simultaneously to breathing through the mouth alone, you will need to raise the upper surface of your velum (soft palate) to close off the airflow to the nose. Many of us are not exactly sure what this action is, even though most of us do it unconsciously when we speak.

To feel the specific action of the velum, continue the breath flow through both the mouth and nose; then close the lips so that the breath flow moves through the nose alone, then on an exhale (breathing out) close off the breath flow to the nose also. You have just raised the velum to close off the **velopharyngeal port,** the place that divides the nasal cavity from the nasopharynx.

There is a complication, though: there are two completely different places where you can close off the airflow under these conditions; one is the velum raising to close the **velopharyngeal port** (this is the action we want to take); the other is the space between the vocal folds, called the **glottis**, closing as it does when we start to cough. By contrast, the velopharyngeal closure and opening by the velum feels rather like snorting. If you are closing at the velum and continue the airflow out with your lips still together, your cheeks will puff out, but if you are closing off the airflow at the glottis no air will come into the mouth.

When you can feel the specific action of the velum as it raises to close off the air- flow through your nose, allow the lips to drop apart and exhale through the mouth. You now are breathing entirely through your mouth.

Tidal breathing. Sit or stand with the spine in alignment and the head floating upward at the end of your neck toward the ceiling or sky as though it were a helium-filled balloon. Exhale fully and then inhale fully. Do not close off your breathing at your throat, nose or anywhere else. Then simply allow the breath to release out as much as it "wants to", while keeping the glottis and the rest of the vocal tract completely open. Just stop breathing, but make sure that you are not "holding your breath" by bracing any of your breathing muscles.

By the way, what does the breath really "want"?
It wants to exist at the same air pressure as the air outside the body and will move on its own (if there is nothing to stop it) until air pressure equilibrium is achieved. This current tidal breathing exploration allows you to do this. Its only minor disadvantage for the maintenance of life is that when this equilibrium is reached, the air stops moving and you stop breathing in and out. So your exploration of air pressure equilibrium will not last very long.

After about five to ten seconds of breathing inactivity, your body will start breathing again. It will be a very gentle in-and-out breathing action with pauses in between the breaths. Allow the breathing action to happen – don't make it happen. If you want to pull a lot more air into your lungs on the inhale, you could do so. If you want to push a lot more air out on the exhale, you could do that. But at the moment you are doing neither: you simply are allowing the breathing cycle to happen. This easy, gentle, non-controlled breathing is called **tidal breathing.** While life exists in your body, this normal breathing is as inevitable and cyclical as the ocean tides.

Another thing that this exploration shows us is that the breathing mechanism, when completely at rest, finds naturally a place of repose approximately halfway between full inhale and full exhale. This may be a revelation to those who may have believed that breathing relaxation is achieved with all the breath exhaled. Not so.

Exploration 3

Your first vocal tract noise. With your jaw dropped open in a relaxed position, breathe comfortably and easily through your mouth. If your mouth starts to get dry, swallow to lubricate the passage and continue your easy normal tidal breathing through your mouth.

You will probably notice that there is little or no sound from the air passing through this open "pipe" from your lungs to your lips, either on the inhale or on the exhale.

Now, *without moving anything in your mouth or throat* (this is very important), start to pull more air into your lungs on the inhale and push more air out on the exhale. Use your torso muscles to get the air in and out, but DO NOT TIGHTEN YOUR THROAT as you perform this action. And keep your jaw relaxed open.

🔊 **Audio track 4:** *Increasing breath flow.*

As you increase the speed and volume of air flow, you will start to notice that you can feel the air moving through your throat and mouth. You should be able to register the feeling pretty evenly with all the tissues of the mouth and throat. You will also start to hear a rushing sound of the air (or, more accurately, a rushing noise of air) as you breathe. You will hear it as equally loud on both the inhale and the exhale.

Explore this "breathy" noise for five breath cycles. Then relax and return to easy tidal breathing. If, at any time when increasing the air flow, you feel at all dizzy, stop the exercise until the dizziness passes.

This experiment tells us a few very useful – if very basic – things. It tells us that producing any sound or noise though the mouth or nose always requires some sort of airflow. It tells us that merely breathing normally through an open, unobstructed mouth and throat produces little or no noise at all. It tells us that in order to produce any sound or noise through an open passage using only a flow of unvoiced air, we will need to breathe a lot harder to produce even this most simple and crude kind of noise. It tells us that this breathy noise is equally possible while breathing in (inhaling, an **ingressive** flow) as when breathing out (exhaling, an **egressive** flow). Finally, it tells us that we are still a long way from having a full set of spoken language skills, but it points the way that we must go.

Voicing

In order to produce more variety of sound (and to avoid passing out frequently from over-breathing), we will need to do one or both of two things. If the flow stays unvoiced (just air moving through a pipe) we will need to be able to obstruct that flow to a degree that will produce a distinct noise even when we are not breathing more heavily; also we will need to obstruct the flow in different places to produce different noises.

Or, we will need to voice the flow. This means bringing the vocal cords together with enough tension to allow the flow passing between the folds to be chopped up into very rapid pressure waves. We can still obstruct the voiced flow if we want to, but we do not need to do so to produce different sounds. Instead we can vary the sounds simply by shaping acoustically the unobstructed (but voiced) flow.

We will appreciate the feeling of voiced sound all the more if we explore the sounds that we can produce on the way to voice.

Exploration 4

Heavy breathing, creaky voice, phonation. The vocal folds themselves are articulators we can use to obstruct the flow as long, because they haven't gone into their rapid vibratory action that produces pressure waves of voice.

If you bring the vocal folds together a bit, you start to hear and feel a localized noise as the breath flow becomes obstructed. The noise is that of the classic Darth Vader imitation, or on an even more banal note, the classic telephone heavy breather. Breathe gently, however, unless you contemplate phone-breathing as a career. Notice that you can do your heavy breathing both ingressively and egressively.

◀)) **Audio track 5:** *Partial glottal closure.*

Bring the folds further together – but loosely, so that the sound changes from heavy breathing to a slow, low-pitched creak, with the vocal folds flopping loosely against one another in a very slow vibratory pattern. With a little practice you can produce the creaky voice both egressively and ingressively with ease. Be aware that this creaky voice should be distinguished from the infamous (to speech teachers) glottal fry. The glottal fry is a somewhat similar sound but is usually softer and is produced with a lot of vocal-cord tension, giving it a nice sizzling quality, usually at the end of spoken phrases. It tells voice and speech coaches that you lack sufficient breath support in the abdominal muscles.

◀)) **Audio track 6:** *Creaky voice and glottal fry.*

Try the Creaky Voice ingressively as well as egressively. It is worth practicing, partly because the resulting sound is so wonderfully odd and partly because, if you learn to do it well, it means that you have let go of excess residual tension in the muscles of the vocal folds.

◀)) **Audio track 7:** *Ingressive creaky voice.*

If you bring the vocal folds together a little more tightly and then allow the cords to become slightly tauter, the slow creak suddenly changes into a very rapid vibration that produces a sound of a specific pitch with resonance overtones above and below the fundamental pitch. This is the action of full voice, or phonation.

◀)) **Audio track 8:** *Phonation.*

Resonance

If we imagine the area located between the larynx and the lips as a very flexible pipe that can change its shape or diameter to produce different language sounds, then we are focusing our attention on the **vocal tract**. The vocal tract can be shaped by the muscles that attach to the walls of this tube to produce different voiced sounds without obstructing the flow. A voiced flow of vibrations is a coherent sound, as distinct from the unvoiced airflow that would be more properly defined as *noise.*

Coherent sound vibrations passing through the vocal tract can be shaped acoustically through **resonance:** as the size of different areas of the vocal tract change, certain parts of the complex voiced pressure wave are **amplified** or cancelled. The exact process, while very interesting in itself, is not necessary for us to explore in any detail here; but we do need to know that resonance within the vocal tract accounts for three things in our voices: amplitude (or loudness), vocal **quality**, and the formation of the acoustic patterns that we recognize as vowels.

Let us explore what shapes in the vocal tract have various effects on these three aspects of resonance.

Exploration 5

The sound of stupidity. Begin as in Exploration 1. Make sure that your jaw is relaxed open and that the tongue is very relaxed also, with the tip of the tongue just touching the back of your lower teeth. Once you have established a normal, unobstructed, silent breathing rhythm, bring the vocal cords (also called vocal folds) together to produce a voiced sound on the outbreath. It will sound something like "uhhh". A nice dumb "uhhh". If it sounds like "ahhh" it means that you are retracting your tongue root. Relax the tongue completely: "uhhhhhhh."

◀)) **Audio track 9:** *Relaxed vocal tract sound.*

This is the only completely relaxed sound in language. So it follows that any sound that you make that differs from "uhhhhhhh" requires some muscular work.

Exploration 6

Vocal gurning. To "gurn" is to make strange faces, and the more bizarre they are the better. Occasionally in tabloid weekly papers (particularly in Britain) one can see photos of the winner of some gurning contest. Usually it is some ancient codger who has no teeth and can pull his lower lip up over his nose or produce some equally weird facial distortion.

Try gurning. Just by itself it is a wonderful exercise program for your face. Smoothly and easily stretch or contract every muscle of expression in your face that you can persuade to participate.

Figure 15. The gurning tradition: *Les Grimaces,* Louis-Léopold Boilly (1823)

Extend your gurning into the vocal tract so that you are engaged in the same tensing/stretching action inside the oral cavity (including the tongue), the pharynx and – as much as you can – up into the nasal cavity. Now start to make voiced sound. Without favoring one sound over another, allow yourself to make faces and surprise yourself with the sounds that come out. Or in, for that matter, if you try gurning with an ingressive sigh.

◀)) **Audio track 10:** *Vocal gurning.*

Anything goes. Any sound is permissible. But keep the sounds voiced: vibrating air, not just air. If you need a tactile reminder of which is which, put one hand lightly on your larynx and feel whether there are vibrations happening all the time.

Slow-motion gurning. Now slow the movements of your facial muscles. Keep the vocal energy going and the gurning as extreme as before, but do it all in slow motion. The sounds will now be changing more gradually, so that you can analyze them more readily. Analysis and gurning might seem to be incompatible, but actually you can do both easily.

What kinds of sound changes are happening as you shape the vocal tract in this rather extreme way? Probably everything that can change is changing. You are making different – and very likely strange – vowel sounds. But sometimes your actions briefly obstruct the flow; when this happens you are actually doing **consonants**. (But more about this later.)

◀)) **Audio track 11:** *Slow-motion vocal gurning.*

Also, you may notice that the kind of tone you are producing is changing, from twangy to hollow, from thin to ample, even from softer to louder, just by the shaping of the tube from your vocal cords to your lips. These are changes in the **amplitude** or loudness of the voice and (even more important for us right now) changes in the tone **quality**. We are not using the word "quality" here to mean good or bad; we are using it to indicate a unique tonal resonance.

All the articulator-shaping we can do contributes to forming our tone quality, but, at the risk of generalizing, most of our quality and amplitude change is caused by changes in the pharynx, the part of our vocal tract that goes up the back of the throat from the glottis past the mouth to the nasal cavity.

Focusing on vowels. Try gurning again on a voiced egressive sigh. Change the gurns slowly. This time, let the back and side walls of the pharynx relax so that they are no longer part of the process. In addition, try not to obstruct or impede the flow of voice on your sigh by bringing the articulators too close together. Within these limits, let the gurning be as free-form as possible.

◀))) **Audio track 12:** *Acoustic vowel shaping.*

Every so often in mid-gurn, at least once per sigh, freeze the articulators. Feel and hear the single sound result that is coming out. Note that sometimes the vowel sounds you are producing will be familiar ones and sometimes they will be very unfamiliar indeed.

◀))) **Audio track 13:** *Move/freeze/move.*

Practice this exercise for at least five minutes. Start getting used to these new sounds and register the way they feel in your mouth, throat, or nose. As you experience these new sounds, note that the physical "posture" of the vocal tract is determining the sound; this is the opposite of what usually happens, which is to imagine a sound and then shape the articulators to produce it. Continue to explore the possibilities of shaping the flow without getting in the way of it. As you do so, keep letting go of any muscle actions that do not directly affect what we would consider "vowel-sound change". Keep playing between freezing the articulators to focus on a new sound possibility and feeling the gradations of sound change as we move through the free-form shaping actions on a voiced sigh.

Gradually, as we play attentively through this more focused form of gurning, we find that we can live comfortably and confidently with all these new sounds and sound actions, and become less and less dependent on the relatively meager set of "vowels" with which we started.

Exploration 7

Toning. Repeat the same focused shaping of a voiced sigh that you found in Exploration 6 above, but explore the feel of the sounds while lying comfortably on your back, directly on a wood floor if possible. Feel the flow flowing through all of your body as you explore the multitude of sounds you can sigh by changing the shape of the tube from the larynx to the lips in every way possible without obstructing the flow. Freeze the articulators and explore the resultant sound flow for at least thirty seconds. Then move on to something else. Continue to let action lead sound rather than vice versa. Let yourself be surprised by the sounds that result.

Note as you feel the different sighed sounds focusing their vibration energy in different parts of your head and torso.

Vibration energy?

The term "vibration" has a variety of interpretations in voice and speech work, and this can cause some confusion. The most literal definition of vibration is a purely mechanical one: it is the oscillation of an object back and forth through a mid-point of equilibrium. A clock pendulum is a decent – and slow – example; a tuning fork, such as a musician uses to determine pitch, is a good and fast example. At the other extreme we find the purely metaphorical: "He's got bad vibes." Or, quadruply positive, the Beach Boys' "Good, good, good, good vibrations." In between we often find gradations and combinations of these two possibilities. Musical sound begins with mechanical oscillation, whether it is the oscillation of a guitar string plucked with a finger, or an oboe's two reeds oscillating against one another, or the oscillating action of the human vocal folds in the larynx.

In all these examples, the mechanical **oscillation** is converted into pressure waves in the air. These, too, oscillate from **condensation** (air molecules pushed together) to **rarefaction** (air molecules pulled apart). It is reasonable to call these "waves" rather than "vibrations", and some voice scientists refuse to term them vibrations, ever. But when these pressure waves encounter the ear drums of a living creature, the process turns back into a mechanical and physiological oscillating action. In the same way that we perceive sound through the mechanical response of oscillation at the eardrum, so we feel sound waves – within the vocal tract or through sympathetic resonance in the body – as a mechanical oscillation response of mucous membrane, bone and cartilage. Or, to put it simply, yes, we do feel "vibrations" and can perceive "vibration energy".

Exploration 8

Egressive or ingressive. Standing or sitting, with the head floating upward and your spine lengthened, explore the shaping of voiced flow as before. This time, however, instead of the usual unvoiced inhale in preparation for the next voiced sigh, explore staying on voice as the breath flow moves egressively (outward) and then also ingressively (inward).

Ingressive speech has a long and noble history. In the Renaissance, there apparently was a tradition of young lovers using ingressive speech to disguise their voices during romantic trysts. Somehow, imagining Shakespeare's Romeo saying "But soft! What light through yonder window breaks?" or Juliet's "O Romeo, Romeo. Wherefore art thou Romeo?" ingressively takes a little of the bloom off the romance, but perhaps a really authentic production would do it that way. It probably will happen. According to some scholars, the tradition of disguising the voice by ingressive flow continues in various cultures to this day.

◀)) **Audio track 14:** *Ingressve speech.*

What is not a matter of debate is that ingressive sounds are a part of today's languages from Swedish to Japanese to Argentinean Spanish, and others as well. In singing, ingressive vocal production (induction?) is often heard as an "extended vocal technique". In voiceover work, ingressive techniques are used in producing unusual character voices or in imitating animal sounds – dog barks, horse whinnies and the like. And as with the Creaky Voice done ingressively, full ingressive phonation is an excellent way to release residual tension in the vocal folds and also to explore efficient rib action, diaphragmatic action and abdominal release on the inhale.

Another thing to explore on ingressive voicing is the feel of the tube resonance in the sub-glottal pipe (**sub-glottal** simply meaning "below the vocal folds") of the trachea, or windpipe, leading from the larynx down to the bronchi (the pipes to each of the two lung)s. In my – admittedly minority – view, the enhancement of amplitude and low overtone resonance experienced during ingressive speech argues for the possibility of genuine resonance in the thoracic cavity. For most voice scientists, genuine resonance is limited to the vocal tract itself.

Terms to know

Turbinates (conchae)	Resonance
Velopharyngeal port	Amplitude
Cavity resonance	Vocal quality
Ingressive flow	Vowel formation
Egressive flow	Consonants
Unvoiced/voiced flow	Toning
Heavy breathing	Oscillation
Creaky voice	Condensation
Glottal fry	Rarefaction
Phonation	Sub-glottal
Gurning	

4 The muscles that shape sound: the tool kit

Consonant articulators

Articulation is the process of shaping the flow of air or vocal vibration so that it forms differentiated sounds that can be clustered in sequence to convey meaning. This is a somewhat dry way of putting it, because we are considering only the physical actions themselves without investing these actions with the ideas, the impulses, and the passions that can make intelligible speech a fully human, rich, and beautiful experience.

But passionate words or complex ideas that are shaped by articulators frozen into narrow habits of use are always diminished. By allowing ourselves to rediscover the physical basis of individual speech actions, we can move past the arbitrary limitations that we have often placed upon our own ways of speaking our language. We gain the skills of shaping sound.

We can make a distinction between **articulators**, which are the parts of the vocal tract that can move through muscle action to vary the sound, and **points of articulation**, which are fixed, unmoving places in the vocal tract toward which the articulators move to obstruct the flow.

Articulators
Jaw
Lips
Tongue (tip, blade, front, middle, back, root)
Velum (or soft palate)
Epiglottis
Vocal folds (or glottis)

Points of articluation
Teeth
Lips
Alveolar ridge (gum ridge behind upper teeth)
Palate (or hard palate)
Velum (or soft palate; it is also an articulator)
Uvula (the "little grape" – in Latin – hanging
from the back of the velum)
Pharynx

Vowel articulators

The big difference between the articulation of consonants and the articulation of vowels is that consonant articulators always act to obstruct the unvoiced or voiced flow, but vowel articulators shape the unobstructed flow (usually voiced), thereby changing the acoustic properties of the sound. These same vowel articulators also shape the unobstructed flow to produce changes in voice quality and amplitude.

Articulators
Jaw
Lips
Cheeks
Tongue
(primarily the front, middle, back, and root)
Velum
Pharynx

(Note that the pharynx is a point of articulation for consonants but that each of the three sections of the pharynx – the nasopharynx, the oropharynx, and the laryngopharynx – can be active articulators is shaping vowels, and even more important in shaping vocal quality and amplitude.)

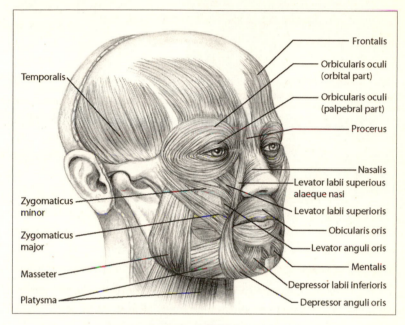

Figure 16. The facial muscles that shape speech.

Warming up the muscles

Put most simply, muscles do one thing: they tense. This is an electrochemical action (it produces an actual electrical charge, measurable in microvolts) that is triggered by voluntary or involuntary brain function. When the muscles tense, they bulge – this is what the body-builder does when he or she poses. If the muscle is tensed more, it shortens along the direction of the muscle fibers; this action is what the body-builder (or anyone, for that matter) does when she or he changes from one pose to another, moving the skeleton around.

A better term for the **bulging** action is **bracing**, and a better term for shortening is **contracting.** Both the bracing action and the contracting action are important in the physical action of vocal production, and both are also important in shaping the vocal tract for speech actions.

When you contract a muscle, you draw the structures to which the muscle is attached closer to one another. These structures could be bones or cartilage, or they could be other muscles.

There is a second thing that muscles can do that derives from the first: they can let go of their tension and relax. When muscles relax, they thin and lengthen. A muscle with the greatest range of action is one that can move from relaxation to full tension and then can release back to full relaxation. In today's society, most of us go through life with unhealthy amounts of residual tension in our muscles, which means that our range of muscular action is limited.

Many of the human facial muscles and the muscles that change the shape of the vocal tract attach at one end to the bones of the skull and at the other end to other muscles. This is why our faces – and our voices – are capable of so many variations. These muscular attachments are accomplished by **tendons**, bands of strong, flexible fibrous tissue that attach to the muscle, then to bone or cartilage, or to other tendons. No muscles attach directly to each other without the helpful presence of a tendon at each end of the muscle.

By the way, what's the difference between a tendon and a ligament?

A **tendon** attaches muscles to bone, cartilage or to other muscles.

A **ligament** attaches bones to other bones. It provides a flexible attachment that permits movement, as in joints. Bones can also attach directly to one another in rigid, complex structures. When they do, they are said to be "knit together".

Both tendons and ligaments are made of strong, fibrous tissue that is largely composed of collagen.

So a warm-up for the facial muscles and the articulator muscles should involve tensing (thickening and shortening) and relaxing (thinning and lengthening). Here are some possibilities.

1. Use both hands. Spread your fingers apart. With the tips of the fingers massage the face with a circular action and moderate pressure, just enough to know that you are moving the muscles around underneath the skin and on top of the skull. Start behind the hairline in your scalp and move down to massage your forehead. Massaging the tension out of the **frontalis** muscle that covers the forehead is an excellent – and speedy – way to let go of tension throughout the body. Continue to massage around your temples and around your ears, then massage the sides of the nose and cheekbone. (Use this massage to help define "the skull beneath the skin".) Continue the circular massage to the jaw hinge and jaw muscles in front of your earlobes and then complete the massage at the cheeks and around the mouth.

2. Let all your facial muscles relax. Let your jaw drop open. Close your eyes. With your fingers spread apart, draw the tips of the fingers directly downward on your face, with almost no pressure, from your hairline to your jawbone. Repeat at least five times. When you have finished, try to sense the weight of your face as it is attached to your skull.

3. Close your eyes. Place the palms of your hands over your eye sockets. Do a very easy circular massage with light pressure. You are massaging the **orbicularis oculis** muscles that ring the eyes sockets.

4. **Gurn.** Gurn slowly. Then gurn swiftly. As you do so, note that you are contracting some facial muscles and – by so doing – stretching others.

Articulator isolations

These exercises, some of which may seem rather odd, are a very important part of our work and should become a part of your warm-up routine. You should practice them with the same sense of form and attentiveness to the experience that you would bring to the basic discipline of learning a musical instrument or training muscles for a sport. These actions form the skills basis for everything that follows. The object here is to explore the mobility of the articulators *in isolation from one another*. It is very important that you pay attention to using the muscles we are focusing on actively. It is equally important that you pay attention to *not* using muscles if they are irrelevant to the focused action.

You should first do each of these exercises without sound, after which it is useful to do them again while releasing a voiced sound, hearing – and feeling – what sound changes are produced and (equally interesting) what sounds stay the same.

Bilateral symmetry

With only a comparatively few exceptions, all the members of the animal kingdom, from tigers to tarantulas, form their physical structure of bone and muscle according to bilateral symmetry. Imagine a line down the middle of your body: the structures on one side of that line mirror the structures on the other. So you have a left arm and a right arm, a left nostril and a right nostril, and so on. There may be minor variations in the mirrored structures, but the principle applies. So when we talk about a muscle on one side of your face, or a bone on one side of your head, there's also a similar bone or muscle on the other side. Note, though, that bilateral symmetry applies only variably to internal organs: you have a left kidney and a right kidney, but you don't have left and right livers. And a number of sea creatures exhibit radial symmetry.

The jaw

We all know what the jaw does: it opens downward away from the skull and also raises upward to meet the skull when our teeth come together to chew. When we think about the jaw, we are really considering the "jaw bone", more accurately termed the **mandible**. Anatomically, the mandible is not a part of the skull, even though it functions in relationship to the skull in all its actions. The mandible contains all the lower teeth and its principal function in movement is to bite and chew food.

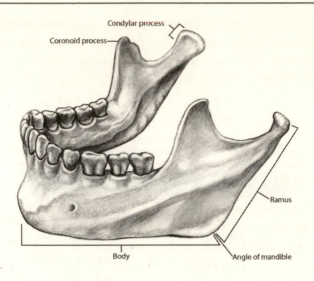

Figure 17. The jaw bone or mandible.

Place the fingers of both hands on the outside of your mandible at the front of the chin, with your thumbs underneath the chin and the rest of your fingers on top. Gently feel the bone as it curves back on the right and left sides of the chin along the **body of the mandible**. Eventually you will feel an angle where the edge of the mandible turns upward. This area of the mandible is called the **ramus** (Latin for "branch") of the mandible. The ramus ends in two very differently shaped **processes** or bony projections. The rear one is the **condylar process**, which is a rounded knob covered with cartilage. It acts as the "joint" for the jaw, fitting into a shallow depression in the **temporal** bone of the skull. However, the condylar process needs to be tied to the skull at this shallow **temporomandibular joint** with ligaments, so that the joint is secure, but also capable of a great variety of movement.

There is another unique feature of the temporomandibular joint: in between the condylar process and the temporal bone is a small disk composed of fibrous cartilage called the **articular disk**. It allows the joint to take two actions simultaneously when the jaw opens: the first is the expected rotation of the condylar process, such as occurs in most joints, like your hips; the second action is the sliding of the condylar process forward as the jaw

opens. There is a great advantage in this double action: it allows the mandible to drop open, a little further away from the skull than would be possible
if there were only a rotational action. It also helps to keep the pharyngeal
area of the vocal tract open and unconstricted.

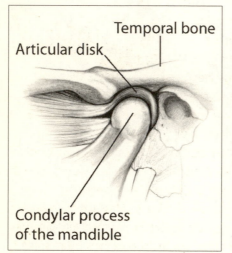

Temporal bone

Articular disk

Condylar process
of the mandible

Figure 18. The articular disk.

Explore this sliding action.
Place your index fingers at the
very top of the mandible, right
in front of your ears. Easily drop
the jaw open (don't force it!)
and feel that the condylar process of the mandible moves
very slightly forward. When you
bring the mandible up to close
it, feel the bone move back.

Dropping the jaw open is a
relaxation action. Gravity does
the work for you. You can open
the jaw further, but to do so
requires muscular action and all
the muscles that pull the jaw open also retract the jaw at the same time,
which constricts the laryngopharynx and the larynx itself — not a useful result
for open, free vocal production. Forced opening of the jaw also can cause
strain at the temporomandibular joint.

Since gravity drops the jaw open very efficiently, it follows that the main
muscles that attach to the mandible are used to raise the jaw upward
against gravity. These muscles are very powerful, since they are used primarily
to bite and chew food.

Place the fingertips of both hands on your cheekbones. You are feeling
bone structures of your skull that actually arch away from the rest of the
skull so that some muscles and tendons can function underneath. The
anatomical name is the zygomatic arch even though part of the always-
versatile temporal bone also forms the **arch** along with the **zygomatic bone**.

Now move your fingertips slightly downward and close your jaw. You can feel muscles brace into your fingers; these are your **masseter** muscles, the primary external muscles of human jaw closure.

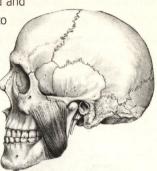

They are short and thick, with broad attachments around the angle of the mandible at one end and into the zygomatic arch at the other. These are powerful muscles that can exert several thousand pounds of bite pressure meas-

Figure 19. The masseter muscle.

ured in pounds per square inch (psi). Because they are powerful, they can store a lot of residual tension, which is one reason we often keep our mouths clamped shut when we're frustrated and why many of us grind our teeth at night while we sleep.

So it is useful to be able to let these muscles go. Massage the masseter muscles with your fingertips, using a circular action and moderate pressure. As you do this, direct the muscles to let go. You should think it, not speak it (lest you need to use your jaw to give the direction!), but it should be an actual word or phrase and it should be framed in a positive form: "Let it go" or "Relax" or "The jaw bone feels heavy" but *not* "Stop tensing" nor "Don't clench your teeth." We tend to understand autosuggestion (suggestions to yourself) only as positive formulations, so "Don't tense" can translate as "Tense!"

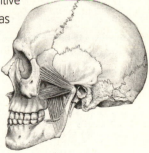

There are internal muscles that also raise the mandible; these are the **medial ptery-goid** muscles that have a similar attachment, but on the inner surface of the mandibular angle. They work with the masseter muscles to raise each side of the mandible like a pair of slings. The other muscles that you see in Figure 20 are the **lateral pterygoid** muscles

Figure 20. Medial and lateral pterygoid muscles.

43

that serve to pull the mandibular joint forward, thus helping to open the jaw and also to protrude the jaw. When tensed individually, they also move the jaw from side to side, with some participation by the medial pterygoids. All lateral jaw actions are more useful for the chewing process than they are for the process of speaking.

The final paired muscles that help the jaw bite with force are the **temporalis** muscles. These muscles attach to the front tip of the ramus of the mandible at the knifeblade-like **coronoid process**. This is a very narrow or focused attachment, using a tendon that extends from the coronoid attachment upward through the space between the zygomatic arch and the rest of the skull. The muscle

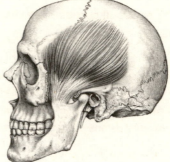

Figure 21. Temporalis muscle.

fibers then fan out in a very broad attachment onto the temporalis bone, the **parietal** bone and the **sphenoid** bone of the skull.

Place your fingertips, with the fingers spread apart, onto your temples on either side of your skull so that you can feel your temporalis muscles, beginning this exploration with your jaw relaxed open. Now bring your mandible up to **occlusion**, with your teeth together as though you were going to bite down (well, "bite up" is more accurate, isn't it?) onto something. You probably don't feel a lot of action at the temporalis muscles while the jaw is closing, because your masseter muscles are doing most of the work. But as soon as you bite "up" and apply pressure at the teeth, you will feel the temporalis muscles pop out, showing that they have braced and thickened.

So we have a pair of muscles with a very broad attachment at the top, meaning that the attachment is going to be very secure – a lot of muscle tissue but with short muscle fiber length. This means that a lot of force can be utilized over a very short distance, and a tendon attachment that focuses and multiplies this muscles force into a part of the mandible that can act like a lever – using the versatile joint at the condylar process as a fulcrum – that *further* amplifies the biting power. No wonder we are omnivores. No wonder we wear our molars down throughout life. No wonder people who grind their teeth in frustration get tension headaches focused at the temples!

The great all-purpose jaw release exercise

1. Crook your thumbs at the first joint so that they can bend around the angles of the mandible on either side. Place your thumbs there; feel the thumbnail resting against the large diagonal muscle that extends from your skull behind the ears down and forward to your collarbone. Very gently pull the jawbone slightly forward. Leave your thumbs where they are, resting in that depression between the muscle and the ramus of your mandible.

2. Now place your spread fingertips on the temporal muscles as before. Apply slight pressure with your fingers and with the thumbs to encourage the muscles to let go and the mandible to stay unretracted.

3. Slide your hands downward until the thumb-tip of each hand reaches the angle of the mandible.

4. Turn your hands, pivoting at the wrists, so that they follow the line of the body of the mandible forward and down. Your fingers will briefly massage your masseter muscles on the way. Your thumbs continue to use the line of the mandible as a guide.

5. Continue the gentle pressure with your fingers as you complete the action of stroking the body of the mandible forward and down, right out to the tip of the chin. Repeat the entire action at least five times.

This exercise encourages a relaxation of the jaw forward as well as downward, which is the natural opening action of the mandible. It massages your temporal and masseter muscles, encouraging them to release any residual tension. As you do this exercise, continue to focus autosuggestion on telling your jaw to let go.

Explore the range of jaw action

> **Advisory:** *Do not attempt this next set of five exercises if you have any pre-existing problems with your temporomandibular joint!*

1. Slowly bring the jaw up to occlusion of your teeth for biting, as you did when you were exploring the temporal muscle action. Let it relax open again. Make sure that you do not retract the mandible. Imagine the "energy flow" of gravity as being downward and very slightly forward.

2. Bring the jaw up again, but this time bring the upper front teeth and the lower front teeth very gently together. This is the action that the jaw generally takes when it raises in the process of articulating speech sounds. Relax the jaw as before.

3. With the jaw relaxed open, gently protrude the mandible. *Do not force it.* Relax.

4. With the jaw relaxed open, gently retract the mandible. *Do not force it.* Relax.

5. With the jaw relaxed open, gently move the tip of the chin to the right. *Do not force it.* Then move the tip of the chin leftward. Return to center.

Combining these actions, you can move your mandible in a circular action, which is very useful for chewing but not particularly useful for speech. In fact, you can move your mandible so that your chin describes three different circles on three different axes. What might they be? Can you demonstrate them? And lest we forget, *do not force it.*

Now that you have explored the anatomy and physiology of the jaw bone (the mandible) I can reveal to you that in most of the work that follows, the jaw's primary responsibility will be to do nothing whatever except – and this is very important – remain relaxed, but not forced, open. In the English language, the jaw is required to raise for only six consonant sounds. They are "s" as in "see", "z" as in "zoo", "sh " as in "show", "zh" as in "Zsa-Zsa", "ch" as in "church", and "dzh" as in "joy". It does not need to raise upward for any other consonants or for any of the vowels or diphthongs that form speech in English. From a descriptive standpoint, of course, we all use our jaws a lot more frequently in almost all our speech sounds to lessen the activity of the other articulators. But precisely because we are in the habit of sharing our tongue and lip actions with the jaw, I will ask that we explore the separation of the actions by allowing the other articulators to enact their full range of motion. Variable jaw positioning is important in forming accents, but in most of our work here we will want to let the jaw go, and only use it for those six consonants – which in English is often enough.

Maintaining a relaxed, open jaw position as "home base" for the mandible while speaking has another qualitative advantage: it allows for a more naturally open vocal tract, which enhances complex resonance of the voice; most of us are fairly good at keeping our mouths shut – literally if not metaphorically – but actors and other professional voice users need to be able to let our very individual voices flourish.

The lips and cheeks

The simplest way to describe the muscles that control the lips is to think of them as resembling a child's drawing of the sun. The ball of the sun here is a simple circle, but to emphasize the sun's importance we have drawn this circle as a double line. Radiating out from the "sun" are its "rays of light", lines going straight out in different directions from the circle.

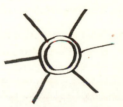

Figure 22. A child's sun.

The muscles of the lips work in a similar way. The circle of the "sun" is the muscle that goes all the way around the lips; it is called the **orbicularis oris** muscle. Actually this muscle is divided into an inner ring, located at the "roseate" part of the lips (the part that we usually identify as the lips), and an outer ring that fills much of the rest of the upper- and lower-lip area. (Interesting note: the discovery that the orbicularis oris muscle has inner and outer rings is a fairly recent one. One doesn't often find recent discoveries in the field of human anatomy.) The "rays of the sun" are attached at one end to one or both of these rings, and at the other end to skull bones or to other muscles, allowing the "ray" muscles, through contraction and release, to change the shape of the rings – the lips.

47

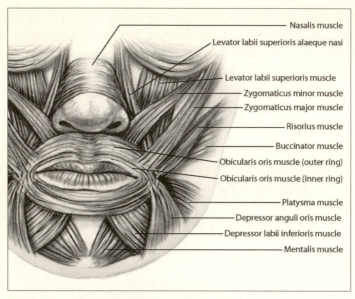

Figure 23. The facial muscles that control the lips.

That is the simplest description – perhaps a little too simple. After all, we know very well that we have an upper lip and a lower lip, both of which can

Figure 24. Lip action possibilities.

move independently, and that there are lip corners at the right and left sides of the mouth that are controlled by more muscle "rays" than the rest of the simple circle we have described before. So the "simple circle" can be pulled into many different forms by the muscles around it.

Warming up the lips

Hook the little finger of each hand around each lip corner. Let your lips relax. Gently stretch the lip corners apart and forward to stretch the orbicularis oris muscle, as in Figure 25. Gently pull the corners upward with your fingers; then gently pull them downward.

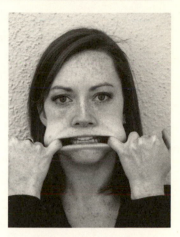

You can also exercise the orbicularis oris muscle by tensing against the action of the fingers with your orbicularis oris muscle. Try to pull your fingers toward one another by using your lips muscles.

Figure 25. Lateral lip stretching.

Unhook your fingers, and blow through the lips in a loose trill, first unvoiced (the classic horse imitation) and then voiced (the classic "I'm cold" expression).

1. Lip isolations

Begin all of the following exercises with lips relaxed and jaw dropped. Between isolation exercises it is a good relaxation to blow through the lips, unvoiced and voiced, keeping the lips and the cheeks very loose.

a **Lip corner retraction** (single). Pull one corner of your lips, on either the right or the left side, directly back toward the back or ramus, of the mandible. Isolate the action. Then release. Try it again using one lip corner, then the other, alternately.

Figure 26. Lip corner retraction.

b **Lip corner retraction (double).** Pull the corners of the lips directly back toward the back of the jawbone. The effect produced is that of a hideous, mirthless grin, stretching your lips tight across your teeth. If you wish to obtain the full psychotic effect, bug your eyes out simultaneously. Don't pull the corners up into an ordinary, commonplace, traditional grin. Relax. Repeat.

Figure 27. Right and left lip corner retraction.

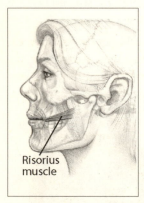

Risorius muscle

Figure 28.
The risorius muscle.

The muscles we use to retract the corners of the lips are the **risorius** muscles.

They attach in front to the **orbicularis oris** muscle at the corners of the lips; in the back they attach to the ramus of the mandible. When engaged, they draw the lip corners directly toward the back of the mandible.

You can also exercise the risorius muscles by gently pushing your index fingers into your cheeks just behind the orbicularis oris muscles, then pulling the lips corners back as in Exercise b, providing resistance to the risorius action.

c **Lip corner protrusion.** Push the corners of the lips directly forward but not intentionally inward toward one another. Relax. Repeat. Make sure that you isolate the action to the lip corners only and do not involve the rest of the lip. (See Figure 29.) When you do this action, you are tightening the outer circle of the orbicularis oris muscle but leaving the inner circle relaxed; as a result the inner circle is pushed outward.

d **The "aside".** Simultaneously engaging the
outer circle of the orbicularis oris muscle and
one of your risorius muscles, protrude one
corner forward and pull the other corner back
at the same time. Alternate. This exercise has
the effect of moving your entire mouth
around to one side of your face, which is
useful when you wish to confide something
to the person next to you without other
people reading your lips. (These other people
may, however, notice that your mouth has
seemingly disappeared.) This action is also
useful if you are imitating a flounder, although
expert flounder-imitators supposedly can
also migrate both eyes over to one side of
the skull, a more challenging task.

Figure 29. Lip corner protrusion.

e **Pursing the lips, 1.** With the jaw relaxed open and the lips naturally dropped
apart, bring the upper and lower lips together. Release them apart. Repeat. Do
not take any action with the lip corners. When you do the action of pursing, you
are tensing the inner ring of the orbicularis oris muscle while bracing the muscles
that attach to the lip corners.

f **Pursing the lips, 2.** Without using the
corners of the lips, curl the lips inward
around the teeth and into the mouth as
far as possible, like a bad imitation of a
person with no teeth. From this position,
swing the lips out and away from the
teeth as far as possible, like a trumpet.
Then swing them back into the mouth.
Repeat. When you perform the action of
lip-curling inward, you are tensing the
inner ring of your orbicularis oris muscle
without bracing any of the other muscle
"rays" extending from the periphery. When

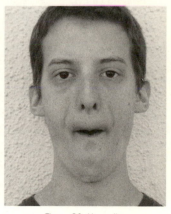

Figure 30. Lip curling.

you swing the lips outward, you are tensing the outer ring and also bracing some of the other muscles that raise and lower the edges of the lips.

g **Isolating the upper and lower lip.** Begin as with (e), but after the lips are stretched in, swing just the upper lip out, leaving the lower lip in. Then follow with the lower lip, isolated, swinging out. With both lips out, swing only the upper lip in, and then the lower lip. Repeat.

h **Changing the pattern.** Explore variants of (g), leading with the lower lip rather than the upper lip, going to complete lip relaxation between actions, repeatedly working one isolated lip, etc.

i **Full lip-rounding.** Push the corners of the lips forward as in (b) and keep them forward; then purse the lips until they touch (as in a kiss), with the lips fully closed. Relax the pursing action but keep the corners of the lips forward. Repeat. The overall effect is that of the traditional fish imitation, generally embellished by its best practitioners – four-year-olds – with the hands at the ears to imitate gills. (This may remain optional here.) After five repetitions relax the corners of the lips. Repeat the entire action. Full lip-rounding is a combined use of the outer and inner rings of the orbicularis oris muscle.

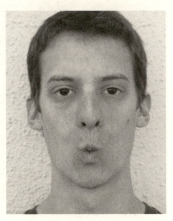

Figure 31. full lip rounding.

j **Bilabial speech action.** Do a few "p" and "b" sounds, feeling the muscular action of bringing the lips together in a pursing action until the flow is stopped; feel the build-up of air pressure behind the closure and then the release of the muscles aided by the release of the compressed flow as the flow is "exploded" out of the mouth.

k **Lip corners up.** The comic mask. Pull the lip corners directly upward toward the very front of your cheekbones. To enact this action you are using the **levator anguli oris** muscles. This is not a smile that you will want to use on your friends. Relax the muscles.

l **Lip corners down.** The tragic mask. Pull the lip corners directly downward (Figure 32). Here you are using the **depressor anguli oris** muscles. Relax. If you wish to explore tragi-comedy, try raising one lip corner and lowering the other.

m **The genuine smile.** This time allow the lip corners to move diagonally upward toward your cheekbones (Figure 33).

Figure 32. The tragic mask.

Here you are using your **zygomaticus** muscles. Of course, in order for this to be a genuinely genuine smile, you also need to have friendly feelings for its object.

Figure 33. The genuine smile.

n **Lip corners diagonally downward.** Unlike the tragic mask, where the lips corners are pulled directly downward, if you pull the lip corners diagonally downward, you will note a lot of muscle fibers tensing in your neck (Figure 34). This is because you are now using your **platysma** muscles, which attach to the lip corners and then fan out in thin sheets on either side of the neck to a broad attachment at your collarbone (or clavicle).

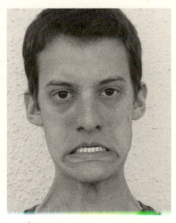

Figure 34. The platysma pull.

There are other "rays" extending from the orbicularis oris muscle that can raise or lower portions of the upper or lower lip. Although they are important in the communication of facial expression, or when you want to imitate a rabbit or Elvis, they have less importance in the articulation of speech, and I will not complicate your life further by exploring them here.

I will, instead, complicate your life with the following:

Cheek isolations

a   Cheek muscle release: with the jaw still relaxed open (important!) purse the lips so that they almost touch. Leave the cheeks absolutely relaxed. Blow air out between the lips so that the cheeks puff out; then inhale with equal force so that the cheeks pull in against the teeth. Repeat two or three times; no more than that, however, since you may start to hyperventilate. If you start to feel dizzy, stop breathing for a few moments.

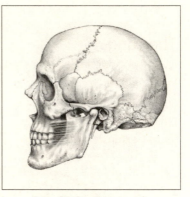

Figure 35. Buccinator muscle.

b   Thicken the tongue to "fill up" one side of the mouth but not the other, so that airflow can escape only around one side and past one cheek. Blow air out with moderate force. This will produce a slow, rather sloppy cheek trill, either unvoiced or voiced. Do the same with the other cheek. (Hint: you may need to advance the lip corner of the "trill" side slightly.) Then shift the tongue to the center and try to trill both cheeks simultaneously. This may take a little practise, but the amusement (or possibly horror) of your friends will quite obviously justify the time spent.

c   With the jaw relaxed open, tense (or bunch) the cheek muscles against the teeth, and then release. Repeat five times. Remember that you are tensing and releasing the muscles only, and not using the muscles to move the cheek area in any direction. When you take this action you are tensing your **buccinator** muscles.

d   Isolate the tensing and releasing action that you did in (c) to the area of the cheeks just behind the lip corners. The cheeks will be tensing into the incisors and/or bicuspids. As always, make sure that you are not using your jaw in this action.

e   Buccinator isometrics. Place the tip of your tongue against the inside of your left or right cheek. Push the cheek outward to the side with your tongue muscles. Then, using the buccinator muscles of your cheek, pull the cheek back in, against the pressure of the tongue action. Do the same exercise with the other cheek.

The tongue

As the next two illustrations show, the tongue is not a single muscle, but many muscles. Some of these muscles exist wholly within the tongue itself and are termed **intrinsic** muscles. Some of them extend from the tongue to other skeletal structures, such as the skull or the hyoid bone. These are termed **extrinsic** muscles.

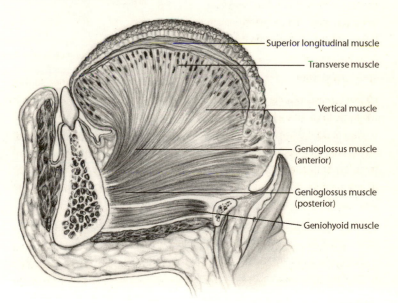

Figure 36. Intrinsic tongue muscles.

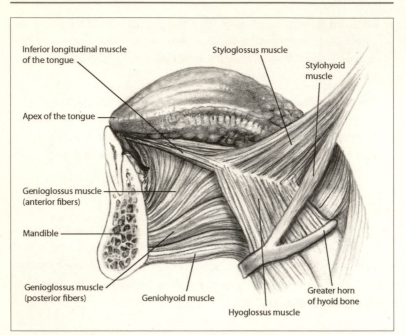

Figure 37. Extrinsic tongue muscles.

Tongue isolations

a **"Stretching" the tongue.** Protrude the tongue-tip and blade straight out of your mouth as far as you can stretch them comfortably. Actually, what you are doing is pushing the tip and blade out of your mouth by tensing (and shortening) the back part of an important tongue muscle that occupies a lot of the rear portion of the oral cavity. As Figure 37, above, illustrates, the fibers of this muscle are attached broadly to the body and the blade of the tongue at one end and are attached to the hyoid bone and – primarily – to the mandible. This muscle is called the **genioglossus** muscle and in protruding the tongue forward you are using specifically the rear or **posterior** portion of the **genioglossus**.

Retracting the tongue back into you mouth uses the forward or **anterior** fibers of the genioglossus muscle.

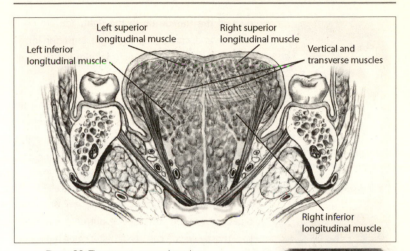

Figure 38. The tongue: coronal section.

b **Raise the tongue tip.** With the tongue protruded from your mouth, curl the tip upward. To accomplish this action you are tensing (contracting) the two **superior longitudinal** muscles of the tongue (Figure 39). As the name suggests, the fibers of these muscles – located to the right and left of the mid-line – run from the tip of the tongue toward the back of the tongue just below the upper surface (in other words, just below your taste buds. Relax the tongue.

Figure 39. Raising the tongue tip.

c **Lower the tongue tip.** Curl the tongue tip downward. Here you are using the **inferior longitudinal** muscles of the tongue (Figure 40). Again these muscles are paired – right and left – and the muscles fibers run front to back. The muscles are located just above the under-surface of your tongue.

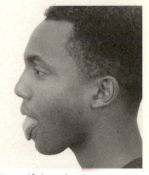

Figure 40. Lowering the tongue tip.

Figure 41. Tongue tip to right.

Figure 42. Tongue tip to left.

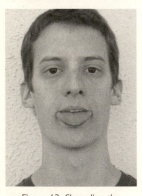

Figure 43. Chaneling the
tongue.

d **Curl the tongue tip to the right.** You are now tensing and contracting the **right superior longitudinal muscles** and the **right inferior longitudinal muscles** (Figure 41).

e **Curl the tongue tip to the left.** As will come as no surprise to anyone who is inclined to recognize patterns, you are now tensing and contracting the **left superior longitudinal muscles** and the **left inferior longitudinal muscles** (Figure 42).

f **Channeling and bunching.** The jaw is relaxed open. Easily slide your tongue out onto the lower lip – mostly so you can see it better. Stretch the side edges of the tongue apart by flattening the tongue; that is, you are bringing the superior and inferior surfaces of the tongue toward one another (Figure 43). In so doing, you are contracting your **verticalis** muscles; as the name implies, the fibers run vertically. When this action is taken, there is a natural tendency for your tongue to "channel" slightly, with the side edges raising a bit and the midline lowering.

Relax the verticalis muscles and the tongue will rediscover its comfortable plumpness. Now you're going to do the opposite action: bring the same side edges of the tongue in directly toward one another, thickening the center of the tongue along the midline (Figure 44, opposite page). Relax. Here you are tensing and releasing your **transversus** tongue muscles that run from one side edge of the tongue to the other.

In bunching the tongue, *do not curl the side edges of the tongue upward* into what can perhaps be described as a rolled fleshy *cannolo* (plural: *cannoli*) as you try to pull those side edges toward one another. Repeat each of these two actions in sequence. The effect is that the midline of the tongue lowers when you are channeling the tongue and raises when you are bunching the tongue.

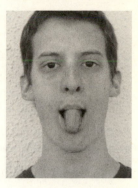

g **Arching and cupping the tongue**. Front: the jaw is relaxed open. Keep the tongue tip at rest behind the lower teeth. Arch the front of the tongue upward toward the alveolar-palatal area to form an "eeeee" vowel. Whisper, but do not voice, the "eeeee." Then cup the front of the tongue sharply downward – keeping the cupping

Figure 44. Bunching the tongue.

action as forward-placed as possible – to form a "flat A" sound; as in, appropriately, the word "flat". Again whisper the sound. Repeat the two actions in sequence, first very slowly moving from "eeeee" to "aaaaa", and then moving energetically from one to the other. Now do the entire sequence voiced. *Keep the jaw relaxed open throughout this exercise*. Here, as you probably realize, you are using your inferior longitudinal muscles to arch the tongue and your superior longitudinal muscles to cup the tongue.

h **Lowering or cupping the back of the tongue.** With the tip of the tongue comfortably behind the lower teeth, isolate the action of lowering the back of your tongue directly downward, then releasing it. Because the superior longitudinal muscles do not function efficiently to lower the greater bulk of the back of the tongue, the action enlists the hyoglossus muscle, which pulls the back of the tongue downward toward this muscle's attachment to the hyoid bone.

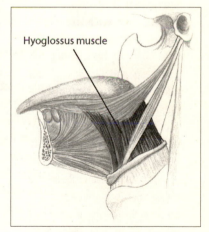

Figure 45. Hyoglossus muscle.

In many speech books and in some speech science texts, you will find the assertion that when the hyoglossus muscle pulls the back of the tongue down, there is also a reactive movement backward by the root of the tongue, thus constricting the pharynx. This is often true as an observation, which is why we hear a lot of people utter a constricted sound when they say "ahhh". Test this yourself: do your best "dentist's office ahhhh" and hear if your voice thins out. But while this constriction *can* happen, it does not *need* to happen. If you use your posterior genioglossus muscle to pull the tongue root forward, this constriction can easily be avoided. (Remember the "professional yawn"!)

i   **Arching and cupping the tongue, back.** Perform the same action as in Exercise g, but this time isolate the *back* of the tongue arched up first to form a long "U" sound, "ooooo", and then with the back cupped down to form a broad "A" as in "aaaahhhh", as in Exercise h. Repeat the sequence from "ooooo" to "aaaahhhhh" first very slowly and then quickly. The rounding of your lips on the "ooooo" helps in the formation of the sound but should not be the focus of your attention; stay focused on the tongue action. *Keep the jaw relaxed open throughout this exercise.*

j   **Advancing and retracting the tongue root, 1.** Without moving the jaw from its relaxed open position, protrude the tongue forward from the back, letting the tongue-tip and blade slide out onto the lower lip. Then pull the tongue root directly back to constrict the laryngopharynx. Try not to tense the tip, blade, or front of the tongue; isolate the action as far back as possible. Relax the tongue-root forward. Repeat. For the retraction of the tongue-root, you are using your **styloglossus**

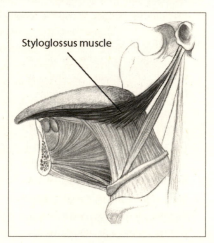

Figure 46. Styloglossus muscle.

muscles, which attach to little prongs pointing downward from your **temporal** bone at the back and bottom of your skull and then loop around the underside of the tongue like a sling.

k **Advancing and retracting the tongue root, 2.** Repeat the previous exercise but this time, allow the tip of the tongue to stay behind the lower teeth. Isolate the action by limiting it to the tongue root itself.

l **Tongue-tip to alveolar ridge and to palate, 1.** Keeping the rest of the tongue as relaxed as possible and the jaw relaxed always open, bring *only* the tip of the tongue up to touch the gum ridge (the "alveolar ridge") just behind the upper teeth. Relax the tongue fully away so that the tip drops down to just behind the lower teeth. Repeat. Now curl the tip of the tongue upward and back so that the tongue tip touches the middle of the hard palate. Can you do this without thickening the rest of the tongue? Relax the tongue fully: does the tip quickly relax down to a position just behind the lower teeth?

m **Tongue-tip to alveolar ridge and to palate, 2.** This time, allow the entire front edge of the tongue, including the tongue-tip, to raise and seal off the airway at the alveolar ridge behind the upper teeth. Make sure that you still isolate this action. Do not involve the jaw in the action. Using a flow of air from the lungs, explode the tongue away from the alveolar ridge back to its resting position, producing a "t" stop-plosive sound. Repeat with a voiced flow, producing a "d" stop-plosive sound. Curl the tongue-tip and the edge of the tongue back to seal off the airway at the palate. Again, use a flow of air to explode the tongue away from the palate producing, this time, an unfamiliar-sounding "t". Repeat with voicing, producing an equally unfamiliar "d" sound. Finally, explore as many possible placements of the tongue-tip and edge between the alveolar and palatal placements as you can. Continue to isolate the action to only those parts of the tongue that must work to complete the action effectively.

n **Rolling the ball.** Imagine that your tongue is cupped to hold a large marble or – a more edible image – a grape, on the blade of your tongue. Slowly roll the imagined marble back along the mid-line of your tongue as far back as you can go before you would swallow it, were it real. Then slowly roll it forward, keeping the tongue fully cupped. Repeat. Don't pull the whole tongue back: just roll the ball.

o **Moving the mountain.** Arch the front of your tongue as though you were about to say "eeeeee". Slowly roll that arch back until the arched back portion of the tongue is just under the velum (the soft palate). Do not retract the tongue in this (or the previous) exercise: the tongue-tip should stay right behind your lower teeth.

p **Bracing.** Channel the tongue, with the midline low and the edges high. Bring the side edges of the tongue up to meet the inside of the upper teeth along the molars and rear bicuspids. Brace the tongue outward against the teeth, pushing laterally. The probable result will be that the midline raises slightly toward the roof of the mouth. Focus the effort of the bracing selectively from the bicuspids to the rear molars.

Practice each of these isolations of the lips, cheeks, and tongue repeatedly, making sure that you focus on only one activity and that you do not tense irrelevant muscles. It is especially important that you try to keep the mandible relaxed open at all times, so that the action is focused into the other articulators. It is more important that you practice the isolations frequently, even if you do not do so for a long period of time in any given work session.

Terms to know

Articulators
Points of articulation
Bracing
Contracting
Tendon
Ligament
Frontalis muscles
Orbicularis oculis muscles
Mandible
Body
Ramus
Condylar process
Coronoid process
Temporal bone
Temporomandibular joint
Articular disk
Zygomatic bone
Zygomatic arch
Masseter muscles
Medial pterygoid muscles
Lateral pterygoid muscles
Temporalis muscles

Parietal bone
Sphenoid bone
Temporal bone
Occlusion
Orbicularis oris muscle,
inner and outer rings
Risorius muscles
Levator anguli oris muscles
Depressor anguli oris muscles
Zygomaticus muscles
Platysma muscles
Buccinator muscles
Intrinsic, extrinsic
Genioglossus muscle,
posterior and anterior portions
Longitudinal muscles
superior and inferior, left and right
Verticalis muscles
Transversus muscles
Hyoglossus muscle
Styloglossus muscle
Clavicle

5 "Phthong" shaping

In exploring the ways we can obstruct the unvoiced or voiced flow to form consonants, we were able to feel a vibratory buzz – or just a rush of air – in specific, very limited areas of the vocal tract. The shaping we are about to re-explore – because we've done it before – will not have that specific focus of feeling within the mouth, but in exchange we will be able to feel the vibrations throughout the body.

I would like you to try to ignore the word "vowel" as a label for this unobstructed voiced flow for awhile, because the word "vowel" suggests the standard "a", "e", "i", "o", "u" (and sometimes "y" and "w") that we use in English. Don't let yourself be limited by this limited selection of sounds. There are infinite gradations of sound change possible here and they all are just as worthy as any others.

Instead we can use the linguistic term **monophthong**. It's a longer word than "vowel", but it's more interesting to say. (I especially like the "phth" sequence.) "Monophthong" means a single voiced, unobstructed sound.

While we are on the subject, we are probably more familiar with the term **diphthong**, which means a glide from one monophthong to another. We use these all the time in words like "voice", "crime", "house" and so on.

We also use the occasional **triphthong**, sliding from one sound to another to a third, as in words like "sour" or "fire".

So the general term that might tie all these more specific descriptions together is **phthong**. This is a word that is not usually included in the linguist's lexicon, but it certainly is easy to remember. It comes from the Greek word φδογγος, meaning "sound". Oh, by the way, voice the "th".

You can explore this work (and this new word) in a standing position, or sitting, or lying down. But make sure that you are "actively relaxed", that your entire body is available to receive and transmit vibrations.

Exploration 1

Focused gurning on tone. You will recall that we previously explored gurning, making strange faces by using all our muscles of expression. Now we are going to use our awareness of articulator isolations to explore the kinds of unobstructed shaping of sound that might be used in language.

Begin by relaxing your jaw open. Leave it open throughout this work. It is easy enough to reintroduce jaw action into the mix of actions, but for now we need to feel the contributions that the other shaping actions are making without the mediation of having the jaw raise and lower to vary the size of the oral cavity.

Begin an *unvoiced* flow of breath, breathing egressively. (But not *agg*ressively! Keep the flow gentle.) Begin to shape that flow by slowly and attentively moving one or more of the "vowel articulators". Make sure that you are never obstructing the flow. Just get used to exploring different shaping actions without having to hear a defined sound result. Don't go back to gurning – use only the vowel articulators. Your lips and cheeks should be the only outside parts of your face that are moving. Everything else is happening inside.

Now let the flow change easily from unvoiced to voiced. But keep your focus on the feel of the movement of the vowel articulators (excluding – for the time being – the jaw): the muscular circle of the lips and all the muscles that radiate from it, the cheeks, the body of the tongue, the velum, the pharynx. Allow the movements of the articulators to be slow and easy as you release vibrations on a series of long voiced sighs.

◀)) **Audio track 15:** *Focused gurn shaping.*

Allow yourself to listen attentively to the resulting sounds. Note the actions that seem to change only the quality of the sound; those that seem to change the loudness; those that seem to change the monophthong sounds (familiar or unfamiliar); and those that seem to change more than one of these categories.

After a bit of exploration, most people generally observe that quality change happens most strongly in pharyngeal actions, that monophthong change is produced most strongly in the mouth through the action of the tongue, lips, and cheeks, and that amplitude (loudness) change can be affected by any of the articulators. But the actual mix is very individual, and all the articulators make some contribution to all the categories.

Go through some "quality" changes on the same monophthong.

◀)) **Audio track 16:** *Acoustic voice quality.*

Play with sounding nasal, denasal (as though you have a head cold), hollow, constricted, and so on. Work anywhere in your pitch range as you do this exploration.

Exploration 2

Isolate phthong change. Sound an easy egressive voiced sigh with your jaw relaxed open. Be attentive to the "vocal quality" – it doesn't matter what it is, but one of your main tasks in this exploration will be to keep that vocal quality the same throughout the work.

Continue to release a series of voiced sighs and start to shape the sound by shaping the articulators – always without obstructing the flow. Keep the vocal quality consistent and also the amplitude so far as possible. Isolate the change to the monophthong sounds you are producing. Try to eliminate actions that don't actually produce some monophthong change.

◀)) **Audio track 17:** *Phthong shaping.*

Probably you will note through the feel of the actions that you are using a more limited set of actions to shape the flow. For one thing, you will note that the tip and blade of the tongue do not contribute much to the variation in the phthongs; the work is centered in the dorsal portion (front, middle, or back) of the tongue. So the tip and blade can stay relaxed. Explore using the dorsal actions *fully*, though. Let the sound always be changing slowly and smoothly through sounds that are new and unfamiliar as well as familiar. You will also note that – with the jaw remaining relaxed open – your lips move from slightly spread at the corners to fully rounded.

Exploration 3

Enter the maraphthong. This isn't a serious linguistic term, but it's a pretty good description of what you're doing right now. It's more than a monophthong. It's more than a diphthong. It's more than a triphthong. It's a marathon glide though constantly changing sound actions on a series of voiced sighs. It's a maraphthong.

Exploration 4

Move/freeze/move. Isolate your action to maraphthong sound change (so you keep the same sound "quality" and the same amplitude. Focus your attention on the physical actions of the vowel articulators as the sound flow changes on a series of easy long-voiced sighs. After about ten seconds, freeze the articulators in place and be aware of the feel and sound of the single monophthong voiced sigh. Hold the articulators in position and register the emotional quality of the sound. Where does it seem to resonate within your body? Where does it seem to resonate within your *psyche*? Enjoy the sound. Get comfortable with the sound. You will probably need this sound – whatever it is – in your work on accents. Resist the temptation to adjust the articulator action and therefore the resulting sound toward a more familiar sound product. Of course you may find that you have frozen the articulators into a familiar sound initially, which is fine. Just make sure it doesn't happen all the time.

◀)) **Audio track 18:** *Move/freeze/move phthlong shaping.*

After you register the isolated sound result by listening and feeling the vibrations, go back to sounding your maraphthong. After another ten seconds or so, isolate the articulator action again. And so on.

Exploration 5

Move/freeze lips/move. Begin the exercise as in Exploration 4. But this time, when you freeze the articulators, freeze the lips only and continue exploring the action of the dorsal part of your tongue. What effect does this selective immobility of the lips have on the experience of the tongue action? What is the effect on the resulting sound? Then go back to the maraphthong and after a few seconds, freeze the lips again in a different position. Repeat.

◀)) **Audio track 19:** *Move/freeze lips/move phthlong shaping.*

Exploration 6

Move/freeze tongue/move. Begin again with your maraphthong exploration but this time, when you freeze the articulators, freeze the tongue action only and continue to explore lip rounding or spreading. Note the effect on the lip action, if any, and on the sounds that result. Then resume the maraphthong and after a few seconds, freeze the tongue action again. Repeat.

◀)) **Audio track 20:** *Move/freeze tongue/move phthong shaping.*

Exploration 7

Sharing the monophthong. If you are working in a group, form a circle. (*Warning:* If you are alone, do not try to form a circle, as injury may result.) Let one person in the circle begin a maraphthong glide on a voiced sigh. Then let that person freeze the articulators into a monophthong release. As this first person holds the mono-phthong sound, a person next to the first person should try to shape her or his articulators so that the same sound is reproduced. Once the monophthong has been "passed" from the first person to the second, the maraphthong-to-monophthong action of shaping a new sound is repeated around the circle until each participant has explored receiving a sound, exploring for a new sound, and sharing that sound with the next person.

6 Obstruents: obstructing the flow

Instinctively we know what makes an "**obstruent**" sound different from a "phthong" sound in human speech, even if we haven't met these terms before. But we may not know why our instinct knows this. In "phthongs" we flow vibrations out of our mouths in an easy unobstructed flow of voiced sound. We may change the shape of the vocal tract (from the vocal cords to the lips) somewhat like the twists and turns of a river: the form changes (in speech when we change one vowel sound to another) but the flow goes on with nothing restricting it.

"Obstruents" are different. When we produce obstruents we move one or more articulators so that they get in the way of the flow.

There is a more familiar term for this class of sounds: **consonants**. But for the time being we are going to use the more archaic term "obstruents" because it is more descriptive of the physicality of the action and also because it is useful for us to think of these actions as something new and unique, not the same limited set of consonant actions that (if English is your primary language) you have already learned so well.

"Obstruents" vs "consonants": some more argument

There are some other reasons to use the term "obstruent" instead of the term "consonant" at this stage of our work. "Consonant" derives from the Latin word consonans *meaning "sounding together". In one of its forms, "consonant" is defined in the* Oxford English Dictionary *as "Agreement or pleasing combination of sounds; harmony, concord." But the physical action here is one that gets in the way of the flow: it is intrusive, it impedes, it obstructs. Obstruent is a more accurately descriptive term.*

So obstruents are defined as articulator actions that get in the way of (i.e. obstruct) the flow – sometimes a lot, sometimes only a little; sometimes so little, in fact, that the obstruents are almost vowels, such as "w" or "y" or "r" or "l" in English.

Try these sounds a few times like this: *wah wah wah, yah yah yah, rah rah rah, lah lah lah*. Can you feel that your tongue is impeding the flow only very slightly? Where do you feel the slight change in the voiced flow within the vocal tract and especially on the tongue?

Sometimes the articulators obstruct the flow so much that it is blocked altogether for an instant. As in "b" or "d" for example.

Say – and make sure you can *feel* – the sounds: *bah bah bah, dah dah dah*. Tie them together on one flow of breath: *bahbahbahdahdahdah*.The action of the flow continues but the stream is blocked until its energy builds up enough to explode past the barrier.

Sometimes the obstruction of the flow is strong enough so that the consonant's quality lies in the flow trying to get past the obstruction. "Z" or "v" or "s" or "sh".

Say out loud *sahsahsahsahsah* then *zahzahzahzahzah*. The "ah" is always voiced, but note that you produced the "s" sound without the vocal cords vibrating and "z" *with* the vocal cords vibrating. So you experience that some of these consonant obstructions of the flow, as in the "s" sound you just made, are strong enough to make their own unique sounds without voicing (vocal fold vibrations) at all.

You can test this. Put one hand lightly on your "Adam's apple" at the front of your larynx. Take a deep breath and on one flow out from your lungs release a long energetic *sssssszzzzzzzsssssszzzzzzzsssssszzzzzz*, turning the vibrations on and off and on again. You can feel with your hand when the vibrations are on and when they are off.

On the following pages you will receive and follow a recipe — a pretty simple one — for making all the obstruent sounds in the world's languages that are powered by a flow of breath energy from your lungs, which is the way speakers around the world form most of their obstruent sounds — though not quite all of them. I am keeping this simple, because I want you to explore freely the possibilities for making as many different obstruent actions as possible.

Ingredients

1   A **voiced or unvoiced flow** of air moving from the lungs through the vocal tract and out your mouth — or sometimes your nose.

2   An **action** by the articulators to obstruct the flow, a lot or a little. Complete stoppage would be one extreme of action, a tiny intrusion would be the opposite extreme, and the rest of the actions would be everything in between. But your listener would have to be able to differentiate the sounds these actions produce.

3   A **place** in your vocal tract (anywhere between your vocal folds and your lips) where the action happens.

Before we can combine the ingredients, we need to know a little more about them, so that when we start to speak obstruents we can go beyond the ones we are used to and actually find some new sounds. The flow can be either a voiced **flow** of vibrations (remember "zzzzzz") or an unvoiced flow of air (as in "ssssss"). That's the only variable in the flow.

Now just *combine* the ingredients. (I said this was a simple recipe.) In other words, start saying some obstruents out loud. To make them easier to say, put a voiced "ahhhhh" phthong after every obstruent. (This is the so-called "broad 'a'", the "ahhhh" sound the dentist tells us to make to get our mouths open.) We also remember that some of our obstruent sounds are formed using a voiced flow of vibration, others using an unvoiced flow of breath.

Put together strings of obstruents on one flow release of breath with the obstruents separated by the "ahhhh" vowel. *Say them slowly but with energy.* These usually aren't going to sound like words as we know them. You are exploring the feel of the articulation actions themselves. There are various names for what we are doing – "doubletalk", "gibberish", "nonsense words", and so on.

🔊 **Audio track 21:** *Free-form obstruents.*

Even if it feels and sounds strange, keep going. Keep the flow energetic. Ignore those puzzled stares from co-workers, fellow students, or loved ones. Don't be limited by the familiar "consonant" sounds you're used to making. Explore the possibilities of new obstruent sounds even if you have never heard them before in any language.

When you have attained maximum variety and audacity of obstruent formation – staying with the phthong "ahhhh" as you do so – turn your attention to the *actions* your articulators are taking. How close together are they getting? Are they interrupting the flow or just getting in the way a little? Do the articulators vibrate against one another repeatedly or touch and bounce away? What path through the vocal tract does the flow – voiced or unvoiced – take? What actions make a consonant sound different from another consonant that is similar to it in other ways? What do these differences sound like and feel like?

Finally, expand your attention to an awareness of the *place* (or even sometimes the *places*) in the vocal tract where the action is happening. Consonants can form anywhere between your lips and your vocal folds (and include both); the only requirement is that the action can obstruct the flow to some degree.

The goal here is to come up with as many different ways of obstructing the flow with your articulators as you can, even if some of the sounds that result are rather nasty. Play freely with these articulatory actions, much in the same way that a very young child explores different vocal sounds on the way to shaping them into language. But play with an adult's sense of attentiveness and an adult's sense of rigor. Vary the tempo of this strange obstruent *mélange*. Vary your pitch inflections. Vary your energy level, but don't let the energy progressively subside. When it stops being play, stop doing it. But come back to it.

Part 2
Finding language

7 Exploring the limits: Outlandish

We now are ready to put together our work in "Obstructing the Flow" and "Phthong Shaping" so that we can produce a sequence of sound actions that resemble a very odd language. It isn't language really, because it doesn't have any direct meaning, except the variable meanings that might be called up by the sounds themselves.

The only limits to this strange "language", which we will henceforth call "Outlandish", are what you can physically enact (without injury!) as vocally produced sound: voiced or unvoiced sound that is produced using a flow shaped or obstructed by your articulators. Outlandish is – and should be – outlandish. Compared to Outlandish, Klingon in *Star Trek* is a language for wimps.

As you speak it, you will be able to collect some useful information about sounds that fit easily into connected speech actions, and those which are so difficult to execute in connected speech that they (and you, and your listeners) would be happier if they stood alone. But as you speak Outlandish, your articulators will get some excellent exercise, and you will be able to express yourself with a kind of perverse eloquence that is fascinating in itself

◀)) **Audio track 22:** *Outlandish.*

You will also start to get some useful information about how "phthongs" (monophthongs, diphthongs, triphthongs, and beyond) and Outlandish obstruents interact in connected speech. Putting obstruents together in a sequence without any phthongs in between is called a **obstruent cluster.** (Well, it's actually called a "consonant cluster" but you have parked the term "consonant" in an unused portion of your brain, haven't you?) You will start to sense the limitations of how long a given obstruent cluster can go on before what you are saying stops sounding like a language at all. You have to throw in a phthong or two fairly frequently. We aren't going to analyze this obstruent–phthong ratio from a linguistic perspective; we are just experiencing it in practice.

Exploration 1

Group outlandish. Imagine that the participants in this exercise are all citizens of the Lost Continent of Outlandis, where all governance is conducted by the group, and all debate at meetings consists of one-word questions and one-word answers.

One Outlandian begins by asking a one-word question in Outlandish to another person in the circle. (We know it's a question because it has an upward inflection.) The person so addressed repeats the question – this is an important tradition! – and then replies with a decisive one-word answer (downward inflection) in Outlandish. The answerer then asks an Outlandish question to another Outlandian in the circle. The process continues until all participants have asked a question and received an answer, at which point, according to the traditions of Outlandis, all discussion ends and it is simply assumed that a decision has been reached. This business method goes a long way toward explaining why Outlandis is a lost continent.

Exploration 2

Outlandish anecdotes. Tell an Outlandish anecdote lasting at least thirty seconds to the group, or to yourself in a mirror, or into a recording device. You should know what the story is, but under no circumstances should you rehearse. Just let the sounds happen. Try to maintain variety of sound production. Or, to put it the opposite way, don't allow yourself to become too fond of only a few sounds. Make sure that you are using both voiced and unvoiced obstruents.

Exploration 3

Outlandish singing. If you or your fellow Outlandians discover that you are still too fond of interminable strings of obstruents, there's nothing like a good song to restore a sense of balance between obstruent and phthong. So sing! Sing the Outlandish National Anthem. Sing some other country's national anthem in Outlandish. (There will be a small prize for the most "melisma" – improvising phthongal vocalization around the melody.) Croon. Rap.

After exploring Outlandish and the physical limits to which it takes us, we are ready to refine our exploration toward those actual language sounds used on the real continents of the world.

8 Obstruents within language

The selection of speech actions that occurs when we move from Outlandish to the repertoire that human beings use in the languages of the world is one that has entirely to do with obstruents. In moving from Outlandish to language, many of the most succulent obstruent sounds reluctantly leave the scene, to be brought back only when we need a special "rude noise". We let them go because for the most part they are simply inefficient to say when a person is putting sounds together in connected speech. In contrast, all those infinite gradations of "phthongs" ("vowels" to the rest of the world) that we have experienced during the preceding explorations do indeed find their way into languages, or into dialects of languages, or into the speech habits of individual speakers.

If you have been paying close attention to the ease or difficulty of various speech actions in Outlandish – and if you haven't, now is the time to review – you may have reached a few general conclusions about the consonant sound actions that do and don't combine fluently with other sounds. Here are some of mine, but you may have more

1   After five consecutive obstruents in a cluster, a "phthong" is very appealing, even if you are speaking Outlandish. If you speak nothing but obstruents, you are an Obstruentian, not an Outlandian, and Obstruentians tend to explode at an early age, a fate you may wish to avoid.

2   Ingressive sound actions are useful in speech only very occasionally, and only if the other actions are all egressive. A few languages do use ingressive sounds to convey specific meanings, but ingressive vocalizations have their greatest utility in singing.

3   Most obstruent sounds are produced easily with the flow moving forward along the midline of the tongue. While there are obstruents where the flow moves around the sides of the tongue ("laterals") this lateral action initiates no further back than the velum.

4   Sounds, voiced or unvoiced, that can only be produced by a radical increase in airflow don't usually occur in languages, but do remain in "rude noises", where radical increase in airflow energy is the whole point. Consistency in airflow helps fluency.

5   Actions using the lips (and there are quite a few in language) only work well in connected speech if the middle third of each lip is active and mostly if the edges of the lips are used. That trill sound, if you can execute it – where your lower lip is slapping against your nose – may look terrific, but it probably won't be used regularly in language.

6   For most people, the tip of the tongue can indeed curl back to touch the velum area, but it is not efficient in connected speech because it's hard to get to the next sound action.

7   The lips do not really want to spend a lot of time behind the teeth. There is only one sound action in the world's languages that begins with the lips (actually, a lip) behind the teeth; and it doesn't stay there long.

You may well come up with other conclusions or even possibly with evidence that counters the foregoing. But we can now explore seriously what the physical actions are that work effectively in language.

9 The physical actions of obstruents in language

The actions

All articulate sound begins with the stream of unvoiced air or a stream of voice – airflow broken into pressure waves – moving through the vocal tract (the tube between the vocal folds and the lips), either in or out, inhaled or exhaled.

Obstruents, the vocal sounds that carry the denotative meaning of words, are always formed by a physical action of the articulators that – in some manner – gets in the way of this flow of air or vibration, not just shaping it, as do vowel actions, but interfering with that flow, like the "shhhh" we hear when a rock gets in the way of a flowing whitewater river. Some obstruent actions intrude on this flow only slightly, and some do so strongly, as with our first category:

Stop-plosives

Also called **plosives** or **stops.** The action *always* begins with the physical impulse for a flow of air or vibration, even if we haven't yet produced a sound. That flow is literally stopped by bringing two articulators together completely, or by bringing an articulator fully into contact with a fixed unmovable point of articulation in the mouth, so that no flow can get past the point of closure. However, the muscular action that produces the flow does not stop. (For most English obstruent sounds, this would be the action of exhaling, with the action initiated in the torso. But not all sounds are English.) As soon as this happens, the air either becomes more dense (the air molecules **compress** closer together) or gets thinner (the air molecules **rarefy** – move further apart), because of the continuing muscular action producing the flow and the natural elasticity of the tissues of the vocal tract. So there is either pressure at the point of stoppage, or a vacuum. Either way, the "dam", the point of closure, is going to burst. When it does, we have the completion of the action of the stop-plosive, in a sudden movement (release) of the compressed air (or voiced sound) through the just-opened space within the vocal tract.

Nasals

We have defined the vocal tract as consisting of a curved tube from the vocal folds in the larynx through the mouth to the lips. But of course there is another option for the voiced or unvoiced flow: through the nasal cavity. In most English consonant sounds, and all English vowel sounds, the nasal cavity does not receive this flow. This is because the upper side of the velum, or soft palate, is usually raised to create its own stoppage, preventing the flow from getting past the nasopharynx. But on certain obstruents – those whose physical action starts out with the initial stoppage of a stop-plosive – the velum is lowered so that the flow impulse can escape immediately through the nasal cavity. Since the nasal cavity itself is pretty much immobile, the shaping of the *differentiated* sound has to be defined by the point of stoppage of the oral cavity (the mouth) during the production of these sounds. Where the stoppage takes place defines the particular acoustic quality of the nasal obstruent. As a result, the nasal obstruents are all voiced sounds, since there cannot be enough differentiation between unvoiced nasal obstruents to be of linguistic use. Nasals are also the first obstruents that can be classified as "continuants", since they can be produced continuously from the beginning of the breath impulse to the end.

> **Are nasals really obstruents?**
> *Well, we certainly are obstructing something: the oral cavity. In fact, we are stopping it altogether. So, yes.*
>
> *But we aren't obstructing the voiced airflow at all, because it is escaping unimpeded through the nose, unless you have a cold. So, no. Still, the International Phonetic Association classes Nasals as "consonants" that require obstruction – i.e. obstruents. Bear this in mind when we start to consider "r"s , "l"s "w"s and "j"s, all of which many phoneticians say are not in any way obstruent.*

Trills

These are all voiced in spoken language, although all of them *could* be produced as unvoiced sounds. Each involves bringing an articulator to the point of closure, as in a plosive, but simultaneously increasing the energy of the flow, so that the articulator(s) are forced rapidly open and shut, producing their own pattern of vibration (but one much slower than the vibratory action of the vocal folds).

Taps or flaps

The same physical action as in a trill, except that the articulator is immediately dropped away from the extreme intrusion into the pressure flow after one (tap) or a few (flap) vibrations.

Fricatives

The largest category of obstruents. All fricatives are **continuant** sounds which can be produced throughout the entire flow of air or vibration. They are also the only obstruent group that can produce differentiated, linguistically useful, sounds – both unvoiced and voiced – in *all* places of articulation in the vocal tract. As the name suggests, fricatives are sounds that derive from a kind of friction: the narrowing of the passage of air or voice flow to the point where there is genuine impedance to the pattern of the flow. So the articulator is brought very close to another articulator or to a point of articulation, without actually closing the space off. One can register the focus of a fricative, unvoiced or voiced, very clearly within the vocal tract

Approximants

These are formed very much like fricatives, but with the articulator intruding only very slightly into the flow of air or vibration. If a fricative is the rock jutting out of the whitewater torrent with the water whooshing around it, the approximant is your toe dipped into the same stream. You can feel it, but it doesn't get in the way of the flow very much. In most cases in connected speech they are voiced because the obstruction is so slight that the unvoiced version does not produce a differentiated sound. But there is still an obstruction: you can prove it to yourself when you enact approximants because – like the toe in the stream – you can just feel the vibratory reaction in the articulator, usually the lips or the tongue, at the point of placement. The tingle of vibration is so slight that most linguists do not class approximants as obstruents, preferring terms like "sonorants" or "semi-vowels." I maintain that even a tiny obstruction is an obstruction.

Laterals

Fricative and approximant. All other sounds can be classified as "central" – that is, the flow proceeds directly down the middle of the vocal tract. But laterals (the "l" sounds) are partially formed by bringing the tongue up to the roof of the mouth, requiring the flow to divide laterally and go around the sides of the tongue. If this action impedes the flow considerably, it is a fricative; if it intrudes only slightly, it is an approximant.

Affricates

There is only one unvoiced/voiced pair of affricate sounds in American English. In other languages there are more sets. Actually affricates introduce no new actions because each is composed of a stop-plosive in which the articulator leaves the point of articulation slightly more slowly than usual, so that the explosion of air or voice registers briefly as a fricative sound.

All the sounds produced so far are **pulmonic.** This means that the flow is moving out of the body through the vocal tract in a muscular torso action that is causing the lungs to exhale. All British and American English speech sounds are pulmonic sounds. However, this is not our only option, and many languages incorporate sounds that are wholly or partially **non-pulmonic.** The only constant physical requirement is that there is a flow in some direction through some part of the vocal tract that can be shaped physically into differentiated sound.

Clicks

These are all unvoiced. They all start with the jaw raised so that the mouth is closed, and the general action of a click is to bring the lips or tongue-tip or tongue-blade or tongue dorsum (body) into complete closure (a "stop") and then to open the jaw quickly with the back of the tongue and the velum (soft palate) or uvula still completely sealed to the roof of the mouth (**velaric closure**), so that air is drawn suddenly into the oral cavity. The articulation energy is put into keeping the differentiating articulators sufficiently tense at the point of articulation so that they lag behind a bit when the jaw is opened, and then spring open instantly to allow the air to fill the oral cavity.

Voiced implosives

These are all voiced sounds, which naturally implies that the flow is coming from deeper in the body than the vocal folds in order to produce that voicing. And so it is. But it is still not pulmonic, because the flow is being pulled by a vacuum created in the oral cavity, not pushed by muscular action from the torso. The action of voiced implosives is much the same as for the clicks: there is a complete closure, or "stop," at some point in the oral cavity, from the lips to the uvula. The velum is raised to stop airflow through the nasal cavity in either direction. However, in voiced implosives the tongue and velum are not sealed together as in clicks, but the vocal folds come together to produce voice, so that, as the jaw is dropped, the voiced flow is pulled up from the lungs.

Before we add the last element, you can practice just this part of the recipe. Bring the lips together (but it could be anywhere else in the oral cavity), raise the velum to cut off the flow from the nasal cavity, put the vocal folds in "voicing position", and then drop the jaw strongly while simultaneously pulling the larynx down, using the extrinsic laryngeal muscles. You can check this by putting your hand lightly on your Adam's apple. As the jaw goes down, you should feel the larynx drop. You will produce an interesting sound reminiscent of a baby alligator still in its egg. (And you never know when, as an actor, you may need to use this.) There is one last step to produce the actual voiced implosive. While you are dropping the jaw, allow the lips (at least in this illustrative example) to drop apart: this last action causes the voiced airflow to be pulled by the vacuum in the oral cavity *inward* in a plosive action at the lips, producing an *imploded* rather than *exploded* sound product.

Ejectives

We are all aware that the muscles around the larynx can be used to pull the larynx up and down. We have just experienced the downward action in the voiced implosive. In English sounds this action is irrelevant, and usually signifies a residual tension pattern in effecting pitch change, especially when singing. But in some languages the sharp upward action of the larynx actually serves to push air out of the vocal tract, without the lungs or the torso generally becoming involved at all. In order to accomplish this, the vocal folds (and probably the false vocal folds also) must be kept tightly closed, so that this is considered a **glottal closure.** All the sounds that result from this ejective action are necessarily unvoiced sounds because the glottis cannot move. All except one are essentially ejective plosives; one is an ejective fricative (though more are physically possible). It is possible to have ejective fricatives as well as ejective stop-plosives

Points of obstruent focus

- **Bilabial.** An action focused at both lips, by bringing to lips to or toward one another.

- **Labiodental.** An action focused at the lower lip and upper teeth by bringing the lip to, or toward, the upper teeth.

- **Dental/alveolar/postalveolar.** The tip of the tongue at the upper teeth, or at the gum ridge ("alveolum") right behind the upper teeth, or just behind the gum ridge on the very front of the palate.

- **Retroflex.** The name means curled back, so that the tongue is curled up and back to give a focal point in the middle or back of the palate. This is the furthest focus back in the mouth that can be accomplished by the tip of the tongue.

- **Palatal.** This is accomplished by focusing the front of the tongue (which is *behind* the tip and the blade) toward, or to, the palate.

- **Velar.** The middle of the tongue is focused toward, or to, the velum (the soft palate).

- **Uvular.** The back of the tongue is focused toward, or to, the uvula, which hangs down from the back of the velum. In practice, unless a trill is desired, the tongue focuses toward the very back of the velum.

Figure 47. Labiodentals. (Cartoon by Bethany Carlson from *SpecGram*, Vol. CLXI, No. 2 (March 2011), reproduced by permission.)

○ **Pharyngeal.** The root of the tongue is retracted toward the back wall of the throat, the pharynx.

○ **Epiglottal.** The tongue root is retracted, almost as though one is beginning to swallow. This brings the epiglottis down in back, where subglottal air pressure can produce either stop-plosive or fricative sounds.

○ **Glottal.** The vocal folds are brought toward one another, or together, in a speech action differentiated from their rapid vibration in voiced sound.

Now we are ready to explore our recipe, to combine these elements:

1 Unvoiced or voiced −

2 The placement, from bilabial to glottal, and finally −

3 The action from most obstructive (stop-plosives) to the least obstructive (approximants)

into the obstruent combinations that form the sounds of language and also the sounds that *could* be found in language. We can always add phthongs between single or clustered obstruents to form full language actions.

There is one final element that can enter our recipe on occasion. Most of the time when we speak, the flow of unvoiced or voiced air travels forward along the midline of the tongue, sometimes narrowly, sometimes broadly. On some sounds, though, we raise the tip upward, or bunch the midline of the dorsum of the tongue upward, so that the flow is divided into two streams that flow around the sides of the tongue. These are the lateral actions, and when they occur we need to note that fact in our recipe also.

10 The empty obstruent chart

The way that the International Phonetic Association has chosen to represent obstruent (*aka* consonant) IPA symbols is by placing them on a set of graphs. The so-called "pulmonic" symbols are displayed on a standard graph with an X-axis and a Y-axis. Each row represents a different physical action used in obstructing the flow; each column represents a different placement or focal point for that obstruction within the articulators.

The rows of different actions start at the top with the most obstructive action (stop-plosives) and end at the bottom row with the least obstructive (the lateral approximants). The columns begin at the left (as though in a left profile of the mouth) with the most forward articulators – the lips – and end on the right with the articulators at the base of the vocal tract, the glottis – the space between the vocal folds.

Each cell in the graph, therefore, represents the possible site of one physical action combined with one placement of that action within the vocal tract. In the actual IPA chart, symbols are placed in many – *but not all* – of those squares. Some squares are empty because the action/placement combination they would represent is considered by the IPA to be physically impossible to produce; some squares could easily be filled with a symbol, but no symbol has been placed there simply because the IPA has not noted its use in any existing language – yet.

Some cells in the IPA pulmonic obstruent chart have two symbols in them, one toward the left side of the rectangle and one toward the right side. The symbol on the left is unvoiced; the symbol of the right is voiced. For now, assume that you might be able to produce both a unvoiced and voiced sound for each cell. This won't always be true, but give it a try.

We don't need the actual symbols yet. All we need to know are these ground rules for the graphs. If you look at the pulmonic chart, you will note that it contains no symbols at all in the squares. However, the information along each axis of the graph will give us all the information we need to fill in the sound actions. We can discover for ourselves which sound actions are possible to enact and which ones can also be easily used in language, even if we don't yet know the language into which they might fit.

Exploring the empty obstruent chart

Starting with the pulmonic chart, and starting with the stop-plosive actions, explore out loud the unvoiced and voiced sound possibilities in each placement. Continue this exploration with all the remaining action/placement combinations in the pulmonic chart. Which action/placement combinations can be performed easily and also provide a clear differentiation of sound for the listener? If the sound meets those two criteria, it probably (though not certainly) has a place in some existing language.

Explore each pulmonic obstruent as though it were the initial obstruent in a one-syllable word, followed by the phthong "aaah",

There are still going to be a few sound actions missing from the pulmonic chart, including an unvoiced/voiced pair that is common in English. For such sounds there is a category in the International Phonetic Alphabet entitled "Other Symbols". Most of them involve what we would consider **co-articulations,** sounds that are produced by using more than one placement of articulators, simultaneously. In the case of the pair of sounds from English,

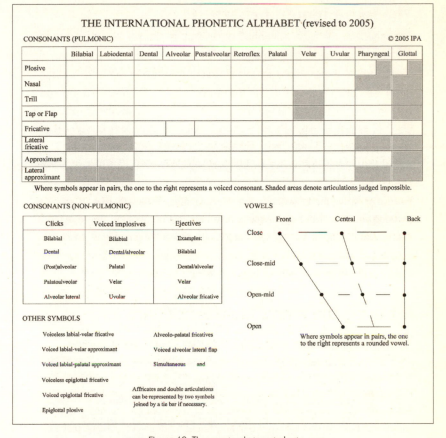

THE INTERNATIONAL PHONETIC ALPHABET (revised to 2005)

CONSONANTS (PULMONIC)   © 2005 IPA

	Bilabial	Labiodental	Dental	Alveolar	Postalveolar	Retroflex	Palatal	Velar	Uvular	Pharyngeal	Glottal
Plosive											
Nasal											
Trill											
Tap or Flap											
Fricative											
Lateral fricative											
Approximant											
Lateral approximant											

Where symbols appear in pairs, the one to the right represents a voiced consonant. Shaded areas denote articulations judged impossible.

CONSONANTS (NON-PULMONIC)

Clicks	Voiced implosives	Ejectives
Bilabial	Bilabial	Examples:
Dental	Dental/alveolar	Bilabial
(Post)alveolar	Palatal	Dental/alveolar
Palatoalveolar	Velar	Velar
Alveolar lateral	Uvular	Alveolar fricative

VOWELS

Front   Central   Back

Close

Close-mid

Open-mid

Open

Where symbols appear in pairs, the one to the right represents a rounded vowel.

OTHER SYMBOLS

Voiceless labial-velar fricative

Voiced labial-velar approximant

Voiced labial-palatal approximant

Voiceless epiglottal fricative

Voiced epiglottal fricative

Epiglottal plosive

Alveolo-palatal fricatives

Voiced alveolar lateral flap

Simultaneous   and

Affricates and double articulations
can be represented by two symbols
joined by a tie bar if necessary.

Figure 48. The empty obstruent chart.
(Please see www.langsci.ucl.ac.uk/ipa/ for original charts.)

the co-articulation involves the lips. Notice that all the "bilabial" actions in the pulmonic chart are performed by "pursing" the lips – that is, bringing the margins of the lips evenly together or close to one another. The common English sound pair we are looking for here uses that pursing action, but combines it with lip-corner advancement (or protrusion) to produce a full lip rounding. This information should be sufficient to allow you to find the sound pair. We can leave the other sounds until we need to learn all the symbols themselves.

The non-pulmonic chart

The graph for the "non-pulmonic" obstruents is simpler as represented in the empty obstruent chart of page 95.. There is only one row across the top indicating the three actions for initiating and obstructing the flow, and then the three columns tell us where these actions are placed within the vocal tract in actual language. There are probably more placements possible, so you can explore vocally beyond the ones shown in the graph. Make sure that you carefully review the actions as described in the preceding section, since these are unfamiliar to most American speakers.

Practice speaking the following recipes for obstruents. Follow them with any phthong you wish. Not every recipe is here but most of them are. Some of these sounds are not found in language, but they are physically possible to enact.

voiced bilabial stop-plosive	voiced post-alveolar lateral approximant
unvoiced velar fricative	voiced post-alveolar fricative
voiced retroflex nasal	voiced post-alveolar tap
unvoiced labio-dental fricative	unvoiced bi-labial fricative
voiced post-alveolar approximant	voiced velar stop-plosive
unvoiced velar stop-plosive	voiced bi-labial implosive
unvoiced uvular fricative	voiced velar approximant
voiced glottal stop-plosive	unvoiced alveolar fricative
voiced post-alveolar trill	voiced labial-velar approximant
unvoiced bilabial trill	voiced bilabial approximant
unvoiced alveolar stop-plosive	unvoiced lateral palatal fricative
unvoiced lateral velar fricative	unvoiced labiodental approximant
unvoiced velar ejective	voiced velar trill (The IPA says you can't!)
voiced dental fricative	voiced bilabial fricative
voiced labio-dental approximant	voiced palatal stop-plosive
unvoiced palatal fricative	voiced epiglottal stop-plosive
unvoiced retroflex stop-plosive	unvoiced labio-dental fricative
voiced uvular trill	unvoiced pharyngeal fricative
unvoiced labial-velar fricative	voiced labial-palatal fricative

unvoiced post-alveolar fricative   unvoiced bilabial ejective
voiced pharyngeal fricative   unvoiced postalveolar click
voiced labio-dental flap   voiced alveolar stop-plosive
unvoiced alveolar fricative   voiced retroflex lateral approximant
voiced palatal nasal   unvoiced dental fricative
voiced retroflex approximant   voiced uvular implosive

11 Making your own language

Omnish and beyond

You now have a full repertoire of the distinct vocal sounds that are used in language. They are not the only vocal sounds that we can make: as we know, even the IPA chart omits some very easy-to-perform sounds. For example, the Voiced Bilabial Trill [ʙ] made it onto the chart in the 1989 revision because linguists observed its use in two languages of New Guinea. But we have been using it as a communicative vocalization to indicate cold ("brrrrr") for possibly thousands of years in many languages. The Unvoiced Bilabial Trill that we often use as a lip release exercise (or to imitate a horse) is not (yet) heard as a phonemic component of language, and so is absent from the IPA chart of obstruents. You have proved that it is possible in the preceding exercises. So we can include the unvoiced version in the work that follows.

We can now begin to explore the feel of these sound-actions when used in combination. This is play, pure and simple, and like all the best forms of play it will inform as well as entertain. It will tell you a good deal about where in the vocal tract you can open your articulators to more active and demanding use. It will tell you what sound combinations are easier or more difficult to enact. No real language contains the entire IPA, so we know that what we are attempting here – using *all* the possible sound actions – is an exercise, not a replication of any particular language.

1 **"Gibberish".**   This is spoken language – here American English – without sense; that is, without meaning attached to any of the "words". Say a "nonsense word" using the obstruent and phthong sounds we use in English. "shleeft, rawv, aglackle, mostawhech, toofler, omzayidge, bopongah" are just a few possibilities. Practice single "gibberish words" until you are sure that you are using only the sound actions we use in English. Now continue this action into connected speech, improvising a conversation with a partner using American English sounds, but not in the usual American English sound combinations. Avoid speaking any actual English words. Keep the jaw relaxed open as much as possible and keep the other articulators active. *Feel* the sounds and be aware of expressing emotional content through the sound combinations. But do not "translate" actual sentences into your "Gibberish". Let impulse take over: observe your partner when she or he is speaking; listen to your partner attentively, to the sounds your partner is making and to the way your partner is saying them. Then let impulse take over and let your own sound combinations respond. You could do this same excercise for any language, but the sound combinations would be different.

◀))) **Audio track 23:** *Gibberish.*

2 **Individual Omnish.**   Relax the jaw open. Begin to speak consonant and vowel combinations using *all* the language sounds possible in the IPA categories of action and placement, including non-pulmonic consonants, whether or not they actually exist in the languages of the world. You will discover that this requires much greater dexterity of articulation than in the previous exercise. After a bit of practice you will discover that you have moved from "Gibberish" to what we will henceforth call "Omnish", from the Latin word *omnis* meaning "all". *Make sure that you observe the restrictions for articulation actions that we find in language. Don't go back to Outlandish.*

◀))) **Audio track 24:** *Omnish.*

3 **Paired Omnish I.** With a partner listening closely to you, speak energetically in Omnish for one minute. At the moment you are not trying to convey specific meaning as you speak, you are just trying to use as many of the sounds of world language as you can in a coherent sequence. Your partner will tell you if you are achieving enough variety – or too much, for that matter. For example, you may repeat several sound actions again and again but fail to move on to other ones. Or you may leave out whole categories of sound actions. Or you may achieve a great variety in consonants but very little in vowels. Or you may find that you are doing a lot of consonant sound-actions that are not found in language at all. Speak Omnish again – just for the sounds – and see if you can correct these limitations so that you are speaking all the actions and all the placements of world language within that one minute.

4 **Paired Omnish II** (*lento*). Speak Omnish *very* slowly. Still pay no attention to "meaning", just to the sounds themselves. Feel and enjoy the new combinations of sound actions. Register in your own mind the actions and placements of the articulators as you are going through them. Get feedback from your partner about variety of sound-action choice as before. If you persist in leaving out certain actions or placements, do some focused practice favoring those sounds, and afterward open out into full Omnish again.

5 **Paired Omnish III** (*presto*). Speak rapidly and crisply as though you were acting in a sophisticated comedy written in Omnish. Your partner will tell you if your variety or fluency is suffering because of your accelerated speech.

6 **Group Omnish I.** The group should form a circle. The person who begins will speak a single Omnish "word" of no more than three syllables in a clear, energetic voice to the next person in the circle. The speaker should speak the "word" slowly as though s/he is trying to teach the sound to the listener. The next person will repeat the "word" back and – if correct – will then generate a new "word" for the next person. The person listening will try to receive the necessary information about the speaker's articulator action and placement from the sound itself and from whatever s/he can observe about the speaker's articulator action.

7 **Group Omnish II** (*added meaning*). The person who begins should advance toward another person somewhere in the circle and say something (but no more than a sentence or two) to that person in Omnish. Try to convey a

specific verbal message in Omnish. Let the physical carriage and gestures support the words. Go further: let the sounds of this rich language shape and move the body, and let yourself feel the sounds center where they will through the entire body. The person spoken to should reply appropriately to the first speaker (*not* repeating what the first speaker said), and then find someone else in the circle and say something to that person. Continue until everyone has been spoken to and has spoken. Keep the exchange moving along, and keep it energized and varied.

Analyze the results, whether from the individual or the group exercises in Omnish. Are the speakers starting to feel fluent using all the sounds in language? Do some sound combinations feel easier to execute than others?

However comfortable it feels – and it will feel comfortable with a little attentive practice – Omnish in a very real sense is an "unreal" language. Why? How do you experience the feel of the language as you speak it? Aside from the greater variety, how does it feel different from Gibberish, or just speaking English, or from speaking any other language you might know?

8   **An Omnish oration** (*adding more meaning*).   As a leading citizen of the nation of Omnia (its national motto translates from the Omnish as "All Things to All People") you speak fluently a language (Omnish) that contains all the sounds that might be found in the IPA. Since you are a candidate for office in the lowest legislative chamber (of twelve) in the Omnian legislature, devise a short (two minutes approximately) campaign speech, spoken entirely in Omnish, that contains the following elements:

a   A short opening joke.

b   A scathing rebuttal to the latest charges from your opponent.

c   A moving tribute to His/Her Serene Omniscience, the King/Queen/President/ Facilitator/Dictator/Chair of Omnia.

d   About fifteen seconds of upbeat generalities about your legislative program.

e   A big finish (balloon drop optional).

Other members of the class should portray your audience and should feel encouraged to respond vocally in Omnish as well.

9 **The Omnish Poet Laureate.** This is an exercise for two persons working together. One person plays the role of a famous Omnian poet visiting an English-speaking country. The other person is the poet's translator.

The translator conducts the proceedings and begins with by introducing the poet in English. The poet then begins reciting a poem in Omnish. After a line or two, the poet pauses as the translator provides a translation into English. This continues throughout the rest of the poem.

Under no circumstances should this exercise be rehearsed in advance.

One of the many virtues of this exercise is that the translator and also the poet will be encouraged by the form of the performance to listen to each other closely and to pick up cues from the other person as to the progress of the poem. These cues will relate primarily to the sounds employed, but will also be found in intonation patterns, timing and gestural signals.

10 **Serious Omnish.** In exploring Omnish it is useful to perform the new sounds as actively as possible because the feeling of the action is easier for us to register. Because these new sounds lie outside our familiar American English repertoire, many of them will seem odd or comic precisely because of that unfamiliarity. Don't let this fact deter you from trying them out. Dive right into this new ocean of sounds and splash about in them. Revel in their unfamiliarity. Let them seem funny – or ugly even: we all have our biases about language sounds and we all make judgments about them all the time. Get all this out of your system.

At the same time, if we stay too long in the ocean we may get swept away by the tide and never get back to firm ground. If we find these new language sounds strange, it is only because we limit ourselves to certain sounds when we speak American English – sounds which, when we speak them, sound equally odd or amusing to speakers of other languages. Language sounds are not *objectively* funny or ugly. It is only our cultural or personal biases that make them seem so. All of the sounds in Omnish are used in one or another of the world's languages to express the entire range of human thought and emotion. They are all taken seriously by somebody.

To move past the barrier of stereotyping language sounds, choose a serious dramatic text in English that is deeply meaningful to you. "Translate" it into

Omnish. Don't actually write down any sounds or memorize a "script"; just let your impulse say in Omnish what the words are in English. Perform it for your class and try to communicate the text in Omnish with as great a degree of sensitivity or profundity as you find in the original.

The skills of Omnish

Just as we practice and gradually perfect the skills of speaking any language, so we can practice and perfect the skills of Omnish, a task made considerably easier by the fact that we don't have to deal with precise vocabulary or grammar. There is a real benefit in becoming a fluent Omnian, however. Omnish, if done correctly, is possibly the best articulation warm-up that we can try. It provides greater muscular activity than any repetition of "tongue-twisters" and it does so in a way that works to free you from the habitual patterns of articulation formed by your own native accent without negating that accent. Tongue-twisters, however enjoyable they are to say, focus on only a few sound combinations of English or another language (most languages have tongue-twisters). They don't really invite you to embody new possibilities. Furthermore, Omnish is more physically demanding than any individual language; it strengthens articulators and frees them simultaneously.

In order to give yourself this effective warm-up, you have to make sure that you are really including over (say) a minute of Omnish speaking a complete repertoire of pulmonic and non-pulmonic obstruents as well as all the possible gradations of phthong-shaping. This takes practice. Here are a few ways to do it:

1   As you are speaking Omnish, focus on a few actions or points of placement and make sure that you are including them in the mix. You can actually refer to your Empty Consonant Charts (pulmonic and non-pulmonic) as you are speaking. If you are in a class, your teacher may call out actions or focal points as a coaching technique. Remind yourself to use both unvoiced and voiced obstruents. Some actions and placements that commonly are ignored are:

  a   Palatals

  b   Retroflex

  c   Trills

  d   Uvular

  e   Nasal (including nasal phthongs)

  f   Pharyngeal

  g   Approximants

  h   Clicks

  i   Voiced implosives

  j   Ejectives

II If you find that you are starting to sound as though you are speaking a parti-cular language in "double-talk" – nonsense words to feign another language – you are focusing too much on certain sounds. This usually means that there is a held tension pattern in your vocal tract that needs to be released. It can also mean that you are using a limited repertoire of phthongs.

III Really pay attention to keeping your speech actions in the world of Omnish. It is very tempting to slip back into the extravagance of Outlandish. Be careful about this.

IV Just as in fine dining, where the waiter brings you a little sorbet between courses as a "palate-cleanser" to free you from the taste of the sautéed sweetbreads and to ready you for the roast buffalo, so you can cleanse your palate (not to mention your velum) in Omnish by throwing in a word or short phrase in English just the way you'd speak it every fifteen seconds or so, as though the Omnian you are embodying is a really good mimic of the real you. This simple technique is really useful for getting you away from Outlandish.

Outward / inward

The progression from Gibberish to Omnish is a progression into a greater variety of articulator action. We have been opening out our possibilities. The next step is to reverse the process and move from more variety to less. Our purpose is to focus in on the physicality of real languages. For the time being we will leave Outlandish out of the picture; it is a very useful exploration for character voices or for imitations of sounds that go beyond human speech, but because we are going to explore the feel of accents and languages as they exist in the real world we will focus back in starting from Omnish.

11 **Finding a new language from the feel of the sounds: "Double-talk".**

Create for yourself a physical focus of tension and relaxation in the articulators, using basic variables, such as:

a   Jaw height.

b   Jaw advancement or retraction.

c   Tongue-arching or cupping. Forward or back, high or low.

d   Tongue root-advancement or retraction.

e   Channeling (widening and flattening) or bunching (narrowing and thickening) the tongue.

f   Relaxation or tensing of the cheeks into the teeth.

g   Advancement or retraction of the lip corners.

h   Pursing or relaxation of the lips.

i   Raising or lowering the velum.

j   Bracing the side edges of the body of the tongue against the teeth.

Remember that not all these variables will necessarily be in play. Especially at the start, it is easier to focus on only a few and hear what effect they produce on sound change. What you will come up with, though, is something that every language and every dialect of every language has: a characteristic vocal tract **posture**. This is the pattern of muscular tension and relaxation within the vocal tract that provides the "home base" to which the muscles would naturally return. The posture has an effect on everything connected with articulation: what obstruents you use, what phthongs you use, and the resonance patterns of your speech.

Less is more. If you overdo these changes, you will always come out with a result that sounds more like an individual with a speech pathology issue than someone with an accent. It is useful to try to make minimal changes in posture and then to see what effect these have on your speech. Understand that every change, however small, will change the sound pattern if you allow it to do so. This takes some trust in letting the physicality lead the process. It also takes some practice.

Start with the single phthong that the posture produces. Let it release with easy but supported vocal energy. Then **shimmer** the posture. This means that you should start to produce micro-movements of the articulators around that phthong without losing the posture as a "home base" for the action. Then gradually increase the activity of the shimmer to add obstruents.

Now begin to speak connected sound combinations fully – a new sort of gibberish. Just let the sounds come, and feel how the actions of the articulators – especially the lip and tongue actions – tend to start self-selecting their own preferred sounds. Feel and enjoy the sounds that your articulators seem to want to say; gradually you may let go of the sounds that your articulators don't seem to want to say very frequently.

Make sure that you do not hold the articulators tightly or rigidly in these postures. If you do you, may not be able to talk at all! The sound actions your articulators take can move away from the chosen posture; they should simply favor moving back toward them and favor sounds that are nearer to these articulator postures. You should still be able to speak as fluently and easily as you did in Omnish – more easily, actually, because your articulators will favor some sound actions over others.

You have now formed a new (non-sense) language physically in a way that is much more real than Omnish or Outlandish, and one that probably has a very definite and characteristic feel or focus to it. It may sound to you like some "double-talk" version of an existing language that you have heard, or it may sound completely new.

Finally, keeping the same focus, the same interplay of muscular tension and relaxation that you just used for your newly created language, begin to speak in English. If you are clear about maintaining the focus, you will definitely produce some sort of "foreign accent". Maybe you will recognize it; maybe you won't. It may even turn out to sound more like an accent pattern from a dialect of English. But you are still experiencing the dynamic tug-of-war between the original language focus (and sounds) and the English focus (and sounds) which is characteristic of all foreign accent speaking.

🔊 **Audio track 25:** *Create an oral posture language.*

🔊 **Audio track 26:** *Create an oral posture accent.*

12 **Finding an accent.** Create a new vocal tract posture, quite arbitrarily, and see what happens when you start to speak through it in English. Is it a recognizable – or nearly recognizable – accent of English from wherever English is spoken as a primary language? Or is it another foreign accent? What physical changes do you need to make to fine-tune it to a recognizable accent in English or a foreign accent?

13 **Finding the "posture" of an accent.** Do an imitation of an accent, in English or from another language, which you can mimic but which is not your own. Speak in that accent for at least a minute. As you listen to yourself, pick out the most important or unique sound changes, the sounds that are strongly different from the way you usually articulate vowels and consonants in your own everyday speech. Now repeat each of these unique sounds several times. As you do so, feel what each one of them tells you about the comfortable posture of that action in your mouth. What is the larger pattern of muscular tension and relaxation in the articulators that requires the sound to be produced in that way?

And now the big question: what do these individual patterns of tension and relaxation have in common for each unique sound action? They might, for example, all work better if the jaw is raised quite high and if the tongue is tensed with the front section strongly cupped. Or another combination might be with the jaw very slightly raised, the tongue tip retroflex, and the buccinator muscles of the cheek slightly braced. Continue to speak in the accent, but stay with the feel of the focus, rather than thinking constantly about the succession of individual sound changes.

Individual sound awareness can remain a very useful corrective when the focus of an accent starts to go astray, but allowing yourself to feel the overall posture of the accent allows you to focus on the many other important elements of the acting process. Finding the posture of the accent helps you to act through the accent rather than getting lost in its mechanics. A postural approach allows the accent to become a physical embodiment of your character's speech – just as your entire bodily posture is an embodiment of your character's movement onstage. So you can focus on behaving as the character, not on enacting the accent.

A world of possibilities opens to us.

But alas, this is not a book that will focus on accent acquisition. So, while it is a wonderful enterprise to use the physical skills that you have acquired to explore many different accents and different language pronunciations based on the characteristic posture of each accent, we will focus in to a narrower area for the remainder of this text. Our language will be English, and more specifically American English. We will apply all these skills to the variable possibilities of speaking American English to others.

We have actually acquired a formidable array of physical skills in articulation. Now the question arises: how do we communicate those gradations of sound-change to others in an efficient manner, and how do we record them for ourselves?

An interlude

A daily articulation warm-up

1   Stand or sit so that your spine is aligned and your neck is released into length. Your head should be balanced at the top of the spine at your occipital joint. Relax your jaw open into a nice, dumb expression. Let all your facial muscles relax.

2   Massage your muscles of expression, starting on your scalp, working downward with circular fingertip massage. Massage the orbicularis oculi muscles with the palms of your hands. Then continue with the tips of your fingers around your nose, around your ears, into your cheeks and lips, ending at the masseter muscles of the jaw. Massage the masseter muscles of the jaw with moderate vigor, reminding yourself to let the jaw release open with a forward-and-down "energy flow".

3   Spread the fingers of both hands and gently stroke directly downward on the face with your fingertips from scalp to jaw bone. Repeat at least five times.

4   Repeat the "Great all-purpose jaw release exercise" at least five times.

5   With the jaw relaxed open – its "home base" for speaking – focus your attention on your natural, easy tidal breathing. Feel the even sensation of the air moving ingressively and egressively through the vocal tract. It you feel the air flow focusing at any point in the vocal tract, focus your attention on letting that area release open.

6   Send a slightly greater volume of egressive and ingressive unvoiced air flow through the vocal tract and use the articulators to engage in "unvoiced

111

phthong shaping". Note if you start to feel any obstruction of the flow at all, and adjust the articulator action to avoid it.

7 Send egressive voiced flow through the vocal tract. Without obstructing the flow, explore moving everything that will shape the sound. Do not change the "voice quality." Do not change the amplitude deliberately. Focus on "phthong shaping". Lead with the physical action: appreciate the resulting changes in sound product but do not look for any specific phthongs. Start with a slow-motion use of the articulators and then move the changes faster; finally, slow down again.

8 Start to obstruct the voiced egressive flow. Explore all the possibilities for obstruction, from stop-plosives to approximants and everything in between, while you continue all the phthong possibilities that you had in 6. You are now doing Omnish.

9 Speak for at least one minute in Omnish in the slow-motion version.

10 Speak for at least thirty seconds in fast Omnish.

11 Speak for at least one minute in Omnish at a normal conversational rate. Relax.

Part 3
Phonetics

THE INTERNATIONAL PHONETIC ALPHABET (revised to 2005)

CONSONANTS (PULMONIC)

© 2005 IPA

	Bilabial	Labiodental	Dental	Alveolar	Postalveolar	Retroflex	Palatal	Velar	Uvular	Pharyngeal	Glottal
Plosive	p b			t d		ʈ ɖ	c ɟ	k ɡ	q ɢ		ʔ
Nasal	m	ɱ		n		ɳ	ɲ	ŋ	ɴ		
Trill	ʙ			r					ʀ		
Tap or Flap		ⱱ		ɾ		ɽ					
Fricative	ɸ β	f v	θ ð	s z	ʃ ʒ	ʂ ʐ	ç ʝ	x ɣ	χ ʁ	ħ ʕ	h ɦ
Lateral fricative				ɬ ɮ							
Approximant		ʋ		ɹ		ɻ	j	ɰ			
Lateral approximant				l		ɭ	ʎ	ʟ			

Where symbols appear in pairs, the one to the right represents a voiced consonant. Shaded areas denote articulations judged impossible.

CONSONANTS (NON-PULMONIC)

Clicks		Voiced implosives		Ejectives	
ʘ	Bilabial	ɓ	Bilabial	'	Examples:
ǀ	Dental	ɗ	Dental/alveolar	p'	Bilabial
ǃ	(Post)alveolar	ʄ	Palatal	t'	Dental/alveolar
ǂ	Palatoalveolar	ɠ	Velar	k'	Velar
ǁ	Alveolar lateral	ʛ	Uvular	s'	Alveolar fricative

OTHER SYMBOLS

ʍ Voiceless labial-velar fricative	ɕ ʑ Alveolo-palatal fricatives
w Voiced labial-velar approximant	ɺ Voiced alveolar lateral flap
ɥ Voiced labial-palatal approximant	ɧ Simultaneous ʃ and x
ʜ Voiceless epiglottal fricative	
ʢ Voiced epiglottal fricative	Affricates and double articulations can be represented by two symbols joined by a tie bar if necessary. k͡p t͡s
ʡ Epiglottal plosive	

VOWELS

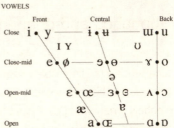

Where symbols appear in pairs, the one to the right represents a rounded vowel.

SUPRASEGMENTALS

ˈ	Primary stress
ˌ	Secondary stress ˌfoʊnəˈtɪʃən
ː	Long eː
ˑ	Half-long eˑ
˘	Extra-short ĕ
ǀ	Minor (foot) group
ǁ	Major (intonation) group
.	Syllable break ɹi.ækt
‿	Linking (absence of a break)

DIACRITICS

Diacritics may be placed above a symbol with a descender, e.g. ŋ̊

̥ Voiceless	n̥ d̥	̤ Breathy voiced	b̤ a̤	̪ Dental	t̪ d̪
̬ Voiced	s̬ t̬	̰ Creaky voiced	b̰ a̰	̺ Apical	t̺ d̺
ʰ Aspirated	tʰ dʰ	̼ Linguolabial	t̼ d̼	̻ Laminal	t̻ d̻
̹ More rounded	ɔ̹	ʷ Labialized	tʷ dʷ	̃ Nasalized	ẽ
̜ Less rounded	ɔ̜	ʲ Palatalized	tʲ dʲ	ⁿ Nasal release	dⁿ
̟ Advanced	u̟	ˠ Velarized	tˠ dˠ	ˡ Lateral release	dˡ
̠ Retracted	e̠	ˤ Pharyngealized	tˤ dˤ	̚ No audible release	d̚
̈ Centralized	ë	̴ Velarized or pharyngealized	ɫ		
̽ Mid-centralized	ě	̝ Raised	e̝	(ɹ̝ = voiced alveolar fricative)	
̩ Syllabic	n̩	̞ Lowered	e̞	(β̞ = voiced bilabial approximant)	
̯ Non-syllabic	e̯	̘ Advanced Tongue Root	e̘		
˞ Rhoticity	ɚ a˞	̙ Retracted Tongue Root	e̙		

TONES AND WORD ACCENTS

LEVEL				CONTOUR		
e̋ or	˥	Extra high	ě or	˩˥	Rising	
é	˦	High	ê	˥˩	Falling	
ē	˧	Mid	e᷄	˦˥	High rising	
è	˨	Low	e᷅	˩˨	Low rising	
ȅ	˩	Extra low	e᷈	˧˦˧	Rising-falling	
↓		Downstep	↗		Global rise	
↑		Upstep	↘		Global fall	

Figure 49. The International Phonetic Alphabet.
(Please see www.langsci.ucl.ac.uk/ipa/ for original charts.)

Introductory

Phonetics and phonemics: the obstruent version

The International Phonetic Association has assigned one written symbol to represent each differentiated sound that is used in language. One symbol = one sound. This makes phonetics completely different from the way we use symbols when we spell a word, even though many phonetic symbols are the same ones that we are familiar with in spelling.

If we allow that voicing or unvoicing is a physical action, we could go further and say that *each phonetic symbol equals a single, unique physical action.*

But the International Phonetic Association, in determining what actions get to be represented as symbols of the IPA, has established another parallel category: each IPA symbol must represent a single, unique unit of meaning within the larger combinations that comprise any given language. The study of **phonetics** is the study of articulator actions as they are used in languages and dialects of language in all their detail and subtlety of differentiation. This attention to detail causes it to differ from the broader study of **phonemics** or **phonology** in that scholars who focus on these latter terms are interested in articulation actions at the level of *meaning.* A good example of the difference as it relates to obstruents would be the "k" sound we produce at the start of the word "keel". We know that if we change the action to produce a "p" the actual meaning of those clustered sounds that we call a word would change, and would become "peel". Or we could change the action again and have "feel" or "seal" or "reel". Or we could let the obstruent sounds remain the same and change the phthong between them, and the meaning would change: "keel", "kill", "call", "cool". (Remember that those "k" and "c" spellings represent the same sound.) So in each case we would be making a *phonemic* change, and each one of those individual sounds that combine to form a word would be called a **phoneme**. When we change the symbol within word units, we change the meaning. So the symbols exist as representations of phonemes, not as their more dialectically detailed subdivisions, which are termed **allophones**.

But if we feel the placement of the "k" sound as we go through that progress of "keel", "kill", "call", "cool", we can register – by where the dorsum of the tongue touches the roof of the mouth – that the placement changes. The "k" in "keel" is certainly touching the back of the palate. The "k" in "cool" clearly is well back on the velum, almost at the uvula. Such allophone changes, though small, will be of great use to us in developing a regional or foreign accent, and they are all phonetically different from one another, which is why we study detailed phonetics in this text. But phonemically those allophone sounds are the same because they all convey that "k" contribution to the meaning of the word.

Sometimes we notate these subtle phonetic differences by using a different phonetic symbol, and sometimes we use smaller symbols above or below the line (called **diacritics**) to show the physical change of articulation in the mouth, nose, or throat. Sometimes, also (and mostly with vowels) we devise a map of the phonetic "territory" of a phoneme, so that the viewer (and the listener) can perceive visually where the allophones of that phoneme might live.

These two terms, *phonetic* and *phonemic,* are not always mutually exclusive in their application, but they obey different rules. Two similar but slightly different sounds that might be phonemically distinct in one language – actually changing the meaning of the word – might have a *phonetic* (but *not* phonemic) significance in another: despite being different physical actions producing slightly different sounds, they "mean" the same thing within the language and often are not perceived as being different at all by the listener and even by the speaker. We tend not to perceive differences if they are not important to us. Conversely, sounds that – in English, let's say – we would perceive as exactly the same, in another language may have a phonemic difference. In some Indian subcontinent languages, the difference between a voiced retroflex stop-plosive and a voiced alveolar stop-plosive is *phonemic* and changes the meaning of a word; in English, it's just a "d". The listener might think that the speaker of the retroflex version "has an accent", but we wouldn't question the meaning.

In practise, the fact that there are two parallel descriptions of what a phonetic/phonemic symbol is – a unique physical action or a meaning unit – doesn't get in our way too often. That's the good news . . .

Cartoon theories of linguistics

Figure 50. Phonemics.

Figure 51. Phonetics.

(Cartoons by Trey Jones from *SpecGram*, Vol. CLIII, No. 4 (September 2007), reproduced by permission.)

12 Writing it down

We now possess awareness and detailed experience of the physical actions and the physical placements of obstruents that produce sounds that we can hear as different from one another. We have also, in a more free-form way, explored the unobstructed shaping of voiced sound flow that we have been calling "phthongs". In the practice of Omnish, we have not limited these configurations of obstruents and phthongs to the sounds that are actually used in the languages of the world, but explored ways to limit them to the sounds that *could be* found in language.

But we know that Omnish is not where speech sounds live for speakers in the real world. Eloquent as Omnish is in its way, it doesn't actually mean anything that the speaker and the listener can agree on. In order to communicate commonly understood meaning, we have to combine the obstruents and phthongs into syllables and then into words. These words convey *conventionally understood* meanings within a given language – sound combinations that are filled with meaning. In moving into the articulation of actual language, we will find it very useful to be able to describe these more complex actions to others, and we will want to be able to write these descriptions down so that we can keep a record of these actions for our own use and also share our analysis with others.

We already have a recipe for the production of pulmonic and non-pulmonic obstruents, and a fair sense of what the articulators, especially the tongue and lips, do to shape phthongs; but trying to write down our perceptions using our current vocabulary would be extremely difficult and tiring. If we had to write "voiced bilabial stop-plosive *plus* strongly cupped (or open) unrounded front phthong *plus* unvoiced alveolar stop-plosive" in order to signify to the reader that we have written the English word "bat", the effort would discourage us from trying to communicate anything.

So it is obvious that we will need to reduce these lengthy descriptions of sound actions to single symbols that will convey the same information in a much more economical way. Our first conclusion might be that we already have just such a set of symbols: the Roman alphabet that we use every day in writing English.

But writing "bat" as "bat" has its problems, too; big ones. Assuming most readers of this book will be speakers of American English, we probably have a general agreement as to how those three letters (i.e., symbols) − "b", "a", and "t" − should be pronounced, at least in this word. But if we want to communicate the actual sounds that we are using to a person who does not know spoken English well, we could be giving that reader some non-precise information. The letter "a", for example, could be pronounced as a "short a" as in "ham", or as a "broad a" as in "calm", or as a "short e" as in "any", or even as a "short i" as in "average",

The classic illustration of the imprecision of English spelling (the technical term for "spelling" is **orthography**) was suggested by the famed Irish playwright George Bernard Shaw, who was an early advocate of simplified spelling. He pointed out that the word "fish" could as easily be spelled "ghoti", using the sounds found in the words "cough", "women", and "nation". English orthography is full of letters that have multiple sounds attached to them, as well as individual sounds that can be pronounced in multiple ways. If we really want to communicate what we are doing when we speak − let alone what we are doing when we speak in an accent −

we will have to come up with some system on notation that is more useful: a system of symbols that assigns a single symbol to every physical action of articulation that produces a sound that can be used in language. This is where the International Phonetic Alphabet comes in. And on page 114 we see what it looks like in its latest revision.

This is the complete chart of the International Phonetic Alphabet, hereafter the IPA. Your first reaction upon gazing at that chart might well be that it is incredibly complicated. But take heart: it really isn't. For one thing, if you're still practicing your Omnish, you're already doing nearly everything on the chart and you know the action recipe for each one of the sounds represented by all those symbols. For another thing, there aren't really that many symbols to learn. Take a close look at these charts: the entire Roman alphabet is contained within them, and it forms a large percentage of the total number of IPA symbols. I might even go so far as to claim that the most important skill you can bring to learning the IPA will *not* be learning new and unfamiliar symbols, but instead *ignoring* those ambiguities that are found in English spelling – because in the IPA each symbol stands for only one unique articulator action and placement. This is worth repeating, prominently:

Each IPA symbol stands for only ONE unique articulator action and placement

So, if we can ignore the different sounds for the spelled vowel "a" or the consonant "r", to take just two examples, we can easily use the Roman alphabet symbols that are already contained in the IPA charts.

Sounds to syllables

We all understand – intuitively and through our experience with language – what syllables are. This knowledge is valuable and will save us a lot of time and effort because the subject is still a source of debate among linguists and voice scientists. So any attempt at a technical definition of a syllable will probably be deficient in some way, certainly deficient to some expert in the field. Far better that we rely on our intuitive understanding and leave it at that.

We do know that a syllable can be as short as a single vowel, as in the "a" in "about". A syllable can form one monosyllabic word, as in "put" (with a very few sounds) or "clasped" (with more sounds). A single syllable can also be one part of a very long word, as in the *Mary Poppins* invention "supercalifragilisticexpialidocious". If we count the syllables is that word, we would all agree that there are fourteen of them, even if we haven't defined what a syllable is.

13 Writing the consonants

Now that we are focusing on writing down the symbols, we can let go of our word "obstruents" and go back to the more familiar term **"consonants"** to describe voiced or unvoiced sound actions that obstruct the flow. We start with consonants, rather than with "phthongs" ("vowels") because consonant actions physically are very clearly defined and differentiated from one another. Vowels (or phthongs) are more elusive – and therefore even more interesting. We will get to them soon.

What do we already know?
Take a good close look at the pulmonic consonant chart on the next page, now filled, or nearly filled, with phonetic symbols. Your first reaction may well be dismay. Our eyes are naturally drawn to the unfamiliar; and a lot of these symbols, at first glance, appear very unfamiliar indeed. But if you focus your attention on finding symbols that you already know, you will make a comforting discovery. So take another look.

	Bilabial	Labiodental	Dental	Alveolar	Postalveolar	Retroflex	Palatal	Velar	Uvular	Pharyngeal	Glottal
Plosive	p b			t d		ʈ ɖ	c ɟ	k ɡ	q ɢ		ʔ
Nasal	m	ɱ		n		ɳ	ɲ	ŋ	N		
Trill	B			r					R		
Tap or Flap		ⱱ		ɾ		ɽ					
Fricative	ɸ β	f v	θ ð	s z	ʃ ʒ	ʂ ʐ	ç ʝ	x ɣ	χ ʁ	ħ ʕ	h ɦ
Lateral fricative				ɬ ɮ							
Approximant		ʋ		ɹ		ɻ	j	ɰ			
Lateral approximant				l		ɭ	ʎ	ʟ			

Figure 52. IPA pulmonic consonant chart..
(Please see www.langsci.ucl.ac.uk/ipa/ for original charts.)

Good news. In bold face below, you will find that twenty-four of these IPA symbols are ones with which you are very familiar as either lower or upper case letters of the Roman alphabet that we use in printed English.

	Bilabial	Labiodental	Dental	Alveolar	Postalveolar	Retroflex	Palatal	Velar	Uvular	Pharyngeal	Glottal
Plosive	**p** **b**			**t** **d**		ʈ ɖ	**c** ɟ	**k** **g**	**q** ɢ		ʔ
Nasal	**m**	ɱ		**n**		ɳ	ɲ	ŋ	**N**		
Trill	**B**			**r**					**R**		
Tap or Flap		ⱱ		ɾ		ɽ					
Fricative	ɸ β	**f** **v**	θ ð	**s** **z**	ʃ ʒ	ʂ ʐ	ç **j**	**x** ɣ	χ ʁ	ħ ʕ	**h** ɦ
Lateral Fricative				ɬ ɮ							
Approximant		ʋ		ɹ		ɻ	**j**	ɰ			
Lateral Approximant				**l**		ɭ	ʎ	**L**			

Figure 53. Bolded Roman alphabet symbols in the pulmonic IPA chart.

I can't claim that every one of them is used in exactly the way we do when we spell English words, but most of them are. So, not only do you know, from the work you have already done, how to produce *all the actions represented by all the symbols* and then some, you also know over a third of the symbols already

More good news. We actually know even more. If you look further, you will find that almost all of the remaining symbols represent some variation on Roman alphabet symbols. Sometimes the symbols have little hooks or other embellishments attached to regular Roman letters. Sometimes the

Roman letters are turned or flipped around. But we can still see what they are; and in every case we can get some very valuable clues about what the sounds are that these symbols represent.

In bold face, here are all the symbols that are Roman alphabet letters *or are derived from Roman alphabet letters*. Now your real search through it will be trying to find the *un*familiar symbols.

	Bilabial	Labiodental	Dental	Alveolar	Postalveolar	Retroflex	Palatal	Velar	Uvular	Pharyngeal	Glottal
Plosive	**p b**			**t d**		**ʈ ɖ**	**c ɟ**	**k g**	**q ɢ**		**ʔ**
Nasal	**m**	**ɱ**		**n**		**ɳ**	**ɲ**	**ŋ**	**N**		
Trill	**ʙ**			**r**					**R**		
Tap or Flap		**ⱱ**		**ɾ**		**ɽ**					
Fricative	ɸ β	**f v**	θ ð	**s z**	**ʃ** 3	**ʂ ʐ**	**ç ʝ**	**x** ɣ	**χ ʁ**	**ħ** ʕ	**h ɦ**
Lateral Fricative				**ɬ ɮ**							
Approximant		**ʋ**		**ɹ**		**ɻ**	**j**	**ɰ**			
Lateral Approximant				**l**		**ɭ**	**ʎ**	**L**			

Figure 54. All Roman alphabet-related symbols bolded.

Getting specific about the symbols

We will start with something very familiar, in the upper left-hand box, or cell, of the chart, the **bilabial stop-plosives**, as we can tell from the descriptions on the X (horizontal) and Y (vertical) axes. (Today, in a graph like this we would describe the "X-Axis" as a line, and the "Y-axis" as a column.) What general information about writing phonetic symbols can we get from just these two symbols? Don't be afraid to give *very* simple, obvious answers and don't look at the next page until you have some.

Some answers

1   The symbols are printed, not written in cursive script. There have been systems for phonetic transcription that used unconnected or connected cursive script, but they have not been used by phoneticians for nearly a hundred years.

2   The symbols are written as lower-case, not upper-case capital letters. There are no "capital letters" in phonetic symbols because we are only concerned with representing sound actions; we don't need to bother about marking proper names, or the the start of a sentence, or – as in German – nouns.

3   The symbol in the left half of the cell is unvoiced. The symbol in the right half is voiced, even though in other respects they are pronounced the same.

4   The symbol on the left / **p** / as printed has a vertical line that goes below the line on which the symbol "sits". The symbol is therefore called a **descender**. Look at the other symbols in the pulmonic chart to see which ones are also descenders. The part of the symbol that descends does not need to be a vertical line, of course; it can be curved or slanted as well.

5   The symbol on the right has a vertical line that goes above the general height of most lower-case letters. The symbol is called – unsurprisingly – an **ascender**. Try to find other ascenders in the pulmonic chart. Then try to find some symbols that are both ascenders and descenders. And finally, find some symbols that are neither, which is most of them.

As we start to print phonetic symbols, we shall use the old line system that we used in childhood (well, I did) to learn to print the Roman alphabet that we use in English, just to make certain that the symbols have the right relationship to each other in a line of transcription. We have first the base line on which the letter sits; above that is a dotted line to indicate the common height of many lower-case letters. Once we learn the proper proportion of the symbols, the dotted line can disappear, as it does by the second grade of grammar school.

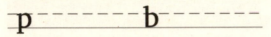

Next pick some other ascenders from anywhere in the pulmonic chart and write at least four of them on the line below.

Write four descender symbols.

Write four symbols that fit between the baseline and the dotted line above, that are neither ascenders nor descenders. These will include symbols that look like capital letters, but they are all **lower-case capitals**.

Next, find four symbols that are *both* ascenders and descenders and write them appropriately above and below the lines.

And finally, write a sequence of at least ten consonant symbols with each symbol different as to ascender/descender characteristics from the one that precedes or follows it.

Now we know the way in which the printed lower-case symbols are written, their size and placement relative to one another. We already know well the recipe that tells us what the physical action is that is represented by the sound. So we can proceed through the rest of the symbols in the pulmonic consonant chart easily.

To help us get into the idea that we are writing sound actions, not "spelling" words, here are a few examples of consonant symbol use. These all derive from the governing principle that one symbol equals one unique sound action, and only one:

The **voiced velar stop-plosive** represented by the symbol / g / looks like one form of the letter "g". When we spell words in English with the letter "g" we could either mean a "hard g" as in "gag" or a "soft g" as in "ginger". But we know from our recipe for sound action that this symbol / g / represents only the "hard g" form. The "soft g" will have to be represented in another way, with other symbols. This is why we need to add consonant symbols to the existing Roman alphabet for phonetic transcription.

We recognize the symbol / c / as a familiar looking character in English spelling that can represent two different sounds in English, just as we found with / g /. However the unvoiced velar stop-plosive, what people often call a "hard c", is already represented by the symbol / k /. Similarly, the unvoiced alveolar fricative, often called the "soft c", is represented by the symbol / s /. So the / c / has lost its usual jobs. Fortunately it is utilized in the IPA to represent a sound action not usually found in English, the **unvoiced palatal stop-plosive**.

Perform this sound action. It sounds a lot like a / k /, but there is a slight difference in the sound produced. In addition, there is a very slight breathy offglide after the plosive action that sounds a little like a "y" (as in "yes"), only unvoiced. Why does this offglide tend to happen with / c / but not with / k /? There is a good reason, and it relates to the anatomy of the roof of the mouth. And I'm not going to give you the answer right away. Write your reason opposite or on a separate sheet of paper.

Assuming you have either figured out a plausible reason for that offglide or else simply given up, we may proceed onward. Take another look at the entire pulmonic chart and also the non-pulmonic consonant chart and see if you can notice other patterns in the way the symbols are written that might give you useful information. Write your conclusions below and please don't turn the page until you have done so.

Some things we find

1   All the symbols in the "Retroflex" column of the pulmonic chart have a hook depending from some point at the bottom of the symbol and curving to the right. So we know that / ɳ / is the Roman alphabet letter "n" with a retroflex modifier. The action, then, is a voiced retroflex nasal, a sound that we find in many Indian subcontinent languages. Curl your tongue tip back and speak it. The same principle applies to all other retroflex sounds. So speak all of them in the column, from top to bottom. The form of the symbol gives you all the information you need. (Except notice that the "r" is written upside down. We will deal with this very soon. But it's still clearly an "r", especially if you're standing on your head.)

2   All three symbols in the "Tap/Flap" line have a rightward-extending hook from the top of the symbol that is still within the lower-case limits; that is, the symbols are not ascenders. Speak them, putting them between two phthongs.

3   All the voiced uvular symbols are printed as lower-case capital letters. That means that they are capital letters written between those two lines that we were using earlier. So if it's a lower-case capital letter, you know that you are using a voiced uvular sound. The IPA can afford to do this because capital letters do not need to be used to indicate grammatical or syntactic features, such as the start of a sentence in English or a noun in German. Their lower-case status in the IPA confirms their non-grammatical use. You know what the letter is in English, though. So speak it as a uvular consonant, using this information.

Look at the non-pulmonic consonant chart opposite. All the "Voiced Implosives" have a **right-curving hook** growing upward from the top of the symbol, making them all ascenders; some have descenders also. So you know that all those sounds are voiced implosives. You know them already; so speak them, from top to bottom.

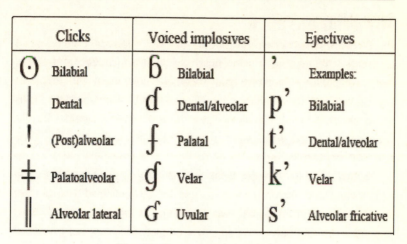

Clicks		Voiced implosives		Ejectives	
⊙	Bilabial	ɓ	Bilabial	'	Examples:
|	Dental	ɗ	Dental/alveolar	p'	Bilabial
!	(Post)alveolar	ʄ	Palatal	t'	Dental/alveolar
ǂ	Palatoalveolar	ɠ	Velar	k'	Velar
‖	Alveolar lateral	ɢ	Uvular	s'	Alveolar fricative

Figure 55. Non-pulmonic consonants, IPA.
(Please see www.langsci.ucl.ac.uk/ipa/ for original charts.)

Also in the non-pulmonic consonant chart, the "Ejectives" column shows Roman alphabet symbols that are followed by an **apostrophe**. An example would be / p' /. Speak all the ejectives in the column. Can you enact other possible ejectives that aren't in this list?

"Clicks" have to be learned individually as symbols, but they do share the characteristic that they are all both ascenders and descenders.

The answer to the question on page 128

The reason the palatal [c] has that little fricative offglide, whereas the velar [k] explodes cleanly, is that the velum, being flexible and containing muscle, can help the plosive action by springing actively away from the tongue. The palate, in contrast, cannot move, so it is harder for the front of the tongue-body to get away from the palate. You can get the front of the tongue away from the palate quickly and cleanly, but you really have to work to do it.

The problem of "h"

The IPA defines the phonemes / h / and / ɦ / which represent the unvoiced and voiced "h" that we find in English, as **glottal fricatives**, and places them appropriately in the Glottal Pacement column in the Pulmonic Consonant Chart. These two phonemes appear in English words always as **prevocalic** consonants that always precede a vowel in a syllable. The "h" appears in spelled words after a vowel, of course, but they are not sounded; or even noised.

We can test this definition. Relax your jaw open and bring your vocal folds toward one another enough to obstruct the unvoiced flow, but not into approximation where you would produce a creaky voice or voiced phonation. You are now doing an unvoiced glottal fricative, our IPA definition. You have already explored this action early in this book when you explored "heavy breathing". Now very carefully use *only* this glottal fricative method of producing an "h" in the words "haul", "how", "have", "hem", "hit", "heel". If you have genuinely done an unvoiced glottal fricative, I suspect that the "h" you are producing bears little resemblance to the way that you actually say "h" in words and phrases.

🔊 **Audio track 27:** *Unvoiced glottal fricative.*

But if we aren't doing an unvoiced glottal fricative here, what are we doing? Go back to the way that you usually say a consonant "h" and feel what seems to be happening as you move from the "h" into a vowel. You can use the same list of six words to practice. Clearly something very different is happening to produce the "h" sound.

In fact, when you enact the "h" in normal speech, you are **preaspirating** the vowel. That is, you are first shaping your articulators to form the vowel – whether it is the "ee" or the "oo" or any vowel in between – then you are increasing the airflow to produce an even turbulence throughout the oral cavity that produces an unvoiced noise. (Remember the "Making your first sound" exploration?) Only then do you start the voicing to produce the vowel. So in a very real sense the "h" is just a modification of the vowel that follows it, not a single, unique consonant action. It certainly is not a glottal fricative.

Speakers have recognized the variable action of "h" for a long time. Ancient Greek represents this preaspiration as a **diacritic**, a mark modifying the action of a phoneme. So the Greek word for the indefinite article "the" is written as "ó", pronounced "ho", with the little diacritic mark above the "o" standing for the preaspiration of the "h". In many ways, this is a much saner way to represent what is really going on.

The so-called voiced glottal fricative / ɦ / is even more eccentric, because it is physically impossible for the vocal folds to produce simultaneously phonation – voicing – and a fricative action, for which the folds cannot be brought together. Only a little attentive exploration reveals that what we are doing when we produce a "voiced glottal fricative" is actually a breathy voiced realization of the vowel that follows, with the same increased airflow that we used before.

◀)) **Audio track 28:** *Voiced glottal fricative.*

Obviously the symbols / h / and / ɦ / should not be located where they are in the pulmonic consonant chart; and very possibly not in the pulmonic chart at all. Or would it be better to go back to the solution in ancient Greek that doesn't use a letter for the "h" sound, but gets by very well indeed with just a diacritic mark?

There are a couple of reasons why it might be useful to keep the symbols, even though they defy the usual IPA requirement that each phonemic symbol should represent a single, unique physical action or placement. The first reason is decently mundane: we are used to the "h" to represent what we do when we utter a preaspirated vowel. Using a diacritic over a vowel would make reading phonetic symbols a little more difficult. The second reason is that even though the placement of the action of "h" is as various as there are phonemes and allophones of "h", there really is a unique physical action that ties all of them together: the increase in the velocity of the egressive airstream that is needed to produce the preaspirated noise.

So / h / and / ɦ / remain in the IPA, having been granted clemency. They really need a new name for their action, however, since they clearly are not fricatives. I suggest calling them **aspirants**, since it is the increase in the air flow that makes them unique. Besides, the term *aspirants* has a hopeful, optimistic tone, which is not a bad attitude for learning phonetic symbols.

Everything else

Turning, inverting and reversing

One of the earliest stated goals of the International Phonetic Association in forming the International Phonetic Alphabet was to use the Roman alphabet as much as possible in forming phonetic symbols. (We might have hoped that one of the first decisions would have been to avoid giving the organization's name and its principal product the same acronym – IPA – but alas, no.) As we know, the IPA (the organization) used the entire Roman alphabet. It also used the capital versions of some of them, in lower case, for voiced uvular consonants and the voiced lateral velar approximant. But if we look again at that column of uvular consonants, we notice that the **voiced uvular fricative** / ʁ / is not only a lower-case capital "R", it is also an **inverted** version of the **voiced uvular trill** / ʀ / , meaning that it is flipped upside down without turning. It's upside down, but it's still facing in the same direction.

Some letters are **turned** (rotated) to make them upside down, which means that the letter is now facing backwards. Good examples are the **voiced alveolar approximant** / ɹ /, which is the way many – but not all – Americans pronounce the consonant "r", and one of my personal favorites, the **voiced palatal lateral approximant** / ʎ /, which you might think is a Greek letter lambda. It isn't, however. It is a "turned y". A lambda would be a reverse image of the "turned Y" and would look like this: "λ". We can find a good example of symbol **reversal** in the pulmonic consonant chart if we compare the **glottal stop-plosive** / ʔ / with its reversed version, the **voiced pharyngeal fricative** / ʕ /.

134

These turned, reversed, and inverted symbols aren't many in number, and about ten seconds of attention paid to each one will fix their correct position in your mind.

If it's **turned**, it is upside down and facing backwards.

If it's **reversed**, it is right side up, but facing backwards.

If it's **inverted**, it is upside down, but it's *not* facing backwards.

And finally . . .

Some of the remaining Roman alphabet modifications can be learned easily with little memory devices. For example, the **voiced velar nasal** / ŋ / looks rather like an "ng" put together into one letter. The same voiced nasal action, produced further forward on the roof of the mouth, specifically on the palate, is written with the "g" hook on the "forward" or left leg of the "n", as / ɲ /. The easily spoken **voiced palatal approximant** / j / becomes tighter, more constricted in its **voiced palatal fricative** version, and it is represented with a symbol, the "curly-tail j" that seems to be attacking itself / ʝ /. The "Fish-Hook r" / ɾ / looks like a fish-hook; but also sonically it looks just like what it is: a **voiced alveolar tap** that is a *part* of a **voiced alveolar trill** / r /, so the **tap** symbol looks like an incomplete **trill** symbol. The slightly abrasive noise of the **unvoiced velar fricative** / x / is sounded as larger and more florid in its **uvular** version, and it is fittingly represented by a descender symbol of more generous proportions / χ /.

The generous proportions of the / χ / are actually the normal proportions of this symbol's other identity – as the Greek letter "chi". This brings us into the category of symbols borrowed from other orthographies, specifically Greek and Old English (or contemporary Icelandic). There aren't a lot of these and they usually correspond closely in their own orthographies to the sounds they are meant to represent in the IPA (the alphabet).

Most of the Greek and Old English symbols are found in the fricatives row on the pulmonic consonant chart. We find them paired in cells where Roman letters to represent these sound actions just don't exist, such as the **unvoiced** and **voiced bilabial fricatives** / ɸ / and / β /. We can see them paired in cells where the Roman letters to represent the sounds do exist

135

The source for the nomenclature of all these phonetic symbols is The Phonetic Symbol Guide, *second edition by Geoffrey Pullum and William Ladusaw (University of Chicago Press). The book is a surprisingly entertaining read and is the definitive reference for all phonetic symbols, living and dead, past and present, major and minor. If you want to be able to bandy about terms like yogh, esh, ash, ram's horn, slashed o, and fish-hook r, all of which can enliven any social conversation, this is the book to consult. The histories of the symbols are diverting too: when things get confusing, the authors frankly admit to the confusion, a refreshing approach, e.g. "Confusingly, the symbol we call Script V looks somewhat more like a Greek upsilon than IPA Upsilon does; and the version of Upsilon used in Smiley 1963 looks much more like Script V than like Upsilon. We regret not being able to terminologize better in this area, but we cannot see a better alternative. (Some phoneticians refer to Upsilon by the name Bucket, but it looks more like an urn to us.)" (page 185).*

but are imprecise or inefficient, such as the **unvoiced and voiced dental fricatives** / θ / and / ð /. The / χ / reclines in solitary Greek grandeur, paired with an inverted Roman partner.

There are very few other symbols left. They have been adapted or invented by various phoneticians throughout the years, submitted to the IPA (the organization) and approved. Their origins are sometimes complex, sometimes murky, and sometimes just wacky. In the **unvoiced** and **voiced post-alveolar fricatives** / ʃ / and / ʒ / we can see some remnants of an "s" in the "esh" symbol / ʃ /,[1] and a bit of "z" in the "yogh" symbol [ʒ], which occurs in Middle English – but as a different sound. Approximant symbols like the "script (or cursive) v" / ʋ / (and you thought it was a Greek upsilon or at least some form of "u", didn't you?) or the "long-legged turned m" [ɰ] (which sounds rather like the name for a water bird or a stick insect) are far less clear in their history and derivation. The "long-legged turned m", the symbol for the **voiced velar approximant**, may not even be

1. This symbol does appear as the "long s" used in typesetting into the eighteenth century, but the "long s" didn't represent this sound.

found as a unique uncombined sound in language. But there it is in print; and approved by the IPA too. And you can speak it.

Other symbols

No graph here. No relative position determined by voicing or action or placement. This is just a list, and its relative disorder bespeaks its status as the orphanage of the International Phonetic Alphabet. This category is the place to put all the symbols for consonant actions that the International Phonetic Association in its collective wisdom couldn't quite fit into either the pulmonic or non-pulmonic consonant charts. Some of the decisions to consign sound actions to the "other symbols" list seem obvious enough; others are more baffling . . . er, interesting.

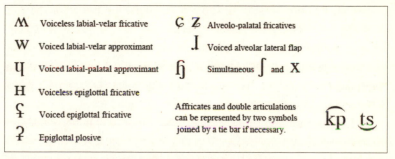

Figure 56. Other consonant symbols.
(Please see www.langsci.ucl.ac.uk/ipa/ for original charts.)

The first two symbols in the left column are very familiar to us as American English speakers. Why are they not in the pulmonic consonant chart? The second of these two symbols is very familiar indeed. It is a / w /, as in the English orthography of the words "wish" "would" and "away". What are we actually doing when we physically enact this sound action? Do you remember the articulator isolations and our separation of the actions for lip corner protrusion and lip pursing that we explored early in the work? If we do *both* these actions simultaneously, we produce full "lip rounding", such as we use in the unobstructed vowel sound "oo". If we continue the pursing action a little further, so that it very slightly intrudes into the voiced flow, we produce a voiced approximant sound. And there we have it: / w /. Or do we?

We notice something else in our recipe description of this symbol. The IPA has listed it as a **voiced labial-velar approximant**. Don't mistake this for a *labio*-velar approximant. "Labio-velar" would mean the lower lip moving toward the velum. If you were actually to succeed in getting your lower lip to arrive in the vicinity of your velum (your soft palate) you might require medical intervention to get it away again. What "labial-velar" means is that the lips are rounded into an approximant obstruction of the flow, as we have just described above, but in addition the middle portion of the dorsum of the tongue is arched up toward your velum to simultaneously produce the voiced velar approximant / ɰ /.

Just say that one sound / ɰ / to remind yourself of the action. So you are doing two separate articulation actions at the same time. Try doing both sound actions – at the lips and at the velum – simultaneously. This is our first experience of a **co-articulated** sound, a really popular feature of the "Other Sounds" category. You are basically doing two articulation actions simultaneously to produce a unique combined sound result.

As it happens, in this *particular* case, I don't believe that this is really an accurate description, so I disagree with the IPA. More specifically, I don't agree that both these actions – at the lips *and* at the velum – *need* to happen to produce the / w / that we know and love. Keep your tongue well away from your velum and just do the fully rounded, mildly intrusive lip action on a voiced flow. See what I mean? The / w / sounds just fine to me without the velar action. There's one vote right there.

The same thing goes for the first symbol / ʍ /, a turned (not inverted – look closely) "w" that represents the speech action of an **unvoiced labial-velar fricative**. Note that it is now a fricative, because unvoiced flow usually requires more obstruction to produce a unique noise without your having to increase the airflow.

Now I allow that a lot of people may raise the tongue toward the velum as a part of speaking the phonemes / w / and / ʍ /. Perhaps most people do so. But some people don't, and don't need to. In my view, the velar co-articulation of / w / and / ʍ / is secondary to the lip action and is possibly irrelevant altogether.

There is something unique about the lip action of / ʍ / and / w /, however – something that doesn't fit into the categories in the pulmonic consonant chart. Compare these fully rounded actions to the unvoiced and voiced bilabial actions of / ɸ / and / β /, and the difference becomes clear: in the bilabial fricatives / ɸ / and / β / the lips are pursed, only with no lip corner protrusion – you're just bringing the edges of the lips closer together. In the fully rounded / ʍ / and / w / the corners are protruded and the lips are pursed simultaneously. But this combined lip action chart doesn't fit into the actions represented along the Y-axis of the pulmonic consonant chart. To get it in there would require a new category of action: lip corner protrusion. Since these are the only symbols that require it, the IPA may well have felt that the effort wasn't worth the trouble for only two symbols.[1]

We know enough about our recipe for consonant production to be able to explore the rest of these symbols with some confidence. We now know that the **voiced labial-palatal fricative** / ɥ / is a co-articulated combination of a / w / and a / j /. It's the sound that the French language uses in the middle of the word "lui" or "huit".

And now the **epiglottals**. The famed linguist David Crystal once described trying to practice speaking epiglottal fricatives and stop-plosives aloud while standing on a station platform in the London tube (subway, to Americans). After only a few seconds of enthusiastic epiglottic exploration he noticed that everyone else on the platform had moved as far away from him as possible. If these sounds have the power to disperse crowds, clearly, performing them has to be fun. The **epiglottis** is the spoon-shaped piece of cartilage covered with mucus membrane that is attached to your tongue root and is poised above your larynx; it drops down to cover the larynx whenever you swallow so that your food is directed to your esophagus and

1. In which case, one wonders why the pair of lateral fricatives, ensconced comfortably in the pulmonic consonant chart, are not listed as "Other Symbols" too. The influence of the powerful Welsh lobby, perhaps?

then your stomach, not down your trachea to your lungs. So all epiglottal sound actions begin with that swallowing action – except that you don't engage the top surface of your tongue as you would when you swallow food. You can tell that there is a real difference from pharyngeal fricatives in the sound when you perform an **unvoiced or voiced epiglottal fricative** / ʜ] or / ʢ /. In performing the **epiglottal stop-plosive** / ʔ / – you'll notice that the IPA is vague as to whether it is unvoiced or voiced – make sure that you are doing the action using the epiglottis and not the glottis; make sure there's an egressive flow, too.

The unvoiced and voiced **alveolo-palatal fricatives** / ɕ / and / ʑ /, as the name implies, involve a fricative channel that obstructs the flow along the midline of the tongue from the top (or **laminal**) part of the tongue-blade (moving upward toward the alveolar and post-alveolar area) to the front portion of the dorsum of the tongue (moving upward toward the front of the palate). Note that the tongue tip is *not* slightly retracted, as it is for the post-alveolar fricatives / ʃ / and / ʒ /.

The **lateral alveolar flap** / ɺ / is pronounced with the tongue-tip held against the alveolar ridge throughout. Then the side edges of the tongue are quickly flapped – using the pressure of the flow – against the side alveolar ridges to produce a very quick closure and release. The action is very similar to something we will explore in a few pages – the action of **lateral plosion**. The difference is that here the action is looser, so that the tongue flaps rather than being held and exploded. In English, it might be used in the pronunciation of the "dl" sequence in the singularly euphonious proper name Dudley, especially if the speaker is slightly drunk at the time, though its principal application with perfect sobriety is in the language KiChaka.

Our last "Other Symbol" is / ɧ /. This is another co-articulated sound action, consisting – as the IPA chart flatly states – of a combined and simultaneous / ʃ / and / x /, an unvoiced post-alveolar fricative and an unvoiced velar fricative. You now have the recipe for this co-articulated sound, so try it. It is the symbol "that dare not speak its name", or at least a name that the IPA dare not speak. Ladusaw and Pullum, always to the rescue, identify this orphan as the **hooktop heng**. It is only used in a few dialects of Swedish, but it's a good exercise to perform, especially because it is tricky to keep the tongue lowered enough in between the obstructions of the / ʃ / and the / x / to keep the flow unimpeded in between.

One other thing: the "Other Symbols" category might be an excellent residence for the "aspirant" phonemes / h / and / ɦ /.

◀)) **Audio track 29:** *The pulmonic consonant chart.*

◀)) **Audio track 30:** *The non-pulmonic consonant chart.*

◀)) **Audio track 31:** *Other consonant symbols.*

Consonant transcription practice 1

Write each phoneme three times in the space provided after its printed version. Speak each sound action as you write it in an initial position followed by a single phthong to form one syllable.

Symbol practice exercise

PLOSIVES

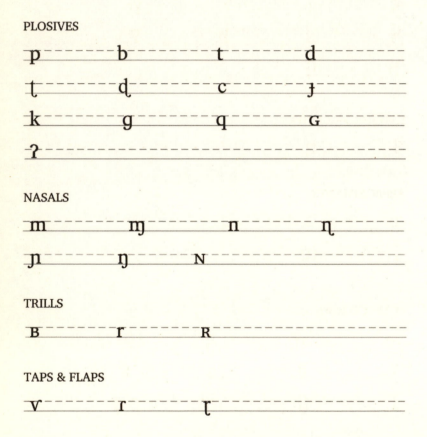

NASALS

TRILLS

TAPS & FLAPS

FRICATIVES

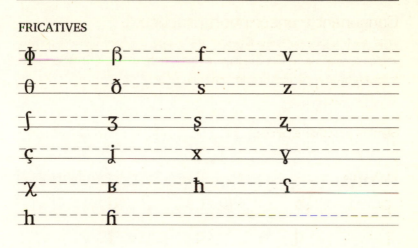

LATERAL FRICATIVES

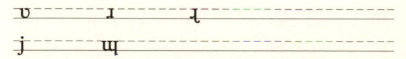

APPROXIMANTS

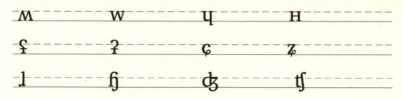

OTHER SYMBOLS

ʍ   w   ɥ   ʜ

ʕ   ʔ   ʢ   ʡ

ɺ   ɧ   ʤ   ʧ

CLICKS

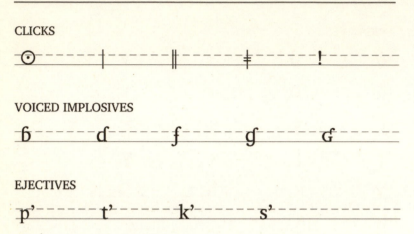

VOICED IMPLOSIVES

EJECTIVES

Consonant transcription practice 2

Now we will practice our consonant IPA transcription of individual symbols by writing the appropriate phonetic symbol for each voicing/placement/action recipe Again, speak the sound action represented by the symbol as you write it:

Voiced bilabial fricative _ _ _ _ _   *Voiced retroflex flap* _ _ _ _ _ _ _ _ _

Unvoiced uvular stop-plosive _ _ _ _   *Voiced palatal approximant* _ _ _ _ _ _

Voiced labiodental nasal _ _ _ _ _ _   *Unvoiced postalveolar fricative* _ _ _ _ _

Voiced alveolar stop-plosive _ _ _ _   *Voiced retroflex nasal* _ _ _ _ _ _ _ _

Unvoiced labiodental fricative _ _ _ _   *Unvoiced uvular stop-plosive* _ _ _ _ _

Unvoiced palatal fricative _ _ _ _ _ _   *Unvoiced dental fricative* _ _ _ _ _ _ _

Voiced bilabial nasal _ _ _ _ _ _ _ _   *Voiced uvular trill* _ _ _ _ _ _ _ _ _ _

Voiced palatal lateral approximant _ _ _   Voiced labiodental approximant _ _ _ _

Voiced velar fricative _ _ _ _ _ _ _ _   Unvoiced palatal stop-plosive _ _ _ _ _

Unvoiced dental click _ _ _ _ _ _ _ _   Unvoiced velar fricative _ _ _ _ _ _ _

Voiced dental fricative _ _ _ _ _ _ _ _   Voiced alveolar fricative _ _ _ _ _ _ _

Voiced alveolar approximant _ _ _ _ _   Voiced labiodental fricative _ _ _ _ _ _

Voiced postalveolar fricative _ _ _ _ _   Voiced palatal nasal _ _ _ _ _ _ _ _

Unvoiced alveolar lateral fricative _ _ _   Voiced pharyngeal fricative _ _ _ _ _ _

Voiced bilabial stop-plosive _ _ _ _ _   Unvoiced velar ejective _ _ _ _ _ _ _

Voiced velar implosive _ _ _ _ _ _ _   Unvoiced glottal fricative[3] _ _ _ _ _ _

Voiced labiodental nasal _ _ _ _ _ _   Unvoiced epiglottal fricative _ _ _ _ _

Unvoiced pharyngeal fricative _ _ _ _ _   Voiced velar approximant _ _ _ _ _ _

(Unvoiced)[1] glottal stop-plosive _ _ _ _   Unvoiced bilabial click _ _ _ _ _ _ _

Unvoiced alveolar stop-plosive _ _ _ _   Unvoiced postalveolar ejective _ _ _ _

Voiced alveolar[2] tap _ _ _ _ _ _ _ _   Voiced labiodental flap _ _ _ _ _ _ _

Unvoiced labial-velar fricative _ _ _ _ _   Voiced palatal fricative _ _ _ _ _ _ _

---

1. Designated as unvoiced by the IPA (the Association) but I question this.
2. Designated as alveolar by the IPA, but I consider it to be commonly postalveolar in both American and British speech. The same is true of [ɹ]
3. I vigorously disagree with this designation by the IPA.

Your teacher, if you have one (if not, enlist a friend; or if all else fails, play Track 32 on the accompanying CD), can now speak individual consonant sounds for you to transcribe. The usual way to speak consonant actions is to use the consonant in an initial position in a syllable, followed by a phthong (usually "ahh". The consonant is then repeated in a medial position as a two-syllable utterance, with the consonant preceded by and then followed by a phthong. Write the appropriate symbol on each short line, paying attention to ascenders and descenders. We include more spaces than there are consonant symbols so that you can do this practice in more than one session.

◀)) **Audio track 32:** *Individual consonant phoneme quiz.*

1   _____   _____   _____   _____   _____

6   _____   _____   _____   _____   _____

11   _____   _____   _____   _____   _____

16   _____   _____   _____   _____   _____

21   _____   _____   _____   _____   _____

26   _____   _____   _____   _____   _____

31   _____   _____   _____   _____   _____

36   _____   _____   _____   _____   _____

41   _____   _____   _____   _____   _____

46   _____   _____   _____   _____   _____

51 _____   _____   _____   _____   _____

56 _____   _____   _____   _____   _____

61 _____   _____   _____   _____   _____

66 _____   _____   _____   _____   _____

71 _____   _____   _____   _____   _____

76 _____   _____   _____   _____   _____

81 _____   _____   _____   _____   _____

86 _____   _____   _____   _____   _____

91 _____   _____   _____   _____   _____

96 _____   _____   _____   _____   _____

The symbols for the consonants spoken on Audio Track 32 will be found at the end of this chapter (page 153). I cannot speak for those teachers and "friends" who have had you filling in all the spaces provided . . .

The Problem of "r"

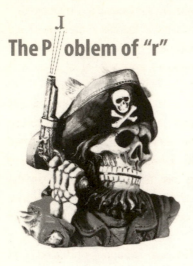

I have alluded to the two parallel definitions of a symbol in the International Phonetic Alphabet: as a unit of meaning called a phoneme, and as a unique physical action. These two definitions maintain a fairly simple relationship throughout most of the consonant graphs and even in the "other symbols" list. But with two of the approximants, things get more complicated.

"L" and "r" both have several symbols that represent very different physical actions that we, as English speakers, would still recognize as the phonemes "l" and "r." (In other languages they might represent phonemic difference.) But in order for us actually to put these letters between the brackets that tell us that this is not a spelled letter, but a phonemic symbol, we have to make a choice. Most of the time, we bow to predominant usage or the preferences of speech teachers: with "l" phoneticians and speech teachers will usually opt for the so-called "clear l," so that the phonemic symbol becomes / l /; this, despite the fact that many Americans pronounce even initial "l" as the so-called "dark l" or / ɫ /. The physical difference between the clear and dark "l" is a slight one: both place the tongue tip at the alveolar ridge, but the dark "l" / ɫ / uses more cupping of the blade and front of the tongue, common in American speech because most Americans relax their jaws open more than speakers do in Britain.

To American speakers, other allophones of the phoneme / l / would certainly sound like accented pronunciations, but they would still be recognizable as "l" sounds.

The "r" is more complicated still. There are recognizable allophonic variations of "r" that extend from the articulation at the lips – the Elmer Fudd "cwazy wabbit" substitution of / w / for the "r" – all the way back to the uvular trill / ʀ /. This variation in allophones covers a lot of vocal tract territory. So which symbol might we use to indicate the phoneme?

One solution that many phoneticians used years ago (and phoneticians still use today for "broad" or less detailed phonetic transcription) is to use the most recognizable form of the "r", the same standard lower-case printed "r" that we are using in this sentence. It has the advantage that if we understand that we are simply using this "all-purpose r" to mean the phoneme, then we have a symbol that is exactly the one that we have been using for spelling "r" words. So our commonly accepted phonemic symbol is / r /, yes?

No. The [r] has the disadvantage that as an allophone (indicated by its placing here in brackets, rather than between slashes), it represents the voiced alveolar trill that is found in some languages (Amsterdam Dutch or Russian for example) and in some accents of English (Welsh, for example), but a trill is hardly all-purpose. Instead, the preferred phonemic symbol for anything other than the broadest transcription is / ɹ /. As you know, this is specifically the symbol for the voiced (post)-alveolar approximant "r", a pronunciation that is regularly employed in English Received Pronunciation ("RP") – often called Standard British – and one that is commonly advocated by American speech teachers as a preferred pronunciation. So there is some history and ideology behind this choice of phonemic representation.

The apparent problem is that many, if not most, Americans don't pronounce "r" using the alveolar placement; certainly not all the time. Yes?

The 800-pound pirate in the room

And no again: that's a problem but it isn't *the* problem. *The* problem is that out of all the marvelous possibilities for allophones of "r" contained in the IPA (the Alphabet) –

◀)) **Audio track 33:** *Allophones of "r".*

149

[w] voiced labial-velar approximant (substitution; can also be another phoneme)

[ʋ] voiced labio-dental approximant (substitution; can also be another phoneme)

[ɹ] voiced post-alveolar approximant

[r] voiced alveolar trill

[ɾ] voiced post-alveolar tap

[ɻ] voiced retroflex approximant

[ɽ] voiced retroflex flap

[ʁ] voiced uvular fricative

[ʀ] voiced uvular trill

– there is no IPA symbol that represents the unique action that is used by many Americans to form the "r" in a prevocalic (before the vowel in a syllable) position; and that is used by *most* Americans – and many other speakers – to pronounce the "r" in a postvocalic (after the vowel in a syllable) position.

Why not? As with the / l / phoneme, the explanation is logical, but logic tinged with a healthy helping of history and ideology. The International Phonetic Association's justification for ignoring the "American r" is that it has no separate existence as a phoneme. Remember that, while the list of "r" allophones above would all be recognized by any English speaker as sharing a general "r" quality and meaning, in certain other languages these same discrete actions and sounds would be recognized as conveying different meanings – making them different phonemes, in fact.

The IPA (the Association) has a good reason for wanting to draw the line somewhere in assigning symbols; there are so many possible variations of consonant and vowel production, especially in accents and in the patterns of individual speakers, that the IPA, early in its existence, established a principle of parsimony, requiring that only phonemes could be assigned symbols, lest the IPA (the Alphabet) sink of its own weight.

But qualifying as a phoneme mostly means arriving early on the phonetic transcription scene. In initially describing the Welsh language, a phonetician might note that the speakers regularly use a voiced alveolar trill / r / in both prevocalic and postvocalic positions. So that's the phoneme for Welsh, which gives the trilled / r / the right to exist as a phoneme in the International Phonetic Alphabet. But we also know that the voiced alveolar trill is used just as regularly in some accents of English (including the Welsh accent of English) where it is considered allophonic because it is not, in English, the approved phoneme for "r."

Let's make the argument the opposite way. If Welsh as a language did not exist and the alveolar trilled "r" did not exist as a sole pronunciation in any other language, then all the speakers trilling away in Scotland or in Amsterdam might find no assigned phonetic symbol to represent what they were doing. The "American r" is actually in the imagined predicament I have just outlined. As a potential phoneme, it has been preempted by the British RP post-alveolar approximant.

But what actually is the "American r?"

"The dog's name"

"Ay mocker. That's the dog's name," says Juliet's Nurse, speaking of the first sound in Romeo's name. And for years in American elocutionary texts, this Shakespearean reference was summoned up to show how inherently ugly the "r" sound can be when actually spoken by actual Americans. The nurse, though, had good reason to characterize the "r" in this manner, because in Shakespeare's time, speakers probably pronounced the "r", in all positions, in a way that sounded closer to a contemporary American pronunciation. In London speech, prevocalic "r" did not center on the post-alveolar / ɹ / until the eighteenth century; and it was not until the 1780s that London speakers slowly lost the postvocalic "r" altogether.

In much regional English speech – especially West Country – and in some areas of the United States, speakers use some version of the voiced retroflex approximant / ɻ / to produce prevocalic and sometimes postvocalic "r". It is this retroflexion that reproduces the classic piratical "Arrrrrrrr" of *Treasure Island* fame. In older American phonetic transcriptions from the 1930s, the / ɻ / was the inevitable symbol for "r" in mid-western and western American speech. It was used because it is the nearest substitute for the real thing. But this symbol / ɻ / does not accurately indicate the action or the sound that most Americans use, especially in post-vocalic positions within a word.

What, then, is this action and its resulting sound? Even if we do not have a phonetic symbol for it, we certainly can describe it. The sound that most Americans (exempting some populations of the Eastern Seaboard) use for postvocalic "r" is what we often call "**r-color**". Technically, it is variously termed a "**molar**", **braced**", or "**bunched r**". And many American use it as their "all-purpose r", even in prevocalic positions.

◀)) **Audio track 34:** *The braced "r".*

I favor the term **braced r**, as it is closest to the the physical action, although the other terms help to complete the description and the degree of bracing can vary. Unlike the alveolar / ɹ / or the retroflex / ɻ /, the tip and blade of the tongue are relaxed down with the tip of the tongue behind the lower teeth and the jaw relaxed open. The middle of the dorsum or body of the tongue is raised and the side edges of the tongue are braced vigorously against the inside of the upper teeth in the area of the rear bicuspids and first molars. Considered in terms of its orientation to the roof of the mouth, this action is taking place in the palato-velar area. The muscular bracing of the tongue has the effect of further tensing and thickening the midline of the tongue, bringing it even closer to the border of the palate and the velum. By varying the degree of bracing the degree of **rhoticity** ("r"-ishness) of the sound can be varied also. So an American can say –

beer, weird, fear, Sears, bare, stair, chairs, large, charm, scarf, bark, torn, court, lore, bore, boor, moor, toured, purr, turf, learn, purse, churn, fire, mire, sour, flour

– with a lot of rhoticity or with just a little by varying the bracing. The "braced r" is a very efficient tool for the dialect actor, because one can easily calibrate the degree of rhoticity. It is also a crucial part of the posture of various Midwestern American accents and, again, subtle gradations in rhoticity help tremendously to localize an accent.

◀)) **Audio track 35:** *Gradations of post-vocalic "r".*

But sadly, there is no "braced r" in the IPA nor is there any diacritic to notate variations in rhoticity, because it hasn't staked out its territory as a phoneme in any language. Since American English has now superceded (for better or worse) RP English as the model for ESL (English as a Second Language) study worldwide, it would seem appropriate for the IPA to revisit this issue. I would even be willing to see a newly devised "braced r" symbol present amongst the "disordered speech" symbols that have been added to the phonetic alphabet for the use of speech pathologists. Certainly the notion of American post-vocalic "r-color" as being pathological would appeal to the English RP zealots and also to many speech teachers in the USA. And dialecticians would applaud, for very different reasons.

There is more to say about rhoticity in a post-vocalic position, but it is best dealt with along with a consideration of vowel transcription. So the suspense can mount.

Answers to consonant quiz (page 146)

(as spoken on Audio track 32)

1. / b /. 2. / k /. 3. / ʒ /. 4. / l /. 5. / s /. 6. / θ /. 7. / v /. 8. / ɲ /. 9. / q /.
10. / m /. 11. / ɓ /. 12. / x /. 13. / ʔ /. 14. / ʁ /. 15. / ɬ /. 16. / ɖ /. 17. / ʃ /.
18. / ʍ /. 19. / tʲ /. 20. / h /

14

Sound to word

"Suit the action to the word"

When Hamlet says this to the players he is, of course, referring to physical gestures when he uses the word "action". But we know that each phonetic symbol represents not only a unique sound product, but also a unique physical action of the articulators that allow the sound to result.

So far we have considered these sound actions more or less in isolation from one another. But now we can start to place them into a sequence that will produce a larger unit of meaning: a word.

Let us consider a typical sequence. If we start with the phoneme / b / and then follow it with the vowel phoneme / i / (a phoneme we will consider soon) and finish with the phoneme / d / we have produced a sequence of actions and resulting sounds that in English symbolically represents a variably small globular object. We have formed the word "bead".

We notice a few characteristics of this particular word, the first word we have described completely in phonemes. For one thing, it is entirely voiced.

Each of the three component sound actions is a voiced one. If we changed the first phoneme from / b / to / s / we would create an entirely different word that is partially unvoiced and partially voiced. The result would represent a variably small object that might be globular or not, but one that could grow into a plant if placed in the ground and watered.

As we move from individual sounds to words, the articulators are learning the first steps of a complex dance inside the oral cavity. The word "bead" starts with a voiced bilabial stop-plosive that explodes into the "close front vowel"[1] that in turn is terminated by the voiced alveolar stop-plosive. Both stop-plosives are stopped and exploded as notated phonetically. But in getting the articulators from one action to another within a word, the speaker may need to change the actions to allow an easy sequence. This is especially true when we articulate words of more than one syllable that require some syllables to be stressed more than others.

Transcription practice

A good way to learn the consonant symbols easily is to write them and speak them as syllables or one-syllable words. The underscore line in the words below represents any phthong (that is, any vowel or diphthong) that you might wish to speak between the consonants. Be adventurous with the phthongs but be accurate with the consonants. We will start in familiar territory with sound actions that are found in American English. Feel free to consult the consonant charts as needed.

Choose each syllable from the phonetic symbols in the pulmonic consonant chart. Some will sound like words you know; some will be nonsense syllables. Do not intrude any other consonant sounds other than the ones printed here:

[b __ t]   [f __ s]   [v __ n]

[d __ g]   [m __ z]   [p __ ɬ]

1. It's the sound we make when we say a "long e", often spelled "ee" or – in this case – "ea". The phonetic symbols for vowels will arrive very soon; do not despair.

[k __ ʃ]   [ʒ __ p]   [j __ θ]
[h __ ð]   [b __ n]   [ʃ __ ŋ]

Now we will add more pulmonic chart symbols that may or may not be found in American English. Don't be shy about checking the chart:

[ʂ __ k]   [ɸ __ l̩]   [g __ ɖ]
[ɹ __ β]   [ç __ z]   [ɲ __ ɢ]
[x __ t]   [ɟ __ β]   [ɱ __ θ]
[ɳ __ ʒ]   [h __ ɻ]   [ð __ q]

The next step is to add non-pulmonic consonants and consonants from the IPA list of "Other Symbols":

[w __ b]   [ɓ __ ŋ]   [ʍ __ χ]
[ʀ __ θ]   [p __ ɣ]   [! __ ɴ]
[ɥ __ ʃ]   [ʐ __ ɱ]   [ɬ __ ʒ]
[ʔ __ ɻ]   [ɾ __ ç]   [ʙ __ ɢ]
[ʤ __ b]   [ǁ __ n]   [ʋ __ l̩]
[ʁ __ t̪]   [ɣ __ ɓ]   [k __ ð]

Two more additions to the mix: consonant clusters (more than one consonant in sequence) and multiple syllables. Whether or not the sound sequences you make mirror actual words, they will still sound more like words, even if they're nonsense.

[ʃ __ p __ lt]   [fl __ ɟ __ ʒd]   [spɟ __ ns __ xt]
[tʃ __ ɸ __ g __]   [c __ βd __ h]   [ɖ __ ɬ __ ndʒ]
[ʀ __ tʃ __ ts __ p]   [ŋ __ ʎ __ ft]   [kl __ vsts]
[ɳ __ dl]   [βʐ __ ʔ __ zb]   [pɥ __ ɣ __ ɱ]
             [tʍ __ zm]   [q __ tn]
          [θw __ ! __ xl __ v __ mʃk]

Two new ideas and two new techniques

The presence of consonant clusters – two or more consonants not separated by a vowel in the same syllable – has (somewhat sneakily) introduced into our transcription of our first words, two new categories of consonant combination. The first is that of the **affricates** – two successive consonant actions in a syllable, the first of which is a stop-plosive, the second a fricative. Exploding the stop-plosive into the fricative can make the succession of two actions sound like a single new sound of limited duration.

In English, there are only two affricates in common use. They use the same action and placement and they are an unvoiced/voiced pair. We have used them in the preceding list. The first is the **unvoiced post-alveolar affricate**, represented in phonetic transcription as / tʃ /. So we know the affricate combination is composed of a "lower-case t" / t / and an "esh" / ʃ /. But the resulting sound combination is really more of a sound mix, because the plosive action of the / t / is still happening as the fricative / ʃ / is formed. So the affricate result may seem to be a new unique sound rather than a consonant combination.

The same observations apply to the **voiced post-alveolar affricate**, represented phonetically as / dʒ /. The "lower-case d" / d / explodes into the "yogh" / ʒ /, producing an apparently new sound result.

In other languages, many other affricates are possible. As just one example, the stop-plosive/fricative combination / ts / occurs in many languages – Greek is one, as in the Greek names Tsouras or Tseckares. In these positions, at the start of a stressed syllable and followed by a vowel, the "ts" combination is truly an affricate, whereas in an English words like "that's" or "sets" it is considered a consonant sequence.

Transcribe the consonants in the following words, indicating the phthong by a subscript line:

chew _____   peach _____

edge _____   jam _____

ratchet _____   surgeon _____

magic _____   situation _____

natural _____   enjoin _____

The second category is **syllabic consonants**. These are consonant clusters (with no vowels in between) that – in themselves, through the physical action of moving from one consonant to another – can form separate syllables. Not all consonants can achieve this feat. The main consonants in American English that can become syllabic are the nasals / m /, / n /, and [ŋ], and the approximants / l / and / ɹ /. Syllabic consonants are often used by speakers when moving from a stressed syllable to an unstressed one; it is the lack of stress emphasis that allows us to take the vowel away and go directly from one consonant to another.

A syllabic consonant is notated with a **diacritic** mark, in this case a stubby vertical line written directly under (the linguistic term is **subscript**) the symbol: / m̩ /, / n̩ /, / l̩ /. It will take a little practice to distinguish syllabic consonants from the same consonants used in a non-syllabic way with a vowel in the syllable. A syllabic consonant might be the only sound in an unstressed word, the / n̩ / in "rock'n'roll" being a good example: we know it stands for the word "and", but we need only the one nasal sound to convey that meaning.

Sometimes we can find two syllabic consonants in a row: "animal" [_nm̩l̩ /. Notice that here the / n / isn't syllabic because it starts the syllable and is not preceded by another consonant. As with other words of this type, "animal" doesn't *have* to be said with syllabic consonants; you could put vowel sounds in between the consonant actions.

Here is a practical example of the use of syllabic consonants. If we wish to transcribe the two-syllable word "chasm", we would write the consonant symbols [k_zm]. As we can easily see, the consonant sequence / zm / forms its own new syllable, without the need to have a vowel in the syllable at all. As I have noted, it is a common practice to add a subscript diacritic, a short vertical line, below the syllabic consonant to identify it as such, as in / k_zm̩ /. This diacritic is not always necessary, but sometimes it is, because a sequence of consonants might be spoken as either syllabic or non-syllabic. The noted science-fiction writer Gregory Benford wrote a novel titled *Cosm* in which the "zm" sequence is syllabic, but if one were effusively to describe the novel as having "cosmic significance" the "zm" sequence would not be syllabic, because the medial consonants "z" and "m" would be drawn into the separate syllables "cos" and "mic".

Here are a few of the many possible words in English that *can* be spoken using syllabic consonants. Say them slowly and feel the actions you take to bring the two consonants together, without any vowel sound in between:

level, pedal, even, cabin, seventy, cobble, rattling, bottled, collect, veneer, prism, Petaluma, eagle, correct, aberration, happen, eaten, satin, schism, potent, second, able, abalone, ballistic, galactic, homonym (two syllabics), *cinnamon* (two syllabics), *rattle 'em* (two syllabics)

◀)) **Audio track 36:** *Syllabic consonants.*

Transcribe the following words, using the format that we have established. There may be more than one way to do the transcription (meaning that there is more than one way to say the word!)

eaten_____   fashion_____

enemy_____   broken_____

happening_____   Manilla_____

fatal_____   huddled_____

seven_____   camera_____

corona _____   medalist _____

garage _____   recollect _____

And the techniques

If you were paying attention to your own vocal tract action as you performed the exercises you just completed, you may have noticed that there are also two new physical techniques that speakers often use to speak syllabic consonants. (And possibly you were doing them.) They allow you to move directly from one consonant to another with no vowel in between.

Nasal plosion. Form an / n / in your mouth – just as you would a / t / or / d /, so that you cannot release any air or vibration through your mouth. Let the / n / sound flow through your nose and feel the vibrations tingling through the pharynx, the back of your throat, and then through the nasal cavity and out your nostrils.

Keep the flow going on another sighed / n /, but this time try to stop the flow somewhere inside the nasal cavity, by raising the top surface of the velum to the top of the nasopharynx, and let the air pressure build up as though you were preparing to expel something through your nose. Note where you feel the contact of the closure. Then let the / n / explode through the nose, as the plosive action helps to bring the velum sharply away from the nasopharynx. (*Note*: Speech work isn't pretty. Deal with it.) Repeat several times until the action of closing and opening the nasal cavity is clear to you (or the Kleenex is full, whichever happens first).

Nasal plosion is notated phonetically by a diacritic, which modifies the stop-plosive that is exploded into the nasal consonant. The small diacritic "n" (for "nasal") is written *above* the baseline of the transcription (**super-script**) and after the plosive symbol. Thus "bidden" becomes [b_dⁿn̩] Or "seven" as it is often pronounced, could become [s_bⁿm̩].

Make sure that you are not substituting a glottal plosion for a nasal one. Do so by trying it both ways, doing the nasal plosion on both an unvoiced and voiced plosive: [tⁿn] and [dⁿn], and then on a glottal plosive [ʔn]. Can you feel that on the glottal plosion you are not raising or lowering the upper surface of the velum at all? All the control is at the glottis.

Practice the same actions on [m] and on [ŋ]. Can you think of any words where you might use a syllabic / ŋ /?

Pair / m / with / b / and pair / n / with / d /: alternate nasal plosion into the / m / with oral plosion into "buhhhh" on one extended flow of vibration: [bⁿmmmm] going right into "buhhhhh". Then do the same thing with an extended / n / and "duhhh". Notice that you can't make the changeover work if you do the closing and opening actions simultaneously: you have to raise the top surface of the velum to stop off the nasal cavity in order to build up pressure for the oral plosion, and similarly stop off the oral articulators to build up pressure for the nasal plosion.

Here are some practice words for nasal plosion. Perform them first un-voiced and then with voicing to feel the physical action before you concern yourself with sound product.

eaten, beaten, Seton, pittance, kitten, retinal, fatten, catenary, button, curtain, cotton, Laughton, oaten, Putin, hidden, bidden, Haydn, redden, madden, badinage, adenoid, sodden, student, couldn't, seven, eleven, making, wrecking

◀)) **Audio track 37:** *Nasal plosion.*

Then write the consonants in each word phonetically. Replace the phthong with a subscript line:

Lateral plosion. Lateral plosion is another articulator strategy for getting from a stop-plosive to the syllabic consonant [l / quickly and easily. In the word "settle" one can stop the [t / and explode it laterally into the [l / by leaving the tip of the tongue touching the alveolar ridge and dropping the side edges of the tongue sharply, assisted by the compressed plosion of the airflow. Phonetically this action is represented by the superscript diacritic [^{l}] modifying the previous consonant, so that "settle" would be transcribed as [s_t^{l}l] or as [s_d^{l}l]. Obviously this means that voiced lateral plosion is equally possible, as in the word "middle", which would be transcribed – lacking only the vowel – as [m_d^{l}l].

Here are some practice words for lateral plosion. Perform them first un-voiced and then with voicing to feel the physical action before you concern yourself with sound product.

beetle, spittle, vittle (also spelled "victual"), *settle, cattle, cuttle, title, portal, mettle, needle, middle, meddle, addle, curdle, puddle, coddle, caudal, modal, feudal*

◀)) **Audio track 38:** *Lateral plosion.*

Then write the consonants in each word phonetically. Replace the vowel with a subscript line:

Go through the phonetic words in the consonant cluster practice list on page 157 and see if you can identify the affricates and the syllabic con-sonants – with or without nasal and lateral plosion. Write only those words phonetically below, this time using the appropriate diacritics; again replace the phthongs with a subscript line. As before, say each word silently and then again voiced before you write it to be certain of the physical action.

We are now writing syllables and words phonetically and we can perceive that the clearly differentiated consonants provide most of the "meaning framework" for our language use. But we now must complete the process by adding those elements that provide even more of the sense, and most of the heart, to our words. These are what we have been calling the "phthongs", but we can now pin them to specific meanings within words. So they may now be termed **vowels**.

15 Writing the vowels

Until now, we have explored the vowels (formerly "phthongs") very freely as simply the acoustic result of our physical shaping of an unimpeded flow of voice. All the gradations of sound change – unfamiliar as well as familiar – are crucial to us in speaking accents. But as fellow speakers of American English, we realize that some of those acoustic results are familiar to us and some are not.

We know that "seat" and "sit" are different words in American English – and British English too – even though the consonants that begin and end the word are exactly the same. These vowel sounds actually change the meaning of the word. So, from our experience with consonant phones and phonemes, we know that the "ea" in "seat" and the "i" in "sit" represent different **vowel phonemes** – vowel sounds that are sufficiently different from one another that the members of a language population will accept them as different and capable of carrying meaning. If that one phoneme in the word is different, the whole word is different.

The symbols in the IPA Vowel Chart represent vowel phonemes just as the symbols in the consonant chart represent (or strive to represent) consonant phonemes in the languages of the world. We shall get back shortly to transcribing the phones, those crucial gradations of sound that we use in accent acquisition, but for now let us consider the simpler category of phonemes and the symbols that denote them.

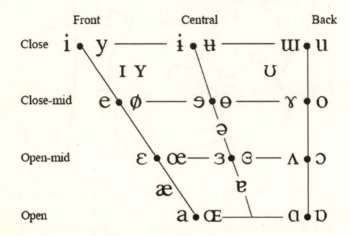

Figure 57. IPA American Vowel Chart.
(Please see www.langsci.ucl.ac.uk/ipa/ for original charts.)

The chart above is called a **vowel quadrilateral** because it is a four-sided figure. In a way it is similar to the consonant graphs that we have encountered before, because the symbols have a special relationship to one another based on physical positioning within the mouth. There is a sort of "X–Y" axes format as well. We see that across the horizontal "X-axis" is written "Front Central Back" and down the vertical "Y-axis" is written "Close Close-Mid Open-Mid Open".

The first thing that we notice about this graph, as distinct from the consonant graphs or charts, is that the left side of the vowel quadrilateral is slanted sharply downward toward the right. There is a reason for this. The vowel quadrilateral is an attempt to provide a schematic representation of the relative position of the articulators while engaging in the acoustic shaping of the vowels.

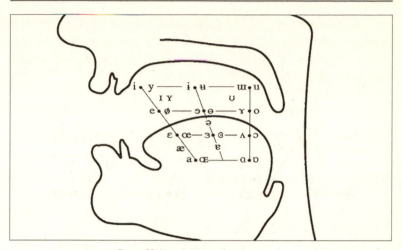

Figure 58. Vowel chart within the mouth.

We know from all our experience with "phthong shaping" that the way to physically shape the acoustic properties of vowel sounds is to arch upward or cup downward the body (dorsum) of the tongue while keeping the tip and blade relaxed and passive to the process. The arching or cupping can take place forward toward (or away from) the palate or back toward (or away from) the velum. The left side is slanted as a mild attempt to show that – because of the anatomy of the oral cavity – "front vowels" are produced further forward in a closed position and a bit further back in an open one.

So the vowel chart represents, roughly, a left-facing profile of the oral cavity. Vowel phoneme symbols near the top of the chart show the highest position of the arched (closed) tongue. The lowest position show the most cupped (open) tongue positions, all in a somewhat arbitrary and imperfect relationship to one another. The front vowels are arched or cupped in relationship to the palate and post-alveolar areas; the back vowels are arched or cupped in relationship to the velum and uvular areas. Note that in our illustration above the tongue in a resting position lies directly through the middle of the quadrilateral, exactly at a symbol lying in the center of the chart. This symbol is a **turned lower-case e** or in our recipe a **mid central vowel** –

/ ə /

– and it represents the first voiced sound that we produced at the very start of our work: the "sound of stupidity", the "uhhhh" that we all utter in the USA when we don't know what we're going to say next. The name of the symbol / ə / is the "schwa". The schwa is the *only* completely relaxed vowel sound that we produce. Everything else requires some tongue effort.

◀)) **Audio track 39:** *Schwa.*

Relax your jaw open. Relax your tongue completely. Sigh out a schwa

[əəəəəəəəəəə].

Then write the schwa several times and say it as you write it:

Every other vowel that we will form will require some muscular effort of the tongue – further forward or further back in the oral cavity, higher and more closed toward the roof of the mouth or further way and open. Enjoy your relaxed schwa while you can.

Vowels require other muscular effort as well. Look again at the vowel chart on page 166. Most – though not all – of the symbols are paired. Often there is a symbol that you might recognize as an English letter paired with a symbol that is quite unfamiliar. The difference is that the symbol on the left is **unrounded** and the symbol on the right is **rounded**. This refers to lip-rounding. So if a vowel is unrounded, the lip-corners stay relaxed and the lip edges stay relaxed apart. In fact, in the high or closed vowels that are unrounded, the lip-corners may actually be retracted very slightly (hello, risorius muscle). In the rounded closed vowels, the lip corners are fully pro-truded and the lips are pursed just short of obstructing the flow.

From the complete relaxation of the / ə / we move to the full muscular use of the closed front and back vowels, unrounded and rounded. Simply experiencing the pair of front closed vowels and the pair of back closed vowels will tell us much of what we need to know about the physical action of vowel formation. Here are the two **close front vowels**:

168

/ i /   / y /

A *probably unnecessary reminder:* when the IPA describes these as "close" it doesn't mean "closed". The articulators are not closed together, nor are they close enough together to obstruct the flow, because then we would have consonants, not vowels. But they are as close together as vowels can get.

The left symbol / i / is formed by arching the front of the body of the tongue strongly upward toward the front of the palate; the lips remain unrounded and may even be slightly retracted. The voiced flow moves unimpeded through this shaping. Our vowel recipe for this shaping is an **unrounded close front** vowel. The resultant sound is familiar to American English speakers and may be found in our first phonetic transcription of a complete word "seat" / sit /.

Speak the following words as they are transcribed phonetically and note that many of them would have different spellings when written in standard English orthography:

[min]   [fɹi]   [bit]   [lis]   [kip]   [plid]   [hip]   [ʃild]
[flis]   [nis]   [tʃiz]   [glim]   [ʌiz]

◀)) **Audio track 40:** *Unrounded close front vowel / i /.*

Now transcribe phonetically the following English words:

read _____   bleak _____   peek _____   zeal _____

keep_____   ease _____   sea _____   wield _____

Review the physical sensation of this vowel by holding the correct tongue and lip position and then breathing unvoiced through the oral shape you have created. Breathe a little more strongly than you would to speak so that you can feel the air on the tongue and the roof of the mouth. Feel it with both an egressive and ingressive airflow. Now do the same with a voiced egressive airflow. It is important to rely even more on the feel of the vowel shaping than on the resulting sound.

Leave the tongue in the same arched position. *Without moving the tongue*, protrude the lip corners and purse the lips into a full lip rounding that still does not obstruct the flow. Send an unvoiced airflow egressively and ingressively through this shaping.

Do the same on a voiced egressive flow. The sound result should be a **rounded close front** vowel. It is represented by the phonetic symbol / y /. We were in very familiar territory with / i /, but the sound / y / is not heard in American English generally, even though we use the symbol in our spelling all the time. But in French, this is a very common vowel, found in such words as "tu" / ty / or "rue" / ʁy /. It is also common in German and in other European languages that feature lip-rounding on vowels.

Try going into the / y / in a slightly different way. Start with a voiced / i / to establish the arched tongue position. As you keep sounding the / i / on a long sigh, go into the full lip rounding for / y /. Hear the sound change, but feel it also. *As you round your lips, make sure that you do not, out of muscular habit, pull the arch of the tongue back at all. We are used to performing a rounded close back vowel in English: this is not it. Keep that tongue arch forward.* Maintaining the close front arch of the tongue, round and unround the lips moving between / i / and /y /:

$$/ \text{i} / \quad / \text{y} / \quad / \text{i} / \quad / \text{y} / \quad / \text{i} / \quad / \text{y} /$$

Write four "nonsense words" using / y / as the vowel(s). Then speak them:

------------   ------------   -----------   ------------

◀)) **Audio track 41:** *Rounded close front vowel / y /.*

Close back vowels

$$/ \text{ɯ} / \quad / \text{u} /$$

The tongue arching for the two close back vowels / ɯ / and / u / is similar to the action for close front vowels / i / and / y /, but with one important difference. The arching action is enacted with the back portion of the tongue body (dorsum), not the front, and the arching action moves upward toward the velum.

170

We can start our exploration of the unrounded and rounded close back vowels with the more familiar rounded version, the **rounded close back vowel**, which is the right-hand symbol in the pair. The action is represented by the symbol / u / and is the sound we make in American English when we say "Ruth" or "bloom" or "route". Phonemically, these various spellings are always represented by / u /.

As with the close front vowels, the tongue tip and blade remain relaxed with the tongue tip just behind the lower teeth. The jaw should remain relaxed open. All the work should be done with the body of the tongue.

To form / u /, arch the tongue up toward the back of the velum and simultaneously round the lips (protrusion plus pursing) fully. Breathe unvoiced through this shaping to feel it before you sound it. Then add voicing to an egressive release of flow

[uuuuuuuuuuuuuuuuuuuuuuuuuuuu]

Speak the following words as they are transcribed phonetically:

[hu] [tʃu] [luz] [ɹum] [ups] [glu] [fud] [ʃuz] [vudu]

Transcribe phonetically the following English words:

doom _____ sleuth _____ drew _____ goo _____

pool _____ blue _____ soon _____ flew_____

◀)) **Audio track 42:** *Rounded close back vowel* / u /.

The **unrounded close back vowel** / ɯ / is not found generally in American speech, although it is becoming more frequently heard in some regional accents, especially among younger speakers, as a substitute for / u /. It has been a familiar feature of Northern English accents for a long time.

Arch the tongue toward the back of the velum as for / u /. Leave the lips unrounded. Speak the / ɯ / on a long sigh:

[ɯɯɯɯɯɯɯɯɯɯɯɯɯɯɯɯɯɯɯɯɯɯɯ]

Make sure that the tongue arching does not slowly roll forward.

◀)) **Audio track 43:** *Unounded close back vowel* / ɯ /.

Keeping the tongue arched toward the back of the velum, alternate lip rounding and unrounding, starting with an unvoiced egressive airflow to feel the shaping. Then do the same thing with a voiced sigh:

[u]   [ɯ]   [u]   [ɯ]   [u]   [ɯ]

Now write four "nonsense words" using [ɯ] as the vowel(s):

------------   --------------   -------------   -------------

Speak the following transcribed English words that use [ɯ] as substitute for [u]

[hɯz]   [tʃɯz]   [slɯs]   [pɹɯv]   [glɯm]   [tɯ]

Open vowels: from arching to cupping

We may be surprised that the efficient speaking of open vowels requires a lot of tongue muscularity. This is because we often speak open vowels by opening the jaw wide—which is fairly easy to do—rather than by using the tongue. Opening the jaw beyond the point of natural relaxation is not a very good idea, though. It can contribute to tempero-mandibular disorder (TMD), for one thing. It also causes us to associate the constriction of the pharynx that accompanies forced jaw opening with the normal formation of some open vowels, a big mistake that even voice scientists can (and sometimes do) make. Open vowels do not require a constricted vocal tract. The secret of successful open vowel production is to use the tongue, not the jaw.

Of course the jaw needs to stay *relaxed* open.

Open vowels use tongue cupping instead of the tongue arching that we have been using for the close vowels. As before, the tongue tip and blade remain relaxed with the tip just behind the lower front teeth.

Open front vowels

$$/ a / \qquad / Œ /$$

These two symbols are found at the lower left of the vowel quadrilateral. The unrounded version / a / is certainly a familiar symbol, a **lower-case printed "a"**. In American English spelling (orthography) the "a" symbol can stand for a lot of different sounds: "cat", "calm", "garbage", for example. In phonetic transcription, as we know, it stands for only one. But what is that one? For most American speakers, it is in none of the three words I just quoted . . .

The easiest way to get at the [a / is to consider the symbol that is right above it in the vowel quadrilateral, represented by the symbol

$$/ æ /$$

This symbol looks like an "a" and an "e" pushed together. It is that is taken from Old and Middle English and its official name is the "aesc", pronounced "ash". (It has been around for well over a millennium, and is still used in the orthography of Icelandic.) It is just slightly less open than the / a /, so the feeling in shaping the two symbols is quite similar. It is a very familiar sound in American English speech.

To form the / æ /, keep the tongue-tip relaxed behind the lower teeth, the jaw relaxed − but not forced − open, and then cup the very front portion of the body of the tongue strongly downward into the curve of the mandible below the lower teeth. Keep the lips unrounded. Breathe strongly ingressively and egressively a few times (don't hyperventilate!) to feel the shaping and then sigh a voiced egressive release

$$[æææææææææææææææææææææ]$$

This is what we often call a "short a' or "flat a", the vowel that Americans use some version of in words like "cat", stand", "map", "dance", "class", "half", "brash", etc.

Say these words using this vowel, and then write them phonetically:
fat, sash, clap, vast, chance, calf, mast

‒ ‒

‒ ‒

Now try to lower the cupping even more. Your well-attuned oral sensors will note that, in doing so, the curve of the mandible at the front of the jaw requires that the cupping action of the tongue rolls slightly back as you cup the tongue further. Breathe silently as before to feel the positioning and then voice the resulting sound. If you have followed the recipe fully, the sound will be / a /. the so-called "intermediate a" or "Italian a".

It is the lowest—most open—front vowel you can make. We find it in American English in the old-fashioned Southern accent single-vowel pronunciation of the personal pronoun "I". It is also the first element of the diphthong that most Americans use to say that same personal pronoun "I". But, in isolation, many American speakers don't really recognize it. You have explored a lot of new territory in your phthong shaping; here's one place where that experience is very useful.

The phonetic symbol for this sound action, as we know, is / a /. Don't be influenced by any previous ideas about a Southern accent, but speak these phonetically transcribed words as the symbols indicate. Keep the cupping action really strong without opening the jaw excessively.:

[fan] [laf] [tʃald] [kand] [mald] [van] [ʌal] [ʃan] [blað] [ɹa] [pan] [vas]

fine life child kind mild vine while shine blithe wry pine vise

◀⟩) **Audio track 44:** *Unrounded fully open front vowel / æ / and / a /.*

We will save the writing of this phonetic symbol for its use in two diphthongs.

Here is the symbol for the rounded open front vowel:

$$/ \text{Œ} /$$

This is an interesting symbol because for some time the International Phonetic Association considered it a more or less theoretical symbol that did not actually occur in any existing language. One can understand why this was so. Lip-spreading (the active form of unrounding) and lip-rounding lessen considerably as we move from the top (close) area of the vowel quadrilateral to the bottom (open) area. So the comparative physical actions and the comparative sound results between [a] and [œ] are both negligible. However, recently Austrian German has come to the rescue, discovering in the proverbial nick of time that the word for rope "seil" is pronounced [sœː]. The wedge-shaped colon symbol, by the way, is a **diacritic** indicating that the symbol preceding it is lengthened; if you've got it, flaunt it.

In producing this symbol, however, we learn something useful about lip-rounding. To move from [a] to [œ], all you need to do is produce the strong tongue cupping of [a] and then protrude the lip corners very slightly. No pursing required. Try writing six nonsense words phonetically using [œ].

_____   _____   _____

_____   _____   _____

and then speak them.

On a voiced sigh, move between [a] and [œ]

[a]   [œ]   [a]   [œ]   [a]   [œ]

Feel and hear that the difference in sound result is negligible. This is a good illustration of the fact that lip unrounding or rounding, while important in the shaping of vowel phonemes, is a secondary action to tongue position – and especially so with the "open vowels".

◀)) **Audio track 45:** *Rounded fully open front vowel* [œ].

Open back vowels

/ ɑ /   / ɒ /

The **script a** and the **turned script a**. The unrounded symbol on the left is not only familiar as another way of writing "a" in English orthography, it is a very familiar sound in American English speech.

Think – and feel – back to the isolation exercise called "Rolling the ball". If you start with the strong front-cupping of the tongue for [a], you can easily "roll the ball" – cupping it all the while – back to a cupping performed by the back of the body of the tongue. To describe it in a slightly grosser way (and why not, I say), cup the tongue as far back and as strongly down as you can without engaging the gag reflex and throwing up. *Do not retract the tongue root as you do this; if you do, you will constrict the pharynx and create an unnecessarily constricted version of the sound result.* The lips remain unrounded – and unprotruded, for that matter. *Do not force the jaw open!* You are now producing the **unrounded open back vowel**.

Breathe ingressively and egressively through this shaping; it is very open, but it is not relaxed: it is a very muscular action. Now sigh egressively through this shaping to form the sound result [ɑɑɑɑɑɑɑɑɑɑɑɑɑɑɑɑɑɑ], the proverbial sigh of relief. Or of discovery. (The two are surprisingly similar, aren't they?)

Speak the following American English words as transcribed phonetically:

[kɑm]	[lɑt]	[ʃɑp]	[hɑt]	[vɑz]	[ɑ]	[dɑk]	[ʃɑk]	[sɑm]
"calm"	"lot"	"shop"	"hot"	"vase"	"ah"	"dock"	"shock"	"psalm"

◀)) **Audio track 46:** *Unrounded fully open back vowel / ɑ /.*

Our word options here are limited. Many [a] vowels occur in "ar" combinations and many in words of more than one syllable that use vowels you haven't yet explored. This understood, try writing a few more one-syllable words with the vowel [a]:

-------- -------- -------- -------- -------- --------

The symbol [ɒ] is termed by linguists the **turned script a** . We know that doing a little lip-protruding will not produce a sound result of great acoustic significance. Even though the **rounded back open vowel** [ɒ] is paired with the [ɑ], it is of insignificant sound difference unless the cupping of the tongue is lessened slightly. This is why many phoneticians commonly render the vowel as placed just slightly higher on the vowel quadrilateral. For the time being, though. practice the action as a very slight lip corner protrusion from [ɑ] to [ɒ]:

$$[ɑ] \quad [ɒ] \quad [ɑ] \quad [ɒ] \quad [ɑ] \quad [ɒ]$$

Now do the same action again and this time, try a slight relaxation of the cupping on [ɒ] to render the tongue position less fully open.

◀)) **Audio track 47:** *Rounded fully (or open) open back vowel [ɒ].*

Filling in the vowel chart

So far our exploration of the IPA's vowel quadrilateral has focused on the pairs of unrounded and rounded vowels that are found at the corners of the vowel quadrilateral. These are the most extreme muscular actions that we take with the tongue and with the lips in shaping the acoustic properties of vowel phonemes. With these skills you can explore all the other actions and their illustrative symbols, using the vowel recipe of physical action. It is another three-part recipe.

1 Unrounded or Rounded.
2 Front, Central or Back.
3 Close, Close-Mid, Open-Mid, Open, and sometimes Fully Open.

Or any shaping in between. *The total space within the vowel quadrilateral represents – in an imprecise, schematic way – the action of arching or cupping of the front, middle or back of the body (or dorsum) of the tongue. It does not involve the tip or the blade.*

To give us a more familiar framework without forcing us into the familiar to the exclusion of everything else, we can now learn quickly the symbols for the commonly accepted American vowel phonemes. This exploration will allow you to experience actions – and sound products of those actions – that we all recognize as conveying definite, unambiguous meaning when contained within a word in American English. They do not, however, necessarily represent the phonemes as they are used in every single American accent.

Rather than learn all the American vowel symbols right now, we will stay with the **monophthongs**, the actions where the articulators are held without moving, to shape the voiced, unobstructed flow into a single sound. We will learn the diphthongs – compound vowel actions – later.

As you **look** at these monophthong symbols, you will see that most of them are Roman alphabet letters that we already use in English. In fact, we have already found some of them in the work we have just completed.

As you **speak** these vowel phonemes, do not worry about minor variations in your pronunciation of the vowel, as long as you and your listeners

177

can clearly understand the correct word in the following list of minimal pairs:[1]

peat-pit   pit-pet

pet-pat   pat-pot

pot-pawt   pawt-put

put-poot   putt-pert

 Audio track 48: *Minimal pairs.*

 Audio track 49: *Minimal pairs using allophones.*

Admittedly a very few of these words are nonsense words in English. We use them here to keep the consonants that begin and end the words the same throughout. If there is any doubt about which word you are saying, alter your shaping of the flow to make the distinction clearly intelligible.

Here, then, are the monophthongal phonemes of American English. They are easy to learn and easy to speak, because you have already had a lot of life practise in doing so. But do not get too comfortable with this inherited skill: the really interesting work for the actor is lies ahead in the myriad of gradations of these shapings: the throng of phthongs that cram the vowel quadrilateral like the proverbial stuffed goose. In other words: the **allophones**, the ingredients of phonetic distinction, the place where accents live.

---

1. "Minimal Pairs" are one-syllable word pairs where the difference in the word meaning is defined by only one phoneme change.

16

American vowel phonemes

In the front

/ i / written / i /

"Lower-case I". Tongue **arched** high and forward, toward the mid-palate. Lip corners unrounded and perhaps slightly retracted. As in "FLEECE,"[1] "mead," "niece," etc.

◀))) **Audio track 50:** / i /.

/ I / written / I / or / l /

"Small Capital I". Tongue **arched** slightly less high and forward, toward the mid-palate: Lip corners slightly retracted. As in "KIT," "give," "chill," etc.

◀))) **Audio track 51:** / ɪ /.

1. Illustrative words in capital letters represent the "lexical sets" devised by J. C. Wells in his book *Accents of English*. Rather than just trying to communicate vocally a single vowel phoneme "I'm saying 'eee'," it is more accurate and convenient to say "I'm saying the 'fleece' vowel.".

/ ε // written / ε /

"Epsilon". Tongue **cupped** slightly down and slightly less forward: Lip corners very slightly retracted. As in "DRESS," "set," "vest," etc.

◀)) **Audio track 52:** / ε /.

/ æ / written / æ /

"Ash". Tongue **cupped** very slightly further down and slightly less forward. Lips unrounded but corners not retracted. As in "TRAP," "BATH," "patch," "half," etc.

◀)) **Audio track 53:** / æ /.

In the back

/ u / written / u /

"Lower-case U". Tongue **arched** high and back, toward the front of the velum. Lip corners forward, lips rounded. As in "GOOSE," "lose," "chew," "true," etc.

◀)) **Audio track 54:** / u /.

/ ʊ / written / ʊ /

"Upsilon". Tongue **arched** less high and back, toward the front of the velum: Lip corners forward, lips slightly less rounded. As in "FOOT," "good," "should," "push," etc.

◀)) **Audio track 55:** / ʊ /.

/ ɔ / written / ɔ /

"Open O". Tongue **cupped** slightly downward in back. Lip corners slightly less forward, lip corners protruded. As in "THOUGHT" (sometimes), "CLOTH" (sometimes), "caught," "bought," "gone," "all," etc. But note that many Americans pronounce these words with a realization closer to the more open phoneme / ɑ / .

◀)) **Audio track 56:** / ɔ /.

/ ɑ / written / ɑ /

"Script A". Tongue **cupped** actively downward in back:
Lip corners relaxed, lips not rounded. As in "LOT," "THOUGHT" (sometimes), "CLOTH" (sometimes), "calm," "father," "cot," "lobster," etc. *But note that not all Americans pronounce all these words using this symbol (i.e. physical action).*

◀)) **Audio track 57:** / ɑ /.

In the center

We begin with the most relaxed central or mid vowel, *the only fully relaxed vowel sound.* All the vowels we have considered so far require some tongue use (or effort): arched or cupped, front or back. And also some lip use, corners spread or forward, lips rounded. Not this one.

/ ə / written / ə /

"Schwa" or "Turned printed E". Tongue completely relaxed in the mouth: Lips completely relaxed. As in "uhhhh," "duhhhh," the unstressed vowel in "COMMA," "relative," or "away," or possibly an extremely de-energized (in articulation) pronunciation of "up," "love," "thumb," etc.

◀)) **Audio track 58:** / ə /.

The two other mid-vowels commonly used in American speech are the subject of some discord amongst phoneticians. I prefer to place them in the vowel quadrilateral as many American speech teachers use them, rather than their IPA placement which is more appropriate for RP British pronunciation.

/ ɜ / *written* / ɜ /

"Reversed Epsilon". The tongue is not so much arched as **bunched** (tensed or braced slightly). The lips remain relaxed. If, while sounding this symbol, the tongue is thickened slightly more, the vowel will start to move into the area of focus for a retroflex approximant consonant [ɻ / , producing a brief "R-color" riding on the end of the vowel. This is represented by the attachment of a [˞ / to the vowel, producing [ɜ˞] for the "R-color" version of [ɜ]. As in "NURSE," "bird," "learn," "worst," "tern," etc. A variety of spellings, and all these words may be said with or without "R-color." I place this sound and symbol slightly higher (more close) in the vowel quadrilateral than the IPA does.

◀)) **Audio track 59:** / ɜ /.

/ ʌ / *written* / ʌ /

"Turned V". In its American form this vowel occurs just below, and slightly back of, the schwa. The IPA gives it more back placement, as an unrounded (slightly lip-spread?) form of [ɔ]. In American use the only difference between it and the schwa in sound is that when we stress the syllable in which the sound appears there is a tendency to flatten the tongue very slightly. So there is a tiny change of physical action, and also a minute change in the sound. We might set the tentative transcription rule then, that the [ʌ] is used in the stressed syllable in a word like "corrupt," while the schwa [ə] is used in the unstressed syllable, "corrupt," (since we pronounce the written "o" like "uh" [ə]). As in "STRUT," "one," "such," "flood."

◀)) **Audio track 60:** / ʌ /.

182

Here is the way many American phoneticians position the central vowels within the vowel quadrilateral:

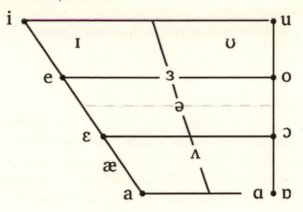

Figure 59. American vowel quadrilateral.

Write the following words in phonemic transcription. Say each word several times before you try to transcribe it. Say it several times after you transcribe it too. Try to write the word the way **you** say it, using the phoneme that does the job best.

think _____

pulled _____

gone _____

shrimp _____

crude _____

perks _____

refreshed _____

manatee _____

phlegmatic _____

probable _____

wheel_____

grassy_____

vexed_____

gauze _____

robs _____

wool_____

above _____

on _____

rationale _____

nauseous _____

(*Note*: Don't just transcribe words off the paper. Say them. Feel them. Then transcribe *your own* physical actions and the sounds that result.)

Here are one or more ways of transcribing the above words:

θɪŋk	ʍil
pʊld	ɡɹæsi
ɡɔn ɡɑn	vɛkst
ʃɹɪmp	ɡɔz
krud	ɹɑbz
pɝ·ks	wʊl
ɹifɹɛʃt	əbʌv əbəv
mænəti	ɔn ɑn
flɛɡmætɪk	ɹæʃənæl
pɹɑbəbl̩	nɔʒəs nɔʃəs nɑʃəs

Your own transcription may not match any of these. But your job is not to match what is printed here: it is *accurately* to represent the way you speak these words. The "right answer" in phonetic transcription is accurate representation, not meeting a standard way of saying something. It is *descriptive*, not *prescriptive*. At the same time, it might be a useful exercise to try these pronunciations anyway.

17

New vowels for diphthongs

. . . and it's [dɪfθɔŋz] not [dipθɔŋz]

A **diphthong** is a sequence of two vowels in which the first is stressed and the second is unstressed, so that to the hearer the sound slides swiftly and almost imperceptibly from the first to the second. There are a few new vowel phonemes in American English that are used primarily in diphthongs.

/eĭ/ *written* / eĭ /

The vowel phoneme [e] is placed just below the [ɪ] in the vowel quadri-lateral. As a pure vowel, it is the sound that we hear in French in "été", and occurs frequently in English dialects but not in most American speech. It forms the first **element** – the first of the two sounds – of the diphthong that we often call a "long a", as in the words "FACE", "take", or "play".

We may not even have thought of this compound sound as a com-bination of two vowels rather than a single one before. The tongue starts with the [e] but before the sound ends the tongue raises very slightly to the [ɪ]. It may seem that the sound is actually sliding higher up to the [i],

185

and perhaps for you it is. Know the difference, however: for most people the fact that the second element is unstressed means that the action won't get quite high enough for an actual [i]. But the fact that the tongue is headed in that direction means that we may *think* that we are producing an [i], when actually we are reaching a high version of an [ɪ].

The "breve" diacritic over the second element [ĭ] means that the symbol it modifies is shortened and pronounced very lightly. We generally notate a [˘] over the second element in a diphthong to show that the two vowels are not spoken with equal stress.

So in [eĭ] the front of the tongue is arched quite high and forward, with the lips slightly spread, and near the end of the sound the tongue arches a bit higher but a bit less forward. As in "say", "rain" "shape", "prey", "lay", "vague". etc. [seĭ] [ɹeĭn] [ʃeĭp].

Alternate saying the diphthong [eĭ] and the vowel [e] until you can feel and hear the difference between them.

Now try doing this in words. The diphthong will probably sound like − or close to − how you say the word in your normal speech. The pure vowel pronunciation will make the word sound like you are speaking with another accent from your own, Irish perhaps, or French. Try each pronunciation twice: once stretching the vowel sound(s) out, and once saying the word as quickly as possible.

"Same"   [seĭm]   [sem]

"Take"   [teĭk]   [tek]

"Fail"   [feĭl]   [fel]

"Chase"   [tʃeĭs]   [tʃes]

"Waste"   [weĭst]   [west]

◄)) **Audio track 61:** / e / / eĭ / .

/ aĭ / written / aĭ /

"I think, therefore I am."

This diphthong is the one we use to assert ourselves in American speech. Quite literally: "I" (or "eye", or sometimes "aye"). The so-called "long i". But as with the "long a" of [eĭ] this is not a single sound: it is a diphthong, a sequence of two vowels. As in "PRICE", "like", "type", "climb".

If we want to distinguish this diphthong clearly from other diphthongs or single vowels, the first element is what is often called an "intermediate a". It is written as / a / just like the lower-case "a" that you see again and again in this text. But it is not pronounced like those spelling illustrations. Many Americans, even those who use this sound in this (and another) diphthong every day, have difficulty initially in hearing the vowel in isolation as different from the vowel sounds around it. But if we approach it physically, the production of the sound is quite easy. And as we produce it consistently, we will get used to its unique sound.

Start with the vowel / æ /. Then cup the front of your tongue *even lower*. Make sure that you keep the tip and blade of the tongue relaxed: the work is happening just behind them. Make sure also that you don't pull the focus of the action back so that you are doing a "broad a" or / ɑ /. Keep the cupping action of the tongue focused forward.

Sigh this new sound on a long / aː /. Hear and feel it without letting it slip into a more familiar sound. In American dialects we use slight variations of this isolated [a] frequently in the so-called "Boston a" of "Paak the caa in Haavud Yaad". Or the genteel old-fashioned Southern of "maaghty faane".

Now we can use the sound in our diphthong. We start slowly with the / a / and gradually raise the front of the tongue from its extreme cupping to a high arch. The lips go from an unrounded open position to a slight spread at the corners. So the sound slides from / a / to a very short, light / ɪ /.

For now it is sufficient that we write the diphthong as / aĭ /. But because the tongue is making a bigger cupping-to-arching action on / aĭ / than on / eĭ /, there is even more of a tendency to slide past the / ɪ / and into an

/ i /. See if you can tell which you naturally tend to do. Then see if you can control that arching of the tongue to produce either one.

There can be other pronunciation differences, too. Many Americans start this diphthong from / ɑ / or even / ɔ /. So "time" is often said as [tʰɑɪm] or sometimes [tʰɔɪm].

Try saying the alternative pronunciations of each element of the diphthong in some words:

> light, chime, fight, while, nice, eye, vie, whine, slice,
> shine, wild, kite, sighed, nigh, ripe, kite, pie.

Now read some words phonetically:

> [faɪnd], [stɹɑɪk], [ʍaɪl], [tɹɑɪ], [gaɪd],
> [laɪs], [smaːɫ], [hɔɪt], [ʃaɪn], [ɹaɪm].

◀)) **Audio track 62:** / aɪ / *with allophones.*

/ aʊ / *written* / aʊ /

In isolation this is the sound of pain: "Ow!" Or as in "MOUTH". "loud", "round".

Most Americans start this diphthong from / a /, the same "Intermediate a" (or "lower-case a" as it is termed in phonetics) that we just explored in / aɪ /. But here the movement of the tongue from cupped to arched goes slightly back, rather than staying forward. And rather than a slight spread of the lips from the first element to the second, the lips round almost fully. The resulting second element is [ʊ], the sound in "good", or "push".

As with / aɪ /, because the cupping-to-arching action is considerable we often have a tendency to overshoot the mark and take the second element to [u], the fully rounded high back placement (as in "two" or "soon"). Say [taʊn] and then [taun]. Can you say both easily while still keeping the second element very short?

An extremely common variant of this diphthong is [æʊ], the bane of prescriptive speech teachers because it starts the diphthong from the "flat a" (in phonetics, the "ash"). If this is the way you pronounce words like "out" or "down", it is not necessary for you to change just to please those few whose ears might be offended; however, you must be able to say the other variants, and to feel the difference in your mouth. To pull students' tongues away from [æʊ̆], speech teachers often mandate that the diphthong be pronounced [ɑʊ̆], with the full sonority of the "broad a" (in phonetics the "script a"). To some, including me, this may sound a trifle old-fashioned, but it does keep the [aɪ̆] and the [ɑʊ̆] completely distinct from one another.

So try saying the following words in their most common variant forms:

"house"   [haʊ̆s]   [hæʊ̆s]   [hɑʊ̆s]   [haʊs]   [hæʊs]

🔊 **Audio track 63:** / aʊ̆ / *with allophones on "house".*

"now"   [næʊ̆]   [nɑʊ̆]   [naʊ̆]   [nɑʊ̆]   [naʊ̆]

plow"   [pl̥ɑʊ̆]   [pl̥æʊ̆]   [pl̥aʊ̆]   [pl̥æʊ̆]   [pl̥aʊ̆]

"bough"   [baʊ̆]   [bɑʊ̆]   [baʊ̆]   [bæʊ̆]   [baʊ̆]

"count"   [kʰɑʊ̆nt]   [kʰaʊ̆nt]   [kʰaʊ̆nt]   [kʰæʊ̆nt]   [kʰaːəʔ˺]

[Just for a change. That strange corner symbol after the glottal stop in [ʰaːəʔ˺] means that it is not exploded, just stopped. And the "h" means that there's a little puff of air after the unvoiced stop-plosive. We'll have more of these decorative symbols soon.]

/ Oʊ̆ / written / Oʊ̆ /

The expression of surprise. Or comprehension. Or perhaps surprised comprehension: "Oh". It is what we sometimes call a "long o" as in "GOAT" or "show" or "hope".

   This diphthong is produced with two "back vowels". In its idealized form it begins with the pure back vowel / o /. Some speech teachers maintain that Americans pronounce the pure vowel (non-diphthong) / o / in words where the "o" receives lesser stress or is otherwise shorter in duration, such as "rotisserie" or "cocaine". I disagree. The action of moving through the diphthong in / oʊ /, from / o / to / ʊ /, is very slight: you arch the tongue a tiny bit higher, and purse the lips – which already should have the lip corners well forward for the / o / – just slightly. We can do this easily even on the shortest syllable and, if one listens closely, that slight tensing during the sound happens almost always in American speech.

The proof is always in the action. Try the alternatives: say / oː / as an extended sound in the following words. Make sure that you don't move the articulators at all during the / o / vowel sound:

Row, know, old, post, vote, most, tone, below, abode, mould,
location, total, lotion, cope, sewed, baroque, shoulder, plosive, demote.

Now, toward the end of the release of sound, add that slight pursing of the lips and that slight elevation of the tongue arching that will take the vowel into a diphthong / oʊ /. Repeat the same words again as diphthongs.

◀)) **Audio track 64:** / oʊ / *with allophones.*

Now say the following sentence as naturally as possible:

"I told you to go over to the boat."

Are you really starting the / oʊ / diphthong with a pure / o /? Possibly; but probably not. Most Americans slide this diphthong in from a mid-vowel. (Most likely a mid-vowel we haven't explored yet.) It's what we call an **on-glide**. So our using / oʊ / to indicate this diphthong is sort of a convention, a way of consistently identifying the phoneme / oʊ / even though phonetically each of us might say it slightly differently.

/ ɔɪ̆ / / written / ɔɪ̆ /

We *know* this one is a diphthong. We *know* that the sound is changing. Even the most unperceptive listener (which you aren't, of course) can hear that weary forward slide from one element to the other: "Oy" – as in the classic Yiddish sigh of resignation "Oy vey" (at least when it's spoken by a non-Yiddish speaker, or maybe a non-New Yorker). Our perception is aided by the fact that here the diphthongal journey is not only from more open to more closed, but also from back to front.

There is much possible phonetic variation for this diphthong, as there was with the ones we have explored above. One might change the first element from / ɔ / to / o /, as in [oɪ̆]. One might slide on through the / ɪ / of the second element onto [i]. One might even intrude a lip-rounded [w] into the diphthong, as in [oŭ.wɪː].

Say the following words as naturally as possible, hearing and feeling what you do:

CHOICE, joy, coy, toy, annoy, boy, coin, voice, ploy, coil, toil, oil, foil, oyster.

◀)) **Audio track 65:** / ɔɪ̆ / *with allophones.*

As with the other diphthongs, this is a notation of the phonemic / ɔɪ̆ /, the approximate way that English speakers say the diphthong to convey a particular defining unit of meaning in a word, "joy" [dʒɔɪ̆] rather than "jay" [dʒeɪ̆].

Try speaking the following sentence using your own usual pronunciation of the / ɔɪ̆ /:

"Joyce's boy-toy loitered noisily in the foyer."

Now try it again definitely using / ɔ / and / ɪ /. (Do the two elements singly, then slide from on to the other: / ɔɪ̆ /.) Now definitely as [oɪ̆]. Now using [oɪ̆]. Explore feeling and hearing the difference, even though phonemically it is the same diphthong.

18

All the vowel phonemes

Unrounded front vowels

We already know all of these, but here they are again:

$$/i/ \quad /\iota/ \quad /e/ \quad /\varepsilon/ \quad /æ/ \quad /a/$$

Speak them again, just for review. Remember that we encountered some of them as the first elements of diphthongs. Speak them all as extended pure vowels. Feel the action of the front of the tongue-body moving from arching to cupping.

Rounded front vowels

We have already met two of the rounded front vowels in our initial exploration of the corners of the vowel quadrilateral. Here are all of them, from close to open:

/ y /

The front of the tongue is arched toward the alveolo-palatal region as for / i /. The lips are fully rounded as for / u /.

/ Y /

The front of the tongue is arched as for / ɪ /. The lips are rounded as for / ʊ /.

/ ø /

The front of the tongue is arched as for / e /. The lip corners are protruded (with slight lip-pursing) as for / o /.

/ œ /

The front of the tongue is slightly cupped as for / ɛ /. The lip-corners are protruded with no lip pursing, as for / ɔ /.

/ Œ /

The front of the tongue is strongly cupped, as for / a /. The lip corners are very slightly protruded, as for / ɒ /.

Unrounded back vowels

We have met two of the unrounded back vowels already. Here are all of them, from close to open:

/ ɯ /

The back of the tongue is arched toward the velum as for / u /. The lips are slightly spread, as for / i /.

/ ɤ /

The back of the tongue is slightly arched toward the velum as for / o /. The lips are very slightly spread as for / e /.

/ ʌ /

The back of the tongue is slightly cupped as for / ɔ /. The lips are unrounded as for / ɛ /.

/ ɑ /

The back of the tongue is strongly cupped as for / ɒ /, indeed, arguably more than / ɒ /. The lips are unrounded as for / a /.

Rounded back vowels

We already know these. Here they all are, in order from close to open:

/ u /

The back of the tongue is arched high toward the velum in a fully close position. The lips are fully rounded, both lip-corner protrusion and full pursing, but without obstructing the flow.

/ ʊ /

The back of the tongue is arched, but slightly less close. The lip-pursing is very slightly relaxed, but lip-corner protrusion remains full.

/ o /

The back of the tongue is only slightly arched. Lip corner protrusion is almost as strong as for / ʊ /.

/ ɔ /

The back of the tongue is very slightly cupped. Lip-corner protrusion is only very slightly relaxed from / o /.

/ ɒ /

Again, in the vowel, quadrilateral this is the "rounded" version of / ɑ /. However I, and many American phoneticians, consider that the actual realization of this phoneme can only happen as a distinguishable vowel from / ɑ / if you slightly uncup the back of the tongue. There is only a very slight lip-corner protrusion in this phoneme, which would not alone change the sound product appreciably. We hear this sound in "short o" sounds as they are heard in a very few American accents, as well as in English RP (Standard English) and in "Good American Speech", the accent that still is often considered appropriate for classical plays in the United States.

The central vowels

Moving the mountain again

In the articulator isolation exercise "Moving the mountain" we explored rolling the arch of the tongue from the alveolo-palatal area of the roof of the mouth to the back of the velar area. The key to this exercise is that the tongue itself does not protrude or retract; like a wave passing through the ocean, the crest of the arched tongue dorsum raises and then relaxes sequentially, thus making the "wave" or the "mountain" appear to move back or forward.

We have now experienced this selective arching and cupping in the formation of the closed and open vowels. To carry this experience into the formation of the central vowels, you can begin with the tongue arched as for / i /. Roll the arch (but don't retract the tongue) *halfway* back toward / u /. When the tongue arch is midway between the two extremes, it is in the correct position for the **close central** vowels.

/ ɨ /

The lips are spread as for / i /.

/ ʉ /

The lips are rounded as for / u /.

For the **half-close central** vowels, lower the arch of the tongue slightly, to the same degree of arching as found in / e / and / o /, but equidistant between them.

/ ɘ /

The lips are very slightly spread as for / e /.

/ ɵ /

The lip corners are protruded with very slight lip-pursing as for / o /.

For the **half-open central** vowels, the tongue is slightly cupped, to the same degree as found in / ɛ / or / ɔ /, but equidistant between them.

/ ɜ /

The lip-corners are unrounded as for / ɛ /. It is commonly realized as [ɝ] in American speech. We have already had a full description of this phoneme as the **nurse** vowel.

/ ɞ /

The lip corners are protruded with no lip pursing as for / ɔ /.

There is one **open central vowel**. The tongue is strongly cupped, to *almost* the same degree as found in / a / and / ɒ /, but equidistant between them.

/ ɐ /

The lips are wholly unrounded.

◀)) **Audio track 66:** *all the other IPA monophthongs.*

19

Combinations

Mid-central offglide diphthongs

Without adding any new vowel symbols or sounds, we can explore ways of combining these basic American phonemes into more diphthongs that play important roles in American speech. The most important category of these combined actions is the group of diphthongs that – in traditional transcription – always end in the "schwa", the totally relaxed "uhh" sound that we have (perhaps unjustly) described as the "sound of stupidity". The phonetic symbol is, as we already know, / ə /. Here, the / ə / is the object of the off-glide and so receives weaker stress than the symbol that precedes it.

There are five mid-central offglide diphthongs in American English. The first one is:

$$/ ɪə̆ /$$

as in "**near**", "steered", "veer", "mere", "tears", "shear", "beer", "here", "tiers", "peer".

As written, we would pronounce these words with a primary emphasis on the first element of the diphthong and then simply continue the vowel (the phthong) action into the complete tongue relaxation of the schwa / ə / as an offglide.

Practice each of these words slowly and pay particular attention to that offglide relaxation, making sure that you always end with complete relaxation and – at the risk of boring repetition – a relaxed mandible. Then practice the words at a normal speed.

But it surely has not escaped your notice that despite the fact that these words have several different spellings, they all have one thing in common: they all have the letter "r" following the diphthong.

Re-enter rhoticity

We have already discussed rhoticity (r-ishness) as it relates to consonant transcription. In this group of diphthongs almost all the words have post-vocalic rhoticity. We even will encounter the classic pirate "arrrrr" as a rhotic mid-central diphthong.

This rhoticity, in a sense, hangs on the mid-central vowels, and for a very good reason: the tongue position is very close to the "braced-r" position; only a slightly greater degree of tongue-bracing tension, and the rhoticity comes roaring through.

As we know – and regret – there is no phonetic symbol for the "braced r". But the International Phonetic Association has allowed rhotic speakers in America, England, and elsewhere a diacritic symbol that can be appended to the weak form second element of the diphthong to indicate some indeterminate degree of rhoticity. If we are using the schwa, as above, the compound symbol looks like this:

$$[\text{I}\breve{\text{ə}}^{\text{r}}]$$

So now you can speak the word list on the preceding page adding that third element of tongue-bracing to produce some degree of rhoticity.

The rhotic zones

We know that the "braced r" is a palato-velar approximant. This recognition, along with our knowledge of other approximant "r" phonemes, allows us to plot a set of three approximant "rhotic zones" along the roof of the mouth from front to back. They would separate other phoneme approximants in the following form:

Tip	Tip/blade	Front	Middle	Back	Back
alveolar	post-alveolar	palatal	palato-velar	velar	uvular
[ʐ]	[ɹ]	[j]	[braced r]	[ɰ]	[ʁ]
	(rhotic)		(rhotic)		(rhotic)

Other vowel options

For most American speakers, the triple action (strong vowel/weak vowel/rhotic bracing) that you enacted in the slow version of [ɪɚ̆] sounds a trifle odd, mostly because the bracing has to take a considerably journey from the complete relaxation of the schwa to the braced approximant rhoticity. For most Americans, the second element of the diphthong would be spoken in a slightly more close position, with the tongue very slightly arched in the middle of the dorsum. From this point, only a tiny bit of additional bracing would bring the tongue into the palato-velar rhotic zone.

The traditional symbol for American speakers is / ɜ /, the "reverse epsilon". While this symbol is rendered on the IPA vowel chart as an "unrounded half-open central vowel, its "phonemic territory" can extend upward to the "unrounded half-close central vowel" position (so, in our physical terms, it is slightly arched, instead of slightly cupped). It was proposed as such to the IPA in the 1930s by the eminent American phonetician John Kenyon, but this proposal was rejected. Nonetheless, American phoneticians have followed this practice since that time. Kenyon also proposed this position for monophthong words like – well – "words". Or:

first, purse, shirt, learn, girth, murk, turn, swerve,
curb, flirt, shirred, gurn, dearth

If the same mid-central offglide diphthong was written in this manner with added rhoticity, it would look like this:

$$[\;\mathrm{I}\breve{\mathrm{3}}^{\scriptstyle\vee}\;]$$

There is another option, though, because if you look at the vowel quadrilateral again, you see that there is another symbol occupying that unrounded half-close central vowel space. We have already established that many of these symbols are theoretical anyway, according to the *Handbook of the International Phonetic Association*. But if we think of these places on the vowel quadrilateral as being roughly equivalent to physical action (and to relative acoustic placement), the appropriate symbol to use for the second element of this diphthong would be the "reverse lower-case e" or / ɘ /, making the appropriate symbol look this this:

$$[\;\mathrm{I}\breve{\mathrm{ɘ}}^{\scriptstyle\vee}\;]$$

One could very well use this symbol for all the monophthongs in the previous word list as well, if one were to choose the option of picking the closest phonetic symbol to the appropriate physical placement, rather than expanding the phonemic territory of the phoneme / ɜ /. Its only disadvantage is that it is not recognized as an English phoneme, but then so few of the central vowels are recognized as actual phonemes in any language!

All of these second-element (or weak-vowel) features can be carried though in the other four mid-central offglide diphthongs, so we do not have to repeat all the explanation each time. Instead, we will simply present all three transcription options.

The second mid-central offglide diphthong is:

$$[\,\mathrm{ɛ}\breve{\mathrm{ə}}\,]\quad[\,\mathrm{ɛ}\breve{\mathrm{ɚ}}\,]\quad[\,\mathrm{ɛ}\breve{\mathrm{3}}^{\scriptstyle\vee}\,]\quad[\,\mathrm{ɛ}\breve{\mathrm{ɚ}}\,]$$

with the first element slightly cupped in the front of the tongue's dorsum, but very forward in placement. As in the words:

    square, care, stair, chair, there, their, lair, eyre. glare, dare

The third mid-central offglide diphthong is:

$$[\upsilon\breve{\partial}]\quad[\upsilon\breve{\partial}^{\iota}]\quad[\upsilon\breve{3}^{\iota}]\quad[\upsilon\breve{\partial}^{\iota}]$$

with the back of the tongue's dorsum arched toward the velum in a position between half-close and close and the lip-corners protruded and rounded in the first element. As in the words:

cure, tour, poor, sure, Coors, boor, lure

The fourth mid-central offglide diphthong is:

$$[\mathfrak{o}\breve{\partial}]\quad[\mathfrak{o}\breve{\partial}^{\iota}]\quad[\mathfrak{o}\breve{3}^{\iota}]\quad[\mathfrak{o}\breve{\partial}^{\iota}]$$

with the back of the dorsum very slightly cupped in the first element in a half-open position and the lip-corners protruded with no pursing. As in the words:

north, force, shore, more, lore, four, pour, store, gore, nor, war, oar

The fifth and final mid-central offglide diphthong is:

$$[\alpha\breve{\partial}]\quad[\alpha\breve{\partial}^{\iota}]\quad[\alpha\breve{3}^{\iota}]\quad[\alpha\breve{\partial}^{\iota}]$$

with the back of the tongue dorsum cupped strongly down in a fully open position with the lip wholly unrounded. As in:

Aaarrrrrrrrrrrrr

(At last.) But also as in:

start, large, farm, cart, hard, carve, charge,
part, mark, shard, carp, farce

🔊 **Audio track 67:** *The IPA dipphthongs* / ɪə̆ / / ɛə̆ / / ʊə̆ / / ɔə̆ / / ɑə̆ /.

Triphthongs

A **triphthong** is a sequence of three vowel sounds in a *single syllable*. The first element (sound) of the triphthong is the only one that is stressed and elongated. The other two are sounded as a sequence of shortened, unstressed **offglides**.

The two triphthongs in most common use in American English are [aɪɚ] and [aʊɚ].

$$[aɪɚ] \quad [aɪɝ] \quad [aɪɚ]$$

As with diphthongs, a triphthong begins with a stressed element. In both the common American English triphthongs, this stressed first element is [a], the lowest or most open of the front vowels, in which the front of the tongue is cupped strongly. The vowel sound raises (closes) rapidly to an unstressed [ɪ] and then relaxes to the **central** mid-vowel [ɚ] with r-color. Some illustrative words are:

fire, mire, sire, tire, wire, choir, hires, liars, prior, inquire, flyer

where the triphthong is spoken as a single syllable, as in "sire" [saɪɚ]. Many speakers, following the practice beloved by rock music lyricists, will commonly change a triphthong into a two-syllable word; so that "fire" is pronounced as [faɪ.jɚ] instead of [faɪɚ]. When that happens, the front of the tongue (not the tip or blade) is raising so much that the vowel / ɪ / doesn't just raise to / i /, it gets so close to the roof of the mouth that the action turns into a consonant, the voiced palatal approximant / j /, because there is a very slight obstruction of the flow.

🔊 **Audio track 68:** *Triphthong/two syllable contrast* / aɪɚ /.

To feel and hear the difference, say the word list again, speaking each word alternately using the / j / and not using it, as in:

One Syllable	Two Syllables
[faɪɚ]	[fai.jɚ]
[maɪɚ]	[mai.jɚ]
[saɪɚ]	[sai.jɚ]
[tʰaɪɚ]	[tʰai.jɚ]
[kʌaɪɚ]	[kʌai.jɚ]
[haɪɚz]	[hai.jɚz]
[laɪɚz]	[lai.jɚz]
[pɹaɪɚ]	[pɹai.jɚ]
[ɪnkʌaɪɚ]	[ɪnkʌai.jɚ]
[flaɪɚ]	[flai.jɚ]

[aʊɚ] [aʊɝ] [aʊɚ]

Most Americans say the first sound of this triphthong as [a]. Many Americans use [æ], and many speech teachers would prefer us to use [ɑ]. Whichever you choose, the effect for a triphthong is the same: the first sound, or "element", is stressed and lengthened, with a closure of the tongue on the first offglide followed by a relaxation of the tongue to the "schwa" [ə]. All three sounds in succession are spoken within one syllable. All of the following words can be spoken on one syllable as triphthongs:

sour, shower, power, cowered, coward, tower, our, bower

It may come as a surprise to some speakers that the words spelled with "-ower" can be spoken in one syllable, since many Americans habitually speak such words with two syllables. Here the lip rounding from [a] to [ʊ] is increased so that there is more lip-rounding than would be necessary for even an [u], and the voiced rounded bilabial approximant [w] is formed, dividing the action into two syllables. Neither the one-syllable (triphthong) version nor the two-syllable version is more correct, but we should have the skills to speak the words either way.

One Syllable	Two Syllables
[saʊɚ]	[sau.wɚ]
[ʃaʊɚ]	[ʃau.wɚ]
[pʰaʊɚ]	[pʰau.wɚ]
[kʰaʊɚd]	[kʰau.wɚd]
[kʰaʊɚd]	[kʰau.wɚd]
[tʰaʊɚ]	[tʰau.wɚ]
[aʊɚ]	[au.wɚ]
[baʊɚ]	[bau.wɚ]

There are other potential triphthongs in American English. "Mayor" or "payer" could be spoken as the triphthong words [meɪɚ] and [pʰeɪɚ]. But "mayor" most often becomes a a homophone for "mare" [mɛɚ], or is spoken in two syllables [mei.jɚ].

◀)) **Audio track 69:** *Triphthong/two syllable contrast* / aʊɚ /.

20

Mid-central offglide diphthongs

Phonetics and phonemics: the vowel version

We know that a phoneme is a speech action that conveys a unit of meaning within a language; it is that commonly understood agreement among speakers of English, for example, that "sit" has a different meaning from "set" or "sat" or "sought" or "suit", all of which, whatever their spelling, have a single, but different, vowel phoneme between the same consonants. We also know – from our free-form explorations of "phthongs" – that there are nearly infinite variations within these vowel phonemes. What is a way to transcribe an accurate version of vowel placement? There are three, actually.

1. Substitutions

Because words exist within larger linguistic structures like phrases and sentences that help to identify meaning, a phoneme may retain its unit of meaning even though its action/sound variation takes it into the territory of another phoneme. Take the two words "get" and "git". In isolation, what do they tell us about their meaning? We might guess correctly that "get" is a verb and that its meaning most likely is "obtain". We might even know that "git" is a noun that is UK slang for "contemptible idiot". We do not use the word much in the USA, despite our adequate supply of idiocy. But we also know, because many of us say it that way, that "get" [gɛt] is very frequently pronounced as "git" [gɪt]; it is even spelled that way often, as in the cowboy song classic "Git along, little dogies". We still know it means "get" though. (And we *all* know that a "dogie" means a motherless calf.)

Such substitutions of one phoneme for another to show pronunciation are extreme examples of what I term "phoneme intrusion" to describe a phoneme that starts to sound like another one but still retains its original unit of meaning.

Advantages. When we are writing vowels and diphthongs phonetically it is a great convenience to be able to use these simple substitutions for accents: [kɛnt] for [kænt] ("can't"), [fɔɪst] for [fɜ˞st] ("first"), and so on. Most speech teachers and many phoneticians represent accents of English or the pronunciation of other languages in just this way: it's not only easy to transcribe, it's easy for the reader to understand.

Disadvantages. The trade-off for this convenience is some degree of crudity. Accents that are taught using only this limited number of phonemes often sound unrealistic because they frequently (though not always) fail to represent the phonetic or allophonic subtleties that most accents possess. But first, we must examine . . .

The territory. When we look at a vowel quadrilateral, divided into sections by lines and populated by symbols in suspiciously orderly array, we may get a hint that we are looking at a theoretical construct. And so we are. When famed English phonetician Daniel Jones established this version of a vowel chart (modifying earlier variants) in 1917, he did so by placing most of the front and back vowels in equidistant intervals from close to open. The few remaining vowel phonemes are also placed with some symmetry in between these so-called cardinal vowels. Jones constructed this formal graph to define the physical territory of the vowel chart, limited to its quadrilateral shape by the limits of vowel articulation within the oral cavity.

By so doing, he was able to define physically the territory within the chart by providing specific points of physical reference, all related to degree of tongue arching/cupping or lip rounding/unrounding, the two chief ways of shaping acoustically the unobstructed flow to form vowels. He did not place the cardinal vowels in these positions because he was in any way suggesting that words using these phonemes must be pronounced at the cardinal positions.

2. Diacritics

The second of the three ways that we can move these theoretically placed phonemes into more accurate positions within the vowel quadrilateral is by using diacritic symbols to adjust the phonemes into their possible allophones. The transcription on page 232 of "clothes" uses diacritics to render the phonetic variety more accurately both in consonants and in vowel transcription.

There's only one small problem, though: you won't be able to decipher these diacritics at this stage of your work. Still, I invite you to marvel at the sentence below in all its diacritical glory.

[spi̱k ðə̞ spit̠ʃ ã̆ɪ̆ pɹ̠e̠ɪ̆ jü | əz aɪ̆ pɹə̃nãʊ̆st ĭt̚ tʉ jü̃ | tɹ̠ɪpɪ̠ŋli ɑn ðə tʰʌŋ ‖]

A few chapters further on, you will be able to read it trippingly on the tongue. For now, it suffices that you know that diacritics can modify both consonants and vowels.

Advantages. Using diacritics allows you to be more varied than does simple phoneme substitution. It allows you to give quite an accurate representation of an accent. That is why transcribers, when listening to native speakers of an accent, use phoneme substitution with diacritic modification more than other methods.

Disadvantages. Most of these diacritics only give the reader/speaker a general direction for this subtle physical adjustment of the phoneme, but do not specify exactly where the vowel allophone is located within the quadrilateral. So one speaker might interpret the diacritic as leading to one position while another speaker – equally correctly, based on the evidence – might interpret it as leading to a slightly different position. This is getting very subtle indeed and may be more than accent learning requires, but it is not yet completely accurate. It also fails to show us readily if there are any clusterings of vowel realization that might give us useful physical evidence of the overall posture of the accent within the vocal tract.

3. Moving the phoneme

This is the last of the methods for transcribing vowel allophones. It requires that the reader/speaker of the transcription consult a separately created vowel quadrilateral that is not a part of the actual transcription in order to note exactly where the phoneme is placed at variance from the cardinal placements.

Here are the vowel placements for a native speaker of Swedish, as recorded in the *Handbook of the International Phonetic Association:*

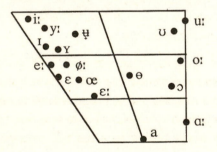

Figure 60. Vowel quadrilateral, Swedish, *IPA Handbook*
(Cambridge University Press, 1999).

We can see that all the phonemes are located away from their expected positions on the cardinal chart, some only slightly and others considerably. We can see also that there is a definite concentration of vowels in comparatively close and fronted positions. All the commonly used rounded front vowels are present also. If these are the vowel positions that are easy for a Swedish speaker to use in informal speech, it suggests something about the characteristic posture of the articulators when speaking the Swedish vowels.

Try to speak each of the vowel allophones as recorded on this chart. Start with [iː] and move down the front from close to open, then to the open central vowel allophone [a] and then up the back from open to close [u]. Finally explore the difference between the mid-central rounded vowel [ɵ] (usually shown as a mid-close central rounded vowel) and the mid-central schwa [ə] that usually appears in this position.

Advantages. This is a more precise way of representing the vowel allophones than either of the other methods. It helps us understand patterns of vowel placement that help us to define the physicality of the accent, whether from an English-speaking dialect, from a primary speaker of another language, or from a native speaker of another language who is speaking in English. It also shows, quite dramatically in this example, the degree to which an allophone may start to occupy the territory of another cardinal phoneme. These boundaries are very permeable. (This permeability, by the way, is another problem in accurate transcription when we are trying to use only vowel substitutions.)

Disadvantages: It is not a technique that lends itself to real-time transcription, as we might try in listening to a contributor performing an accent, or even listening to a recording that you could repeatedly hear. We would have to prepare the allophonic vowel chart quite separately from our actual transcription, which would in itself be a *Catch-22* problem because our phonetic transcription would depend on the existence of the vowel chart. This technique is best utilized by researchers who can gather data from a number of samples and who have the time to subject the samples to acoustic analysis. Finally, at a certain point of departure from its cardinal position, it might be more practical to simply write another phoneme rather than trying to extend the phonemic territory of a phoneme to occupy some distant region of the vowel quadrilateral. The real question is how committed a transcriber is to that unit of meaning that a phoneme represents: if meaning rather than physical placement is paramount, "get" is better represented by a diacritic or by a relocation of the phoneme than by writing it as "git". If simple physicality is at a premium, "git" gits the message across very well.

From a practical standpoint, we should be prepared to use all these transcription methods, depending on the needs and environment. Narrow transcription of accents is not needed in many cases. Narrow transcription is crucial in others. What is crucial for the transcriber is making sure that the reader/speaker knows what the ground rules are.

21

Polysyllabic words

Onset of vocalization

When we whisper something to someone, we know that all the sounds we're producing are *un*voiced; that is, an extra-strong airflow shaped by the articulators is doing the work. In whispering we never bring the vocal folds together to form the vibration action that we call "voice".

By contrast, when we speak "aloud" we often think that we are now fully "on voice", with the vocal folds always vibrating to send our voices through-out a space to all our listeners. But this is not so. If it were, then Hamlet's advice to the players – "Speak the speech, I pray you, as I pronounced it to you – trippingly on the tongue" – would actually sound like this: "Zbeag the zbeedge I bray you az I bronounzed id do you, dribbingly on the dung."

In connected human speech, where we speak one or many words in a single uninterrupted breath, the vocal fold vibration – the voicing – turns on and off many times during the simplest sentence. Of course all the vowels and diphthongs are voiced, but most consonants can be paired in either voiced or unvoiced action, producing sounds very different from one another.

In the unvoiced stop-plosives / p /, / t /, and / k / the flow of air often explodes the articulators apart forcefully, producing a puff of air. If you put the palm of your hand three or four inches in front of your mouth and whisper "puh" energetically you will feel that puff of air sharply on your hand. Now with your palm the same distance away, say a fully voiced "buh". You will feel little or nothing.

Say the word "team". Say it again, and notice that as the / t / explodes there is a tiny fraction of a second where that compressed puff of air has to escape before the voice "turns on" to produce the vowel sound "ee" / i /. It's not "t" followed by "ee", it's "t" followed by a puff of air followed by "ee". Phonetically this action is termed **aspiration** and in American speech the "t" in team is usually (but not always; these are not hard and fast rules) pronounced as an *aspirated* "t". The way to notate this small aspirate pause before that next voiced sound kicks in is by writing a small superscript [ʰ] above and to the right of the stop-plosive that produced the aspiration. So the word "team" as it is pronounced by most speakers would be written phonetically as [tʰim].

The same thing happens with / p / and / k /. The words "path" and "cough" as spoken by many American speakers would be [pʰæθ] and [kʰɔf] when written in phonetics.

What has happened, then, is that the aspirate puff of air has pushed the **onset of vocalization** a little further toward the end of the word.

So do we always put a [ʰ] after every unvoiced stop-plosive that we say? Are we always producing that aspirate puff of air? No. There are a few conditions, based on physical action, that usually govern aspirate unvoiced stop-plosives / p /, / t /, and / k /:

1 The stop-plosive will usually be followed by a vowel, diphthong, triphthong, or in some cases a pause (when it is at the end of a word) in the *same syllable* for aspiration to occur.

2 The syllable is almost always stressed for aspiration to occur. It doesn't have to receive the primary stress, but it has to be stressed somewhat. Or

to put it the opposite way: if the syllable is unstressed, the stop-plosive – even if followed by a vowel – probably won't be aspirate. So in the word "compel" the / k / would probably not be aspirate because the "com-" is not stressed. But the / p / would be aspirate because the "-pel" is stressed: [kəmpʰɛɫ].

3 When an unvoiced stop-plosive occurs before another consonant, whether in the same syllable, in different syllables, or from the end of one word to the beginning of another in connected speech (even if the next word begins with a vowel), the stop-plosive is *not* generally aspirate. The word "inept" would thus probably be spoken as [ɪnɛpt] or possibly [ɪnɛptʰ]. The word sequence "take vows" would be said [tʰeɪ̆k vaŭz], where the [tʰ] is aspirate, but the [k] is not. The word sequence "at odds" would probably be spoken [æt ɑdz] with no aspiration.

4 There are four consonants in American English which are affected by an unvoiced stop-plosive preceding them in a syllable. They are / j /, / w /, / ɹ / and / l /, all **approximants**. Like other consonants, these sounds are spoken immediately after the stop-plosives without any intervening puff of air. But unlike other consonants these approximants allow the aspirate puff of air from the stop-plosive to take place, in effect blowing out their voicing. Two of these approximants, / j / and / w /, have their own unvoiced fricative symbols, / ç / and / ʍ / respectively. So "puke" and "quince" would usually be said as [pçuk] and [kʍɪns]. The voicing doesn't fully come in until the vowel.

The other two approximants have to be treated differently. / l / does indeed have an unvoiced fricative form, [ɬ]. It is pronounced with the side edges of the tongue strongly obstructing the lateral flow of air, producing a very hissy unvoiced "l". This is the sound we hear in Welsh "double-l" words, such as Dylan Thomas's fictional town "Llareggub" in his verse play *Under Milk Wood*. (Never one to ignore a dirty joke, Thomas concocted the fictitious Welsh place-name from "bugger-all" spelled backwards.) For most American speakers, however, the unvoiced "l" is not spoken so tightly after an unvoiced stop-plosive. So instead of the [ɬ] it is more accurate to write the ordinary [l] with a small subscript circle directly underneath it; this diacritic indicates that the voiced symbol it modifies is unvoiced: [l̥]. Thus "plod" could be notated as [pl̥ɑd] or "applaud" as [əpl̥ɔd]. The last of these approximant symbols, [ɹ], has no unvoiced fricative form as a separate symbol, so once again we employ the unvoicing diacritic underneath it to produce the notation [tɹ̥ʌdʒ] for the word "trudge" or [kɹ̥ɪpɫ] for "cripple".

5 There is an exception to this. If the stop-plosive-plus-approximant combination is preceded in the same syllable by an "s", then the **onset of vocalization** is pulled back toward the beginning of the syllable, and the approximant is voiced again. Thus " squeal" is spoken – and notated – as [skwil] not [skʌil], and "strip" would be spoken as [stɹɪp] [stɹ̥ɪp]; note the difference in the voicing or unvoicing in the following word pairs:

> pray – spray   pre – spree   cream – scream   trap – strap,
> queaze – squeeze   cue – skew   plain – explain

6 The conditions we have just explored are not inflexible rules; they are perceptions about common usage. Individual speakers may vary from these guidelines, voicing or unvoicing sounds, intruding an aspiration between a stop-plosive and a vowel, or not doing so, in ways that confound our attempts to organize speech actions into neat right-and-wrong categories. The important thing is to be aware of the possible and probable actions, to listen for them in the speech of others, and to feel them in our own speech.

American vowel, diphthong, and consonant practice

Write the following words in phonetic transcription

1	Place	26	Snafu
2	Noisy	27	Shopworn
3	Broken	28	Clouds
4	Blame	29	Cowered
5	Grope	30	Attire
6	Wouldn't	31	Chicanery
7	Affairs	32	Curdled
8	Grievous	33	Toughs
9	Flange	34	Elevate
10	Snicker	35	Winch
11	Busy	36	Choir
12	Whipped	37	Reigning
13	Languor	38	Appearance
14	Evasive	39	Chopped
15	Pulley	40	Result
16	Abrasion	41	Stench
17	Northern	42	Mask
18	Dirigible	43	Showers
19	Pazzazz	44	Detour
20	Caffeine	45	Garbage
21	Corpulent	46	Enough
22	Neither	47	Placate
23	Dowry	48	Marshal
24	Voracious	40	Soften
25	Pauses	50	Luge

American vowel, diphthong, and consonant practice

With sample transcriptions

Speak each of these transcriptions. Compare the pronunciation of the word with the way you would pronounce it and compare your own transcription wiith the version here. Each answer given here represents only one possible pronunciation. Do not interpret it as the only "right" way to say the word.

1	Place	[pl̥eɪ̆s]	26	Snafu	[snæfu]
2	Noisy	[nɔɪ̆zi]	27	Shopworn	[ʃɑpwɔɚ̆n]
3	Broken	[bɹoŭkən]	28	Clouds	[kl̥aŭdz]
4	Blame	[bleɪ̆m]	29	Cowered	[kʰaŭɚ̆d]
5	Grope	[gɹoŭp]	30	Attire	[ətʰaɪ̆ɚ̆]
6	Wouldn't	[wʊdⁿn̩t]	31	Chicanery	[ʃɪkʰeɪ̆nɝ̩i]
7	Affairs	[əfɛɚ̆z]	32	Curdled	[kʰɝ̩dˡɫ̩d]
8	Grievous	[gɹivəs]	33	Toughs	[tʰʌfs]
9	Flange	[flændʒ]	34	Elevate	[ɛləveɪ̆t]
10	Snicker	[snɪkɝ]	35	Winch	[wɪntʃ]
11	Busy	[bɪzi]	36	Choir	[kʍaɪ̆ɚ̆]
12	Whipped	[ʍɪpt]	37	Reigning	[ɹeɪ̆nɪŋ]
13	Languor	[læŋgɚ]	38	Appearance	[əpʰɪ̆ɚ̆ɹəns]
14	Evasive	[ɪveɪ̆sɪv]	39	Chopped	[tʃɑpt]
15	Pulley	[pʰʊl̩i]	40	Result	[ɹɪzʌlt]
16	Abrasion	[əbɹeɪ̆ʒn̩]	41	Stench	[stɛntʃ]
17	Northern	[nɔɚ̆ðɚ̩n]	42	Mask	[mæsk]
18	Dirigible	[dɪɚ̆ɹɪdʒəbɫ]	43	Showers	[ʃaŭɚ̆z]
19	Pazzazz	[pəzæz]	44	Detour	[ditʰʊɚ̆]
20	Caffeine	[kʰæfin]	45	Garbage	[gɑɚ̆bɪdʒ]
21	Corpulent	[kʰɔɚ̆pjʊlənt]	46	Enough	[ɪnʌf]
22	Neither	[niðɚ̆]	47	Placate	[pl̥eɪ̆kʰeɪ̆t]
23	Dowry	[daŭɹi̩]	48	Marshal	[mɑɚ̆ʃɫ]
24	Voracious	[vɔɹeɪ̆ʃəs]	40	Soften	[sɔfn]
25	Pauses	[pʰɔzɪz]	50	Luge	[luʒ]

Nonsense words

Speak these words that employ only English phonemes. Don't try for fluency immediately; speak each word slowly. Accuracy is more important than fluency. Bu after you are really confident with each word, speak it in a normal conversational pace:

ʒæmsʌtʃ   lipɹɑv   ɔngwɪbz

tɛkʃəwɜ   ɹeɪdsaʊpəglæk   vɜˑnɑdʒ

ʍʊlps   ðʌʃəblɪtʃ   hipɹɛnʒd

lɔɪ̆fɪvl̩   ʒugə   ɛtpɑpt   jæ

m̥ʊndʒəwɛpi   zuvn̩ɑldəjɪŋkt

Now try these words that use phonemes that are not all found in English. Use the same method as above.

qɑɲɒl   væʃɐɫeɪ̆ɸə   ŋɔɪ̆d̺ɪʀɑbl̩pyp

cʌçˈ   zøməɬ̬ʃad   χɔʎəkømzɪpʀɒk

bl̩ʊɢ   ʋɛnɥicastœm   ɠalɔɪ̆ɸ

bɟyɲəwæʃn   aħa   bɯdiwɪç

Don't be afraid to practice these very slowly, referring to any of the charts or explanations you need. Put the words together and then say them several times until they become more comfortable to speak.

Now we will take another major step, moving from single words – real or nonsense – to phrases and sentences; what linguists call connected speech. This step brings in new elements, because we don't always speak words in connected speech in the same way that we do when we say them individually. You can easily prove this. Speak the sentence "What do you want me to say?" first as separate individual words with an inhaled breath between each word, and then as a connected sentence on one breath. Notice what happens to the words.

For this next step, we have to move from "broad" or general phonetic transcription to "narrow" or specifically detailed phonetic transcription.

22

Connected speech

Moving toward "narrow transcription"

"Rumours about the new play had been fanned by Shaw through London."
(Michael Holroyd, *Bernard Shaw*, Vol. 2)

On the next page will be found several different phonetic transcriptions of this sentence, using slightly different pronunciation choices or different degrees of detail in the transcription. In order to represent these three different pronunciations, we will use symbol changes from one phoneme to another and also diacritic symbols to modify individual phonemes into their allophonic variations. But first, here are the diacritics used, each creating an allophone of a phoneme symbol:

[ə̆]
"Breve." The symbol modified is given no stress and is very short.

[ɜʵ]
"Rhoticity sign." The symbol modified ends with a slight tongue-bunching into "r-color " – the "braced r".

[I̩]

"Raising sign." The symbol modified is pronounced with the tongue arching (or uncupping) slightly higher toward the roof of the mouth. Also referred to as being a more "close" sound.

[i̞]

"Lowering sign." The symbol modified is pronounced with the tongue cupping (or de-arching) slightly lower toward the floor of the mouth. Also referred to as being a more "open" sound.

[d̥]

"Under-ring." The symbol modified is pronounced unvoiced.

[t˺]

"Corner." The symbol modified is stopped but not exploded.

[t̪]

"Subscript bridge." The symbol modified is pronounced with a tongue-tip placement on the back of the upper teeth – "dentalized".

['bæt]

"Vertical stroke (superior)." The syllable modified is given primary stress.

[ˌbæt]

"Vertical stroke (inferior)." The syllable modified is given secondary (but still *some*) stress.

Here are the pause symbols:

[|]

A short pause, roughly equivalent to a comma.

[‖]

A longer pause, roughly equivalent to a period.

Armed with this information, say each of these versions of this sentence. The variations are more or less random, although the final version does tend toward a particular accent. Do you have all the phonetic information here that you need to define the accent clearly?

[rumɜ˞z əbaʊt ðə nu pleɪ hæd bɪn fænd baɪ ʃɔ θru lʌndən]

[ɹumɜ˞z əbaʊt̚ ðə nu pl̥eɪ əd̚ bɪn fænd baɪ ʃɑ θɹu lʌndən]

[ˈɹuməz | əˈbaʊʔ˺ ðə ˌnju ˈpl̥e | həd ˌbin ˈfæ̩nd ˌbaɪ ˈʃɔ ˌθɹu ˈlʌndən ‖]

◀)) **Audio track 70:** *Rumours – three versions.*

Speak each sentence slowly and meticulously, letting the phonetic symbols guide you. Then repeat it several times, slowly moving toward fluency without sacrificing the flow of the specific sounds in each version.

Now we can try another pair of short sentences:

"What do you want? Did you settle on a pronunciation yet?

And some different ways to say them:

[ˈʍʌt̚ du ˈjuː ˌwɒnt ‖ ˌdɪd ju ˈsɛt'ɫ ən ə pɹəˌnʌnsiˈeɪʃn̩ ˈjɛt ‖]

[ʍət̚ ˈduː ju ˌwɑnt ‖ dɪd ju ˈsɛtəɫ ˌɒn ə ˌpɹoʊˈnʌnsɹˈeɪʃən | ˈjɛtʰ ‖]¹

[wa də jə ˈwɒnʔ ‖ ˌdɪd̚ dʒə ˈsɛt̚ɫ ˌan ə pɹənʌnsijeɪʃn̩ jɛʔ˺ ‖]

[wə tʃə ˈwɑ̃ʔ ‖ dʒə ˈsɛ˞ʊɫ ɒn ə pəˌnʌsi̥ˈjeɪʃə̥ jɛʔ˺ ‖]

[wə ʃə ˈwɑ̃ː ‖ ʒə ˌsɛ˞ʊ̃ː ɑ̃ː pənə˞ˈseɪʃə jɛ̃ ‖]

◀)) **Audio track 71:** *What do you want – five versions.*

Notice the diacritics with which you are unfamiliar. Consult the list below and try again.

---

* The symbol [ʝ] is called a "curly-tail J" and is a voiced palatal fricative: pronounced much like [j] but with the tongue tighter toward the palate. Here it suggests the speaker's heavy emphasis of the word.

New diacritics

[æ̃]

"Tilde." The symbol modified is pronounced with nasality, accomplished by dropping the upper surface of the velum and letting the vibrations flow through the nose as well as the mouth.

[t̬]

"Subscript wedge." The symbol modified is pronounced with some voicing. This commonly occurs in American speech when an unvoiced stop-plosive – (especially [t] – is said in an unstressed syllable, as in "pretty" [pɹɪt̬i]. The [t] becomes voiced almost – but not quite – to a full [d].

[ɑ̽]

"Superscript cross." The symbol (always a vowel) thus modified is pro-nounced toward the mid-central part of the vowel quadrilateral. In other words, it is relaxed toward the "schwa" [ə]. *This tendency is extremely common in American speech.*

[iː]

"Length mark." The sound of the symbol modified is lengthened. This can happen with vowels and with continuant consonants. In print this symbol consists of two filled-in wedges pointing at one another; in writing a colon (two dots) will do just as well.

[iˑ]

"Half-length mark." The symbol modified is lengthened slightly. As in [wiˑ sɔː ðə mæn] – "we saw the man".

A few other diacritics in common use for American English:

[ä]

"Superscript umlaut." The vowel symbol thus modified is centralized; that is, moved toward the center line without being more open or close. Note the difference from the mid-centralized vowel symbol [ˣ] which is relaxed toward the schwa [ə].

[ạ]

"Subscript umlaut." The voiced symbol thus modified is murmured; that is, pronounced with a breathy voice quality. Any vowel or any voiced consonant can be murmured.

[ọ]

"Subscript tilde." The symbol thus modified is pronounced with a creaky voice. This diacritic can be used to indicate "glottal fry" in a speaker, although in the narrowest sense a "creaky" voice is not a tense sound at the larynx, as the glottal fry certainly is.

[ʊ̞]

"Subscript plus." The vowel thus modified is placed further forward (**advanced**) in tongue position.

[t̺]

"Subscript turned bridge." The symbol thus modified is an action enacted with the **apical** portion of the tongue; that is, with the tip.

[t̻]

"Subscript box." The symbol thus modified is an action enacted with the **laminal** portion of the tongue; that is, with the blade.

[ɛ̱]

"Underbar." The vowel thus modified is placed further back (**backed**) in tongue position.

[ʌ̟]

"Advancement sign." The current IPA usage of this symbol (of which I am not overly fond) is to indicate a pronunciation with an advanced tongue-root (the tongue-root pushed forward). In the good old days it was used to indicate a generally forward placement of the sound, for which purpose the "subscript plus" is now employed. It would seem to me more logical to have the subscript plus sign and underbar used to indicate tongue-root position. But did they consult me? No.

[ʌ̠]

"Retraction sign." Currently used by the IPA to indicate tongue-root retraction (the tongue-root pulled back toward the pharynx). For my complaint about this usage, see above. *Consistent tongue root retraction is common in much American speech.*

[t̺]

"Subscript turned bridge." The symbol thus modified uses the tip (or **apical** – from "apex") portion of the tongue to place the obstruent action at or near the roof of the mouth.

[t̻]

"Subscript box." The symbol thus modified uses the blade (or **lamina** – meaning thin plate) of the tongue to place the obstruent action at or near the roof of the mouth.

Having collected the information that allows us to explore more "narrow" (detailed) transcription, we can now explore it further in recording actual ways that we might speak a text. In this case, it is a classical one. But it could be contemporary as well.

Broad and narrow **phonetics**

hæmlɪt ənd hɛkjŏbə | sɛvɹəɫ tʰaĭmz

Hamlet has just seen the Player King brought to tears while performing a speech about Hecuba's hysteria at the fall of Troy. Now alone, he says:

> oŭ ʍət ə roŭg | ænd pɛzn̩t sleĭv æm aĭ ‖
> ɪz ɪt nɑt mɑnstrəs ðæt ðɪs pleĭɚ hɪɚ |
> bʌt ɪn ə fɪkʃn̩ | ɪn ə drim əv pæʃn̩ |
> kʊd fɔɚs hɪz soŭl soŭ tu hɪz oŭn kənsit
> ðæt frʌm hɚ wɚkɪŋ ɔl ðə vɪzɪdʒ wɑnd ‖
> tɪɚz ɪn hɪz aĭz | dɪstrækʃn̩ ɪnz æspɛkt |
> ə broŭkən vɔĭs | æn hɪz hoŭl fʌŋkʃn̩ sutɪŋ
> wɪð fɔɚmz tu hɪz kənsit ‖ ænd ɔl fɔɚ nʌθɪŋ ‖
> fɔɚ hɛkjubə ‖

◀)) **Audio track 72:** *O, what a rogue – broad version.*

These lines have been written in fairly **broad** phonetic transcription. Fully broad transcription would have nothing but the phonemes. To define pronunciation somewhat, we used the "all-purpose r" that we discussed on page 149 for prevocalic "r" sounds and we noted "r-coloring" as a diacritic [˞] to the phoneme [ə]. We put the "breve" symbol [˘] over the weak vowel sound in diphthongs, half-pause and full-pause marks which serve the function of commas and periods, and we noted syllabic consonants such as [n̩]. We wrote the words with no other modifications, giving full value to the consonant and vowel sounds.

Writing this way has several advantages. For one thing, it's comparatively fast and easy to notate. It gives a clear general picture of how the lines sound when spoken. But it also leaves out a lot of information that might make your speaking of it more precise, and the pronunciations tend to the generic. When you are reading it aloud (and you should *always* read phonetic transcription aloud), if you are really reading the phonetic sounds *as written* (*make sure that you fully explode those stop-plosives!*) and not just translating, you may sound a little stilted, a little idealized. Obviously, even in this broad transcription some decisions about pronunciation have been made and, while they may help you to recognize the words, they may not be the way you would prefer to pronounce them, or even the way you could pronounce them comfortably, no matter how supple your articulators might be.

And some decisions haven't been made – exactly what words to put the stress on, for one thing. Or what our actual speech actions are when we string all these great words together. After all, how we say the words in isolation can be very different from how we will say them in a phrase or sentence. So let's revisit the text and put some more details in. This time we'll add stress marks: ['] for primary stress, and [,] for secondary stress, coming before the syllable they refer to. And no mark at all means that the syllable is unstressed.

We'll also change some of the symbols, such as [r] to [ɹ], to reflect a more specific physical action (in this case, the all-purpose "r" turning to become the voiced post-alveolar approximant). We'll let some of the vowels change because they occur in unstressed syllables. We'll note aspiration after unvoiced stop-plosives [pʰɛznt]. We'll also allow some of the vowel sounds to lengthen [ɑː], and some consonants to become unvoiced [l̥]. Some of the consonants will be stopped but not exploded [t̚], or dentalized – said on the teeth [t̪] – or both.

All these changes are done in the interest of representing more accurately the real speech actions that occur in these lines. Now remember that this will not necessarily be an "ideal" reading, just a more specific one. Go through it slowly, even though some of the changes will make more sense to you when you do them at a normal rate of speed. After you feel all the sound actions precisely, flow the phrase at a normal rate of speech.

> 'oʊ ʍət ə 'ɹoʊg | ənd ˌpʰɛznt̚ 'sleɪ̆v əm 'aɪ ‖
> ˌɪz ɪt̚ ˌnɑt 'mɑnstɹəs ðət̚ ˌðɪs 'pl̥eɪ̆ɚ ˌhɪ̆ɚ |
> ˌbʌt ɪn ə 'fɪkʃn̩ | ɪn ə 'dɹiːm əv 'pʰæʃn̩ |
> ˌkʊd 'fɔ̆ɚs hɪz 'soʊl̥ 'soʊ tʊ hɪz ˌoʊ̆n kən'sɪt
> ðət ˌfɹʌm hɚ ˌwɚkɪŋ 'ɔl ðə 'vɪzɪdʒ 'wɑːnd ‖
> 'tʰɪ̆ɚz ɪn hɪz 'aɪ̆z | dɪ'stɹækʃn̩ ɪnz æ'spɛk̚t̚ |
> ə 'bɹoʊ̆kən 'vɔɪ̆s | ən hɪz 'hoʊ̆l̥ 'fʌŋkʃn̩ ˌsʲutɪŋ

wɪð 'fɔɚ̃mz tə ˌhɪz kn̩'sit ‖ ənd 'ɔːɫ fɚ 'nʌθɪŋ ‖
fɚ 'hɛkʲəbə ‖

◀)) **Audio track 73:** *O, what a rogue – second version.*

Remember, you still may not ordinarily pronounce the phrases the way they are transcribed above, but it is definitely one way you could pronounce them. This is a more **narrow**, or detailed, transcription. It has the disadvantage of being slower – and a bit harder – to write; it has the advantage of giving you a lot more information about the physical actions the speaker is taking in articulating.

We are still being rather detailed also in our pronunciation. (And nothing wrong with that, say I.) If, however, we were to let our speech actions become a little more – how shall we say – fluid and keep our transcription just as detailed, we might come up with something like this:

'oʊ wəd ə 'ɹoʊg ən 'pʰɛzn̩ʔ 'sleɪv əm 'aɪ ‖
ˌɪz ɪʔ' naʔ' 'manstɚs ðəʔ' ˌðɪs 'pl̪eɪɚ̃ hɪɚ̃ |
ˌbʌʔ n̩ ə 'fɪkʃn̩ | ˌɪn ə 'dɹ̥iːm əv 'pʰæʃn̩ |
kəd' 'fɔɚ̃s ɪz 'soʊɫ 'soʊ du ʷɪz ˌoʊn kn̩'siʔ' |
ðəʔ' fɹ̩ʌm ɚ ˌwɚkɪn̩ 'ɔ:t ðə 'vɪzɪdʒ 'waːnd ‖
'tʰɪɚ̃z ɪn ɪz 'aɪz | də'stɹækʃn̩ ɪnz ə'spɛk't |
ə 'bɹoʊk̚ⁿŋ 'voɪs | ən ɪz 'hoʊɫ 'fʌŋkʃn̩ ˌsuʔn̩
wɪθ 'fɔɚ̃mz tə ˌhɪz kn̩'siʔ' ‖ ʔən 'ɔːɫ fɚ 'nʌθɪŋ ‖
fɚ 'hɛkʲəbə ‖

◀)) **Audio track 74:** *O, what a rogue – third version.*

Now what I have written is a more conversational version of essentially the same accent as the versions that have preceded it. You'll notice that a certain amount of linguistic detail by the speaker has been left out, even though there is actually more phonetic detail to the transcription. But we can go further using only the vowel symbols that we have learned so far – and a couple of other diacritics – and take the speech into another sound pattern entirely. Again, go through the sounds slowly, until you are comfortable with all the changes – and have figured out what all those diacritics mean – and then see if you can read it aloud at a normal speed. See if you can experience where all those sounds focus in the mouth: the pattern of tension and relaxation in the articulators that makes this sound pattern inevitable for you when you speak. That is the "feel" of the accent.

'æŭ wəd ə 'ɹæ̆g̊ ən 'pʰɛ̞zn̩? 'sləĭv əm 'aː ‖
ˌɪz ɪ?ʼ naʔ̚ 'mã̆ə̆nstəs d̥ɛʔ ˌd̥ɪs 'pl̥ɛ̞ĭʲə̆ ˌhɪʲə̆ |
ˌbʌd ɪn ə 'fɪkʃn̩ | ˌɪn ə 'dɹɪĭm ə 'pʰæ̆ə̆ʃn̩ |
kəd 'fã̆ʷəs ɪz 'sæ̆ŭɫ 'sæ̆ŭ də ʷɪz ˌoŏn kn̩'sɪĭ?
ð̥əʔ ˌfɹʌm ə ˌwɝ·kən 'aŭɫ ð̥ə 'vɹ̥ə̆zɪdʒ 'waə̆nd ‖
'tʰĭʲəz ɪn əz 'ãːz | də'stɹækʃn̩ ɪnz ə'spɛk̚t̚ʼ |
ə ˌbɹɛŭk̚ⁿŋ 'voʷ̆ɪs | ən ɪz 'hɛ̃ŭːɫ 'fʌŋkʃn̩ ˌsĭuʔn̩
wɪθ 'fɑ̆ʷə̝m̥z tə ˌɪz kn̩'sɪĭ? ‖ ən 'aːŭ̆ɫ fə 'nʌʔn̩ ‖
fə 'hɛ̞k̚ʲəbə ‖

🔊 **Audio track 75:** *0, what a rogue – fourth version.*

What are the new diacritics used, and what do they signify? While we wouldn't need or for that matter want to use this kind of narrow transcription all the time, it is precisely in this degree of specificity that the subtleties of a person's individual accent can be noted for ourselves and communicated to others. Be aware that we have now notated some individual inconsistencies in the way an individual phoneme might be spoken in different contexts. That is what happens in real life when a person speaks. So now we have truly entered the world of phonetics, not phonemics; we are becoming aware of changes in speech that don't just relate to units of meaning, but rather to the unique sounds that are produced in a dialect or accent pattern.

We are also in a world where there are no longer simple "right answers" for making a correct transcription. A good transcription in this context would be extremely observant and detailed, and the physical actions observed would be notated clearly and would be likely ones for a speaker to do from a physiological standpoint. A poor transcription might have the articulators taking actions that they wouldn't or couldn't manage. It might notate actions that were inconsistent with the accent as a whole, or just write the symbols or diacritics inaccurately. It might use one symbol when the writer meant another.

But in a narrow phonetic transcription there may very well be more than one way to express these physical actions. Phonetics ultimately is a skill, not a formula. Or to put it in only slightly more grandiose terms, phonetics is an art, not a science, though it uses aspects of scientific observation and methodology. So our goal is always the most artful transcription, not just the correct answer.

Naturally you don't need the following transcription, but here it is anyway, written in that amusingly imprecise orthography, English spelling:

> O, what a rogue and peasant slave am I!
> Is it not monstrous that this player here,
> But in a fiction, in a dream of passion,
> Could force his soul so to his own conceit
> That from her working all the visage wann'd,
> Tears in his eyes, distraction in his aspect,
> A broken voice, an' his whole function suiting
> With forms to his conceit? And all for nothing,
> For Hecuba!
>
> (*Hamlet*, II, ii, 555–8)

One final note about the transcriptions. In the sixth line, I have taken the reading of "distraction in's aspect" letting the "in his" contract to one syllable, and keeping the line ten syllables long. A lot of actors do it this way (Olivier, for one). It is perfectly reasonable, though, to say the line as written, using eleven syllables and letting the line end with a less stressed syllable, a so-called "feminine ending".

Clothes

I love this text. It's great because Mark Twain is a great writer. It's great because it is rhetorically elegant. It's great because it's true. And, for our purposes, it's great because it has such a wonderful variety of sound use in the English language. Speak on.

What would a man be, what would any man be, without his clothes? As soon as one stops and thinks over that proposition, one realizes that without his clothes a man would be nothing at all; that the clothes do not merely make the man, the clothes are the man; that without them he is a cipher, a vacancy, a nobody, a nothing.

Titles — another artificiality — are a part of his clothing. They and the dry-goods conceal the wearer's inferiority and make him seem great and a wonder, when at bottom there is nothing remarkable about him. They can move a nation to fall on its knees and sincerely worship a man who, without the clothes and the title, would drop to the rank of a cobbler and be swallowed up and lost sight of in the massed multitude of the inconsequentials....

A policeman in plain clothes is one man; in his uniform he is ten. Clothes and the title are the most potent thing, the most formidable influence, in the earth. They move the human race to willing and spontaneous respect for the judge, the general, the admiral, the bishop, the ambassador, the frivolous earl, the idiot duke, the sultan, the king, the emperor. No great title is efficient without clothes to support it.

Is the human race a joke? Was it devised and patched together in a dull time when there was nothing important to do? Has it not respect for itself? I think my respect for it is drooping, sinking — and my respect for myself along with it. There is but one restorative — clothes! Respect-reviving, spirit uplifting clothes! Heaven's kindliest gift to man, his only protection against finding himself out: they deceive him, they confer dignity upon him; without them he has none. How charitable are clothes, how beneficent, how puissant, how inestimably precious! Mine are able to expand a human cipher into a globe-shadowing portent; they can command the respect of the whole world — including my own, which is fading. I will put them on.

Mark Twain, 'The Czar's Soliloquy'

[kl̥ŏŭðz] or [kl̥ŏŭz]

naŭ | hɪɚz wʌn pʰasəbl̥ weĭ tŭ pɹ̩ənaŭns ðɪs tʰekst ‖ ɪts natˀ kəɹekˀt | bət̪
ɪts wʌn weĭ ‖ aĭ wɪl ɪgnɔɚ stɹɛs maɚkɪŋz bikəz aĭ wɒntˀ tŭ əlaŭ jŭ tŭ
hæv sʌm liːweĭ | bət̪ aĭ nɵŭ ðət sʌm sɪlæbɪk stɹɛs wɪl bi ɪndɪkeĭtɪd baĭ
ðə tʃɔɪs of æləfɵŭnz ‖ oŭ jes | ænd aĭ nɵŭ ðæt mɵŭst pipl̩ seĭ kl̥ɵŭz | natˀ
kl̥ŏŭðz ‖

ʍʌt wŭd ə mæn bi | ʍʌt wŭd enĭ mæn bi | wɪðaŭt hɪz kl̥ŏŭðz ‖ ǽz sur̩n
ǽz wʌn staps ənd̪ˀ θɪŋks oŭvɚ ðætˀ pɹ̩apəzɪʃn̩ | wʌn ɹiˑəlaĭzɪz ðǽt
wɪðaŭt hɪz kl̥ŏŭðz ə mæn wŭdˀ bi nʌθɪŋ ǽt ɔːɫ ‖ ðǽt̪ˀ ðə kl̥ŏŭðz dŭ nat
mɪɚˑlĭ meĭk ðə mæn | ðə kl̥ŏŭðz ʔaɚ ðə mæn ‖ ðæt wɪðaŭtˀ ðm̩ | hi ɪz ə
saĭfɚ | ə veĭkənsĭ | ə noŭbədĭ | ə nʌθɪŋ ‖

tʰaĭtl̩z | ənʌðɚ aɚtɪfɪʃɹ̩ælɪtĭ | aʒ̪ ɹə pʰaɚt əv hɪz kl̥ŏŭðɪŋ ‖ ðeĭ ǽnd̪ˀ ðə
dɹaĭgʊdz kənsiˑɫ ðə weɛɹɚz ɪnfɪɹɹɹɪtĭ | ǽnd meĭk hɪm siːm gɹeĭt ǽnd ə
wʌndɚ | ʍen ǽtˀ batəm ðɛʒ̪ ɹɪz nʌθɪŋ ɹɪmaɚkəbl̩ əbaŭt hɪm ‖ ðeĭ kən
muːv ə neĭʃn̩ tŭ fɔːl ɒn ɪts niːz ǽnd sɪnsɪɚlĭ wɚːʃɪp ə mæn huː | wɪðaŭt̪ˀ
ðə kl̥ŏŭðz ǽnd̪ˀ ðə tʰaĭtl̩ | wŭdˀ dɹap tŭ ðə ɹæŋk əv ðə kʰɑˑblɚ | ǽnd̪ˀ bĭ
swalŏŭd ʌp ənd̪l̩ lɔːst saĭt əv ɪn ðə mæːst mʌltɪtçuːd əv ð̪ĭ
ɪnkʰɑˑnsĭkʍenʃ̪z ‖

ə pəliˑsmn̩ ɪn plɛĭn kl̥ŏŭðz ɪz wʌn mæn | ɪn hɪz juːnĭfɔɚm hi ɪz tʰen ‖
kl̥ŏŭðz ənd̪ˀ ðə tʰaĭtl̩ aɚ ðə mɵŭst pʰoŭtⁿnt θɪŋ | ðə mɵŭst fɔɚmɪdəbl̩
ɪnfluˑʷĭns ɪn ð̪ĭ ɚθ ‖ ðeĭ muːv ðə çur̩mn̩ ɹeĭs tʊ wɪlɪŋ ænd spantʰeĭnĭəs
ɹɪspekt fɔ̪ɚ ðə dʒʌdʒ | ðə dʒenɹəɫ | ðĭ æd̪ˀmɚɪɵ̆ɫ | ðə bɪʃəp | ð̪ĭ
ǽmbæsɪdɚ | ðə fɹɪvələs ɚːɫ | ð̪ĭ ɪdiʲətˀ djuk | ðə sʌltⁿn̩ | ðə kʰɪŋ | ð̪ĭ
ɛmpɹɪɚ‖ noŭ gɹeĭtˀ tʰaĭtl̩ ɪz ɹfɪʃn̩t wɪðaŭt kl̥ŏŭðz tŭ səpʰɔɚt ɪt ‖

ɪz ðə çur̩mn̩ ɹeĭs ə dʒoŭk ‖ wʌz ɪtˀ d̪ĭvaĭzd ǽnd̪ˀ pʰætʃˀ tŏŭgeðɚ ɪn ə dʌɫ
tʰaĭm ʍɛn ðɛʒ̪ wəz nʌθɪŋ ɪmpʰɔɚt̪ⁿn̪tˀ tŭ duː ‖ hæz ɪtⁿ nat ɹɪspekˀt fɔ̪ɚ
ɹɪtself ‖ aĭ θɪŋk maĭ ɹɪspekˀt fɔ̪ɚ ɹɪt ɪz dɹuˑpɪŋ | sɪŋkɪŋ | ǽnd maĭ ɹɪspekˀt
fɔ̪ɚ maĭself əlɔˑŋ wɪð ɪt ‖ ðɛʒ̪ ɹɪz bət wʌn ɹɪstɔɚɹətɪvᵛ | kl̥ŏŭðz | ɹɪspekˀt
ɹɪvaĭvɪŋ | spɪɹɪt ʌplɪftɪŋ kl̥ŏŭðz ‖ hevn̩z kʰaĭnd̪lljĭɪst gɪftˀ tŭ mæn | hɪz
oŭnlĭ pɹotʰekʃn̩ əgɛnst faĭndɪŋ hɪmself aŭt ‖ ðeĭ dɪsɪɪv hɪm | ðeĭ çonfɚ

dıgnıti̧ əpʰɑn hɪm ‖ wɪðaʊ̆t̚ ð m̩ hi hæ̆z nʌ'n ‖ haʊ̆ tʃæɹɪtəb ̩l ɑˑ kl̩oʊ̆ðz |
haʊ̆ bɪnɛfɪsn̩t | haʊ̆ pçuˑʷɪsn̩t | haʊ̆ ɪnɛstɪməbl̩i pɹɛˑʃəs ‖ maɪ̆n ɑˑ eɪ̆b ̩l tʉ̆
ɪkspænd ə çuˑmn̩ saɪ̆fɚ ɪntu ʷə gloʊ̆b ʃædoʊ̆ʷɪŋ pʰɔɘ̆tɛ̃nt ‖ ðeɪ̆ kn̩
kəmæːnd ðə ɹɪspɛk̚t əv ðə hoʊ̆ɫ wɝˑɫd | ɪnkl̩udɪŋ maɪ̆ oʊ̆n | ʍɪtʃ ɪz feɪ̆dɪŋ
‖ aɪ̆ wɪl pʊt̚ ð m̩ ɔˑn ‖

mɑɚ̆k tʍeɪ̆n

Remember: Don't translate. Do the articulatory actions and feel the sounds.

🔊 **Audio track 76:** *Clothes.*

Part 4
The skills of intelligibilty

23 Formal and informal speech

This section of the book moves across the line that I have very purposely set up between descriptive and prescriptive learning, between the inform- ation that describes what connected speech actually is and the information that mandates what (under defined circumstances) speech actions should be. But all the skills that you have learned until now will be of crucial impor- tance here and will make the acquisition of any prescriptive pattern easy.

We know – because we do it all the time in real life – that we constantly use different strategies to vary our communication with others, depending on whom we are talking to and the demands of the occasion. So our connected speech never gets stuck in just one set of techniques for stringing sounds together in sequence to form phrases and sentences.

But there is a difference between the physicality of formal and informal speech. We use more formal speech, sometimes instinctively, when we need to communicate to people who might not understand us. They might not share our accent, or they might not hear too well, or they might be listening to us in a challenging acoustic environment, such as a theatre or a lecture hall. Or it might be the communication of very complex text to a listener (although complete formality of speech may not be the best stratagem for this). Or it might be a challenging situational requirement, such as an airplane pilot who does not speak English as a first language communicating with the control tower while landing a plane, or a doctor from another country giving the specifics of a prescription to a nurse in an American hospital – both high-stakes environments for intelligibility.

We use informal or conversational speech when we are speaking fluently to other people with whom we feel comfortable in environments where there are not undue acoustic or textual challenges and where we do not need to impress. The performance of many theatrical works would fall into this category, too. Even in Shakespeare the actor's main goal should not be to impress the audience with one's speech skills; the objective is to make the characters live on stage and to share their life with the audience.

There is another consideration that in a perfect world wouldn't exist, but in our real world does. This is the element of social prestige. For many generations there has existed a social bias in favor of some degree of formal speech. It has diminished considerably in the last fifty years, but I, alas, am of an advanced age that remembers when it was in full flower. During my time in grammar school I well recall being corrected constantly because my speech was considered substandard, especially when, at the age of six, I arrived at school in New England from New Orleans. And many of my fellow students, some of them native New Englanders, suffered this social stigma far more and far longer than I did.

For generations, in America, prescriptive speech training was a major part of elementary, secondary, and college education, although that is no longer true. Stigma in speech pattern today is much more about whether you are speaking in an accent that is easily accepted by the people around you, but prestige based on class is still an active ingredient.

There are many good reasons for learning the skills of formal American English speech. But social prestige is not one of them.

Formal speech actions

You know all of this already — in fact, you have done some of it. Our work here consists in focusing our attention on our arrangement of these sequential speech actions.

1 Try this experiment. Say the following sequence of phonemes as wholly separate actions, with an in-breath between each one. For the vowels, naturally, say the correct phoneme, even though there may be some variation among speakers. For the stop-plosives and the affricates, follow the consonant with a vowel. Use your entire breath flow, unvoiced or voiced, on each consonant and vowel action and be very aware of the feel of forming, feeling and then hearing each sound, whether it is unvoiced or voiced. With the stop-plosives and affricates, make sure that you feel the stoppage and also the explosion. Keep your jaw dropped comfortably open on all phonemes except the phonemes / s /, / z /, / ʃ /, / ʒ / and the combined affricate phonemes / tʃ / and / dʒ /. This is a lot to think about, so do it slowly.

/ b /	/ ə /	/ t /	/ ɪ /	/ f /	/ j /	/ u /	/ m /
/ aʊ /	/ ð /	/ ɪ /	/ t /	/ æ /	/ z /	/ m /	/ ɛ /
/ n /	/ i /	/ ə /	/ v /	/ j /	/ ʊɚ /	/ p /	/ l /
/ eɪ /	/ ɝ /	/ z /	/ d /	/ u /	/ aɪ /	/ h /	/ æ /
/ d /	/ æ /	/ z /	/ l /	/ i /	/ f /	/ ð /	/ ə /	/ t /
/ aʊ /	/ n /	/ k /	/ r /	/ aɪɚ /	/ s /	/ p /
/ oʊ /	/ k /	/ m /	/ aɪ /	/ l /	/ aɪ /	/ n /	/ z /

2 Now do several successive phonemes on one breath. Do this *very slowly*, extending all the phonemes except the stop-plosives and affricates, which no longer need that added vowel. Breathe where you need to; even if you begin to sense words forming sometimes, do not feel that you have to breathe at word endings. Keep each phoneme fully formed, as before.

3 Keeping the phonemes fully formed, as before, do more phonemes on one breath. Make sure that you aren't changing any of the phoneme actions. By this point you surely will have started to perceive larger linguistic units emerging from the sounds – words and even phrases. Feel free to breathe after the ends of words or phrases.

4 If you can still keep each of these phonemic actions formed fully in exactly the same way that you did before, say the entire sentence in two breaths. By now, you may be very aware that you are speaking a sentence from Hamlet's advice to the players: "But if you mouth it as many of your players do, I had as lief the town crier spoke my lines" (*Hamlet,* III, ii).

5 See if you can say the sentence at normal playing speed while still retaining the unaltered identity of each of those phonemes, even in connected speech. This is not easy to enact, and the results may occasionally sound stilted or strange, but do not compromise. Because I have asked you to speak phonemes, there may be some variation in the actions you take for them in some of the consonants and definitely with the vowels and diphthongs – and that one triphthong. For this go-through, that is all right.

Congratulations: you have just produced an extremely instructive parody of formal speech. Even the most rigorous and doctrinaire speech teacher in creation today would not ask you to speak exactly like this, although in years long gone by voice and speech teachers, then called **elocutionists** (along with their pronunciation-specialist cousins, **orthoepists**) came close.

What sounds odd about this speech pattern? Be careful that your answer is *not* "It doesn't sound like the way I talk." After all, the person next to you in class, doing the previous exercise, may not have sounded quite the same as you. No, the thing that sounds odd about it is that the individual phonemes, spoken in more and more closely connected speech, have not altered themselves to allow easy movement of the articulators from one action to another, so the flow of connected speech sounds stilted and over-articulated.

What is useful about the speech pattern you just enacted? The most obvious thing is that everyone can understand easily what you are saying, even if the articulation seems stiff, odd, and lacking in individual character.

Our imaginary "doctrinaire speech teacher" would have yet another perspective about the oddity and the utility of the speech product in the preceding exercise. He or she might allow the student to use altered speech actions to carry her or him with some fluency from one sound to another (within limitations), thus lessening the oddity, but that same teacher would want the student also to eliminate any differentiation within each consonant and vowel phoneme so that each articulation conformed to a required standard that is set by the speech teacher.

The practical problem with this view is that, as long as each speech sound as spoken by real speakers remains within the realm of generally understood phonemes, there is no real problem for the listener in understanding what the speaker is saying. So if intelligibility is the main objective, minor differences within the phoneme – the kinds of things we find in regional accents all the time – do not really matter as long as the appropriate phonemic detail is communicated to the listener by some means.

We can conclude that differentiation between phonemes and the communication of the linguistic information contained within each of them (by some means) is the main characteristic of formal speech actions. Try speaking the sentence you used before in a larger portion of Hamlet's speech. Keep the phonemes fully articulated. Do it twice – the first time following the standards that we established before. Then do it again and try to get all the phonemic information in, but allow yourself to move comfortably from one sound to another. (Note: there is no exactly right way to do this. Experiment.)

> Speak the speech, I pray you, as I pronounced it to you, trippingly
> on the tongue. But if you mouth it as many of your players do,
> I had as lief the town crier spoke my lines. Nor do not saw the air
> too much with your hand thus, but use all gently; for in the very

torrent, tempest, and, as I may say, whirlwind of your passion, you
must acquire and beget a temperance that may give it smoothness.

(*Hamlet*, III, ii)

Your second experiment shows the feel and sound of formal speech
moving in the direction of fluency, and therefore moving in the direction of
informal or conversational speech. If you carry the physical strategies that
you use in fluent formal speech further, your speech will start to become
much less formal. Eventually, using the same strategies, you will start to lose
phonemic detail; and your intelligibility may suffer in some environments.

Fluency strategies

You should not be misled by the binary distinction of "formal/informal".
Most speech in real life, as well as onstage or in front of the camera, lives
somewhere between these extremes, negotiating between them: phonemic detail on the one hand and fluency on the other. Both are desirable
in any speech interaction with a listener: we must be understood, but we
also must be able to achieve this intelligibility with minimal effort.

You have already experienced both the clarity and also the awkward-
ness of excessively formal speech and have instinctively made some
accommodation to fluency. But what actually are you doing when you
move toward fluency? There are several ways that we change our speech
actions to allow our articulators to move easily from one phoneme to another.
The two categories that govern most such actions are called **coarticulation**
and **assimilation**.

Coarticulation

In learning the pronunciation of the phonetic symbols we encountered
several interesting examples of coarticulation, by which we mean forming
a unique sound product in consonants by simultaneously obstructing the
flow at two places in the vocal tract rather than one. Sometimes we
accomplish this simultaneous action by using two different articulators;
sometimes we do it by using the amazing versatility of the tongue muscles.

One example of using different articulators is / ɥ /, which is described by the International Phonetic Association as a "voiced labial-palatal approximant", formed by producing a palatal approximant / j / and also rounding the lips to produce a simultaneous / w /; it is used in French in words like *huit* or *lui*. Another more challenging one, using only the tongue, is the endangered "hooktop heng", endangered because it is found only in one dialect of Swedish and the speakers of that dialect have – for the most part – given it up (not surprisingly, once you have tried to say it). It is formed by producing a / ʃ / and a / x / simultaneously, as you may recall from our study of the IPA. In African languages, we find the simultaneous enactment of / k / and / p / to form the combination / k͡p / and there are several other such stop-plosive combinations.

English has such simultaneous actions as well, but sometimes they are hidden because we are so used to the sound products of the language. It may come as a surprise to us that the / w / is considered by the Association to be a "labial-velar" coarticulation. We are quite used to the "labial" part of it – with some useful lip corner advancement – but the "velar" description may cause some question. It certainly does to me.

The lateral approximant / l / is a better example of a coarticulation. The IPA chart describes it simply as an "alveolar lateral approximant", with no other specification. However, if we consider the muscular action of the tongue in keeping the side edges well down to direct the flow laterally around the tip and blade, while the tip is raised to contact the alveolar ridge, we will sense – with our keen knowledge of the sense and position of the entire tongue – that the dorsum of the tongue is thickened and its superior surface is raised as a natural muscular response to the curling action of the tongue tip and blade. So the middle of the tongue is thickened or arched toward the velum in a coarticulation that is described as "velarization" [lˠ]. The assumption, then, by most phoneticians is that is any / l / is considered to have some degree of velarization or arching of the middle of the tongue toward the velum, in addition to the contact by the tip of the tongue to the alveolar ridge. But in much American and also in much UK pronunciation of English, there Is no contact of the tip of the tongue to the alveolar ridge in the so-called postvocalic / l / positions. What we are left with, in fact, is the arching of the middle portion of the dorsum of the tongue to an approximant version of the voiced velar fricative; as a symbol it is [lˠ]. An even more adventurous way of representing it phonetically would be as the voiced velar approximant / ɰ /. In accents where the tongue root is retracted, such as Cockney, the action becomes uvular; since there is no symbol to indicate "uvulization", the nearest we can come is to honor the tongue retraction by writing – in narrow transcription – the symbol as [lˤ].

The phonetic realization of the phoneme / l / for final "l" has been a source of controversy among phoneticians for years. Some have suggested – wrongly – that the final "l" is always simply retroflex [ɭ]. Others have suggested that it becomes the voiced uvular fricative [ʁ]. Still others have suggested that it becomes a vowel, such as [oː].

As you explore the less formal speaking of text, you will find lots of examples of coarticulation. Because this is a book for actors and speakers, not for phonetics students, we need not explicate all the possible varieties, but informal coarticulation does have two basic sub-categories that deserve some brief mention.

Prearticulation (the linguistic term is "anticipatory coarticulation"). This is the practice of moving an action from one point of articulation to another, so that you can say the next phoneme more easily in connected speech. Prearticulation would be used if we said the word "income" as [ɪŋkʌm] or "utmost" as [ʌpˈmoʊst]. When we say "obvious" as [ɑb̪ˈviʲ.əs] with a dentalized "b", we are stopping the / b / as a labio-dental action to make the transition to the labio-dental / v / easier.

We do **postarticulations** too: actions where a consonant action changes in the second phoneme of a consonant cluster because of the placement of the one just before it. When we say "agree" in American speech, we are almost certainly using the "braced" or "molar" r (for which there is no symbol in the IPA so we will settle for the phoneme [r]) before the / i /, not because of the vowel that follows, not because it needs to be there

244

but because the *preceding* consonant [ɡ] guides the approximant that follows into a placement that is enacted near it with the same portion of the tongue. Postarticulation happens more commonly with the phoneme / r / than with most other consonants.

We do use these coarticulations across phonemes all the time, especially in consonant combinations, because they contribute to fluency without seriously compromising intelligibility, except in those fairly rare cases – rare even onstage – where each and every consonant phoneme must be made completely clear by differentiating that action totally from every other action.

We can do allophonic prearticulations from consonant to vowel as well. When we say "at all" we are probably doing a somewhat more retroflex version of the "t" than we might use in "at ease", in order to prepare the vocal tract for the easy movement to the back vowel of "all", whether that vowel is [ɔ] or [ɑ] in American speech. Or consider the difference in lip position on the "s" in the following words: "seep, sap, sop, soap, soup". For most speakers, the lips move from fully unrounded progressively to fully rounded. This doesn't have a great effect on the identity of the phoneme (we still know well that it is an "s") but it illustrates the physical action of prearticulation effectively because the lips have to do what they have to do.

Assimilation

Assimilation is the monarch of informal speech. Most of the accommodations to efficiency of enactment that we make in informal speech can be included in this generous category. It is the practice of contracting one or more sound actions into another simpler action. We use assimilation all the time and in various forms. A very simple but good example is what we do with individual consonants when we say the two "t" phonemes across two consecutive words in "at that". We commonly stop the first / t / on the back of the upper teeth (phonetically [t̪]) rather than on the alveolar ridge and then we release the voiced dental fricative / ð / from the same place, so that the two consonants move efficiently from one to the other. It isn't quite as linguistically detailed as exploding the "t", but this still conveys the linguistic information of both the phonemes, even though the first phoneme is stopped but not exploded and is also enacted on the back of the upper teeth rather than on the alveolar ridge, the better to release the / ð /. There is an obvious resemblance to the previous category, coarticulation, but it is slightly different because it crosses word boundaries.

We do a similarly simple but not identical action when we divide the stoppage and the plosion of the / t / over two "t" sounds in a row when we say "at times". While it does not involve a change of placement, it does involve the division of a compound two-part action, the stop and the plosive, to convey the linguistic information for each; one "t" is stopped, the other exploded. We do this a lot in English as a practical sequence of actions with "t" sounds in successive words, but we do not do it in doubled consonant words such as "butter". In Italian, though, it is formalized in the characteristic sound of doubled consonants such as the doubled [t] in "stretto", where the first "t" is stopped and the second exploded (the linguistic term is "geminate", from "Gemini", the twins). And "stretto", by the way, is a good description for many assimilated sounds, since it means "compressed or shortened".

Assimilation can also involve the loss of phonemes in consonant clusters; sometimes the loss of combined consonant and vowel or diphthong combinations; and sometimes – in very conversational speech – in the loss of one or more entire syllables or even clauses. It can also involve changing one or more consonants to other ones.

A phonetics text would go through these in considerable detail. But for our purposes here, a few illustrations will suffice.

Yod coalescence. The "yod" is the name for the voiced palatal approximant / j / as in "yes" or "beautiful". When we say an alveolar stop-plosive / t / or / d / in a final position in a word and it is followed by a / j / in an initial position in the next word, as in "that you" or "would you", it is common to let the / t / or / d / expand back from the tip to include the blade (laminal portion) of the tongue forming the post-alveolar fricative / ʃ / or / ʒ /, thus producing in sequence the unvoiced affricates / tʃ / or / dʒ /: "that you" [ðæt ju] turns into [⬚ætʃu] and [wʊd ju] turns into [wʊdʒu] or sometimes [wʊdʒ]. This assimilation is very common in American English speech, which is fairly lax in all its accents when compared to the relative linguistic tenseness of Standard British English or RP. But even RP can do the same (or a similar) assimilation when it and American English speakers who employ the so-called "liquid u" as in "tune" [tçun], "Tuesday" [tçuzdi], "duke" [djuk], or "deuce" [djus] assimilate it to [tʃun], [tʃuzdi], [dʒuk], or [dʒus]. The assimilation could proceed further with the assimilation of "What do you want?" to [wəʃəwɑ̃ʔ]. This phenomenon, also called "palatalization", occurs across word with a final / s / or / z / going into an initial / j /. "Bless you" becomes [blɛʃu], "curse you" becomes [kʰɝːʃu], and "please you" becomes [pl̩iʒu].

Eth / ð / dropping. It is very common, in informal American speech, to change the phoneme / ð / to / d / or more narrowly [d̪]. So "with daring" could change to [wɪd̪ˈdɛɚˈɪŋ] and "but this" could change to [bət̚ˈdɪs]. There is an element of coarticulation in this assimilation change also: these two main categories are not totally distinct from one another.

Schwa / ə / absorption. This is a term originated by J. C. Wells. We have already encountered the phenomenon in a context that is used even in most formal speech: the syllabic consonant, where "even" [ivən] becomes [ivn̩] or with some prearticulation and nasal plosion added [ibⁿm̩]. Its most extreme informality could be [iːm̩]. In an initial position in a connected speech word, the schwa can be absorbed into a syllabic / l / in the famous quote from Dr. Frankenstein "It's alive!" This can be realized as [ɪtsl̩aɪ̆v]. If the doctor is really in a hurry to examine his monster, he might even say [sl̩aɪ̆v]. In a medial unstressed syllable, as in "innocent", the schwa would be absorbed to [ˈɪnsn̩t̚]

Glottal / ʔ / substitution. The most common glottal substitution is to replace "t" in a medial or final position. This substitution is sometimes enacted as a complete replacement, as often occurs in American speech in a final stopped position: "What?" is realized as [ʍʌʔˈ] or [wʌʔˈ]. (Naturally, you haven't confused the glottal symbol [ʔ] with the question mark, have you?)

The glottal [ʔ] can also be coarticulated with the stop-plosive in a final stopped (but not exploded) position. It occurs with / t / but even more commonly with / p / or / k / as in "sip" [sɪpˀʔˈ] or "take" [tʰeɪkˀʔˈ]. While any of these words could be enacted with only the stopped (unreleased) stop-plosive, and, while they would sound almost exactly the same as in the examples above, the "double-stopping" is characteristic of accents in English that exhibit tongue retraction, such as Cockney or many American accents.

Consonant cluster assimilation. A very common action in informal American speech is to eliminate final – or even medial – "t" sounds when they are preceded or followed by another consonant, frequently by / s / or / n /. "That's all" becomes [dæsɔɫ]. "Most interesting" becomes [ˌmoʊsˈinəˌɹəstɪŋ]. "Her fasts are costly" might be assimilated to [hɝˈfæsɪkʰɑsli]. Successions of stop-plosives can undergo assimilation: "beasts" becomes [bis], tastes" becomes [tʰeɪs]. / d / is often dropped after / n /. "Band" could either be enacted as [bæn] or even as [bæ̃], especially if the word is in a final position in a phrase.

Nasalization. Often informal American speech we find / nt / or other post-vocalic nasal consonants or combinations are assimilated into a nasaliz-ation of the vowel, often where the word ends in an unreleased stop. "I can't go" can be spoken as [aɪ kʰæ̃gˈgoʊ]. "Advance" could be [dvæ̃s]. "Vaunt" could be [vɔ̃ʔˈ], "sink" could be [sɪ̃kˈ], "limp" could be [lɪ̃pˀʔˈ].

/ h / dropping. In connected speech we drop the / h / very frequently. Earlier in this book I explained my objection to the International Phonetic Association's recipe for this symbol as an "unvoiced glottal fricative". In English, at least, we can discover with very little experimentation that few if any people actually produce this noise at the glottis. Instead it is a preaspiration of the vowel that follows, its distinguishing physical feature being an increase in pulmonic airflow. I prefer to call it an **unvoiced aspirant.** This increase in airflow means that, in addition to being always prevocalic, the / h / must always begin a syllable that is either fully or partially stressed. If the airflow decreases, as it always does in an unstressed syllable, / h / is going to be dropped unless the speaker makes a special effort to say it. So "Did he leave?" spoken informally usually becomes ['dɪdi'liv]. "Take him away" would become ['tʰeɪkmə'weɪ]. "Leave her to heaven" might be spoken as ['livɜˑ̩ ̩təhɛvn̩] if the Ghost in *Hamlet* was in an unusually nonchalant mood. Note that the / h / remains in "heaven" because the syllable is stressed.

/t / voicing. This is a phenomenon that is very characteristic of American speech in most regional and social dialects. When / t / appears as the first letter in a prevocalic position in an unstressed syllable, as in the words "pre*tt*y", "ci*t*y", or "gra*t*itude", American speakers give voicing to this unvoiced alveolar stop-plosive – to some degree, at least. Some British commentators consider that Americans voice the / t / fully and substitute / d / as though American speakers were saying "sadisfy" or "naughdy". John Honey, makes this point forcefully:

> Some features of American English . . . deserve to be resisted by anyone concerned for intelligibility and clear communication. One of these is the American treatment of the "*t*" sound; . . . If it appears between vowels, as in "le*tt*er" and "ci*t*y" it becomes almost a "*d*", making it difficult to distinguish between *writer* and *rider*, *bidden* and *bitten*.   (John Honey, *Language is Power*, page 248)

There is some evidence for this, since Americans often rhyme the two spellings, as in the banner I saw recently in a printing shop proclaiming "Lordy, Lordy, Al's turned forty." Or the Hooter's employee (and how do you pronounce the "t" in the restaurant title?) who successfully sued her boss for emotional injury because she had won a sales contest that promised, she thought, a "new Toyota" as a prize. Instead she was presented with a small figure of a sage character from *Star Wars: the Empire Strikes Back*. But if Americans truly substitute the phoneme "d" for the phoneme "t" in the way Honey suggests, there would be much more confusion even among Americans about this pronunciation ambiguity, and there isn't. Clearly something else is going on that may escape the ears of some British listeners – and some Americans too.

Many phoneticians suggest that the adjustment of the "t" moves to an alveolar tap / ɾ / with American speakers, so that "dirty" would become [dɝ·ɾi̩]. Aside from the curious juxtaposition of two allophones of / ɾ / in this word, here are reasons to consider that this may not be completely accurate, though it certainly is better than the substitution surmises. A small – but growing – number of phoneticians, with whom I agree, consider that a better transcription of the voicing action on "t" would be a / t / with the subscript wedge voicing diacritic, indicating that the "t" is partially voiced: [t̬] as in "today" [t̬ədeɪ̆], "Saturday" [sæt̬ɝ·deɪ̆], "Fruit of the Loom" [fɹut̬ ə ðə lum], "fatty" [fæt̬i], or "etymological" [ɛt̬əmɑlɑdʒɪkl̩]. I submit cautiously that Americans may be able to distinguish between "bidden" and "bitten" based on the difference between semi-voicing and full-voicing.

Contractions. Many of the preceding verbal actions are, in effect, contractions: enfoldings of speech actions one into another in which both consonants and vowels can be dropped. Their purpose is to provide enough linguistic information to the listener while, at the same time – and in the interest of fluency – not overdoing the action. There are a few other contractions that we have ignored until now only because we know them so well. They have a long (see Shakespeare) and noble history even in the most elevated of English pronunciation. Though contractions are not limited to them, two unstressed or "weak form" words in succession provide a particularly healthy environment for contractions. We know them well: "I've" for "I have", as in the phrase "I *have* a plan", where "have" and "a" are both unstressed. "you're" for "you are", "I'm" for "I am", "she's" for "she is", "what's" for "what is", "they've" for "they have", "that'll" for "that will", "isn't" for "is not" and so on and so on. So useful are these contractions in all but the most formal speech that most of them are used even if the first word in the pair is stressed within a phrase. I've used them frequently in this text to maintain its informal, though hopefully informative, tone.

It is incorrect to characterize informal speech as "lazy" or "sloppy". On the contrary, it is efficient; conforming to the observation that speakers in informal conversational settings instinctively employ minimum (but sufficient) effort to maintain intelligibility, unless they have some overriding reason to conceal their meaning. But minimum effort is not an absolute; the effective minimum for one speech environment might be inappropriate for another. We can also see that there are many different articulatory strategies that speakers can use to be understood always by a listener. It certainly is an error to assume that for all purposes on stage, even within an individual play, an actor has to set a single unvarying level of speech action. The real skill of articulation is learning to sense the kinds of actions that are appropriate to the complex, moment-to-moment conditions of performance and to execute them fully and efficiently.

Formal and informal
Initial practice: back to *Hamlet*

Have a partner for this exercise. One of you will be the formal speaker and one
the informal speaker. The formal speaker, using the criteria for formal speech
(even though we have not yet examined speech skills in detail) will speak the
passage pronouncing every phoneme fully, even if this feels excessively articulated.
Then the informal speaker will speak the same passage, using as little effort in
articulation as possible while maintaining minimal intelligibility (and keeping the
volume up).

> O, it offends me to the soul to hear a robustious periwig-pated
> fellow tear a passion to tatters, to very rags, to split the ears of the
> groundlings, who for the most part are capable of nothing but
> inexplicable dumb shows and noise. I would have such a fellow
> whipped for o'erdoing Termigant. It out-herods Herod. Pray you,
> avoid it. *(Hamlet, III,ii)*

Discuss what the speech strategies were that each of you used. What
information can you trade about intelligibility or appropriate articulatory action?

The formal speaker should do the speech again, moderating the pronunciation
of the text toward less formality, but maintaining as much formality as will make
every phoneme very intelligible to the listener. The informal speaker should
explore putting in the necessary phonemic detail – but as little as possible –
to make the reading not only intelligible, but comfortably so.

Switch roles. Go through the same process, except that this double run-through
will be informed by the last one.

This is our first pass at the formal–informal continuum. When we have
completed our exercise work on the speech skills of consonant and vowel
action we shall try it again, even if you were brilliant this time.

24 Consonant skills

You should be aware by now that the point of view of this book is that formal speech is not intrinsically superior to informal speech, as long as the informal speech is completely intelligible to the listener. However, we have to consider the reality that informal connected speech is a skill in which most American speakers, and most American actors, have a lot more expertise and practice. Since a key premise of this book is that actors can use everything, it is important that we spend some time exploring in greater detail phonemic (i.e. meaning) differentiation through phonetic (i.e. specific and fluent) means. There are real benefits to the actor in exploring the specific actions that provide linguistic detail in our speech.

We already know that complete formality sounds odd because it usually involves more linguistic detail than we as listeners might need. There are other messages that might be contained within such strict formality: the implication that the listener is hard of hearing, or disinclined to listen, or simply stupid. These implied messages limit the fluidity of verbal communication and especially the possibilities for characterization by actors.

But formalism does have its positive uses in actions skills. While we would never go to the extremes of formality (except when performing in an outdoor theatre with terrible acoustics, a high wind, and a train going by) we need to develop our skills in moving toward formality, if only because many of us have never been there. Speech informality is something that we all are really good at already, whereas the skills of speech formality require actions that many students have never explored.

It is a generally accepted precept in language teaching that listeners unfamiliar with the words they are hearing will comprehend better if the words are spoken with a high level of linguistic detail, and with all the phonemes, consonant and vowel, highly differentiated. As language students become more familiar with the vocabulary and grammar, some degree of informal speech strategies can be introduced by the teacher in the interest of fluency. But even a diligent student, newly immersed in the language environment of a given country, may have great difficulty in understanding native speakers of the language when they are conversing with one another.

In the same way, speakers of a common language with different dialect backgrounds will find that they all understand a speaker better if a greater degree of linguistic detail is employed. The actor who is speaking complex text to a diverse audience will find that its group comprehension is usually bettered by judicious increase in the detail of certain speech actions, especially if the acoustic demands of performance are also more challenging.

There is a pitfall in focusing exclusively on formal skills, however separately they may be taught. If all our practice moves inexorably in the direction of formality and increased activity, we can lock ourselves into an inflexible pattern of formality, even if we are trying to keep the skills separate from one another. So it is crucial to practice all the word lists or sentences in two directions – toward detail and then toward informality. By practicing these skills on this kind of continuum, we will have the added benefit of honing our perceptual skills so that we know when a particular set of sounds is or is not communicating effectively to a listener. Eventually this knowledge becomes instinctive, so that an actor does not have to think about any sort of skills set, but feels instead – in every moment – the unique way in which her character wants to communicate with the other characters onstage and with the audience too.

Specific skills

1 All consonants *except* [s], [z], [ʃ], [ʒ], [tʃ], and [dʒ] in American English can be formed with the jaw remaining relaxed open, and with greater muscularity of the other articulators. This is not a new skill for you as we have been exploring this convention throughout our phonetic work. Furthermore it is a natural posture for most American accents. But it also makes good sense in performance. If the jaw is relaxed open, there is more room in the oral cavity for the sound to come from. Getting the jaw out of the formula for articulation allows us to be more varied and specific in our use of the other articulators. For many accents, variation of jaw position will be very important but, for now, keep it relaxed open.

For the six consonants listed above, the jaw needs to be raised and brought forward very slightly toward the upper front teeth. Relax the jaw open again immediately after the sound is completed, so that the relaxed jaw remains "home base" for articulation. Speak the following words and sentences slowly and then at normal pace, being very careful to raise and then release the jaw back to home base as needed. Monitor your jaw with your fingers lightly at the sides of your mandible if you wish.

situate, fashion, Sicily, cashew, seizes, judges, notion, satchel, nausea, versus, contusion, Atchison, contagion, seizure, vicissitude, ration, sideshows, church socials, jerseys, bastion, Xerxes, prestidigitation

She casually spoke with the teacher.
They chided the speaker for his foolish notions.
Imagine a scenic design with no visual elements on stage.
The judge showed his agitation.

◀)) **Audio track 77:** *Jaw action.*

Repeat. But this time, explore what happens if you keep the jaw raised toward the upper front teeth all the time. What works better and what works worse?

2 Just to see how it feels, try pronouncing all the consonants in the following word list with full, precise action. Do this very slowly, with a lot of attention to the complete enactment of each phoneme; then repeat it at normal speed. Be wary of following the spelling slavishly: there are spelled compound consonant sounds but there are no silent letters in the words.

plinths, drifts, crusts, groped, lengths, schlepped, thanked, plagues, clucked, bragged, cthonic, angst, clapped, shelves, dephlogisticated, marsupial, bloviate

The internists inadvertently performed a lobotomy instead of a phlebotomy.
Rustication precludes professional diligence.
The cleric attempted to placate his infuriated parishioners.

◀)) **Audio track 78:** *Pronouncing all the consonants.*

3 Explore making voiced/unvoiced distinctions in the following consonants:
[ʍ] – [w], [tʃ] – [dʒ], [s] – [z], [t] – [d], [θ] – [ð]

Carry this through to the following word lists:

[ʍ] – [w] *which witch, when wen, why Wye, whether weather, whale wail, whit wit, whirred word*

[tʃ] – [dʒ] *charred jarred, choke joke, chain Jane, chaw jaw, etch edge, larch lodge*

[s] – [z] *seal zeal, sit zit, sue zoo, peace peas, Miss Miz, Fess fez, cuss cuz, eased east, cause slides, slays sleeves, close close, picks pigs, drags sacks*

[t] – [d] *feat feed, meat mead, rote rode, suit sued, patty paddy, Pinter Pindar, pant panned, faint feigned, post posed, petty Pedi, mottle model, betting bedding*

[θ] – [ð] *ether either, teeth teethe, sooth soothe, cloth clothe, this'll thistle, Theseus seethes, breathe breath, wreathe wreaths*

Why worry when we wonder which way we wander?
The judge charged the jury in chambers.
He's ceaselessly espoused his causes so zealously.
Matty petted her pretty parakeet and tried to distract attention from her pouty "puddy tat".
Think this uncouth threat through, and then breathe methodically.

◀») **Audio track 79:** *Unvoiced/voiced distinctions.*

As you can tell easily, the distinction between unvoiced and voiced phonemes changes the meaning of the words in the word pairs completely. Speak the word pairs with full attention to a maximum distinction between unvoiced and voiced. Then say each sentence using the same maximum unvoiced/voiced distinction. Say each sentence four more times, gradually moving all the paired consonant phonemes toward full voicing. Then speak the sequence again, gradually moving the paired consonant phonemes toward full unvoicing; the last exploration may sound strange to you.

We know, from our discussion of informality, that / t / semi-voicing to / t / voicing is the most common voicing in American speech. It deserves some extra consideration.

Voiced/unvoiced challenge. The British novelist Martin Amis wrote a story in which the main character, a young boy, is speaking "in sarcastic Americanese" about a tragic event. Can you read the passage exactly as written? It requires voicings of all unvoiced consonants, including those that Americans never voice. Because it assumes that Americans voice all unvoiced consonants, not just "t" sounds, it is "sarcastic". But it is also informative about the British perception of American speech.

Note that the "th" sounds are the only written letters for which there is no orthographic way of indicating whether the phoneme is unvoiced or voiced. It could be / θ / or / ð /. But in context, it is certainly / ð /. When Amis knows that a written / s / would be pronounced in a particular word as / z /, he doesn't change the spelling. Note also that Amis changes the spelling of the "short o" sounds, represented in Standard English (or "Received Pronunciation") as / ɒ /, to "a", even though to an American that might suggest a more fronted vowel.

Try to read the passage exactly as written. Then, translate the text back into the way Americans actually speak, noting now the feel of the unvoicings or voicings define the meaning.

A derrible thing habbened do me on my haliday. A horrible thing, and a bermanend thing. I won'd be the zame, ever again.

Bud virzd I'd bedder zay: don'd banig! I'm nad zuvvering vram brain damage – or vram adenoidz. And I gan wride bedder than thiz when I wand do. Bud I don'd wand do. Nod vor now. Led me egsblain.

I am halve Englizh and halve Amerigan. My mum is Amerigan and my dad is Englizh. I go do zgool in London and my bronunziazhion is Engizh – glear, even vaindly Agzonian, the zame as my dad'z. Ameriganz avden zeem zurbrised do hear an eleven-year old who zbeegs as I zbeeg. Grandaddy Jag, who is Amerigan, admids thad he vinds id unganny. As iv zuj an agzend reguirez grade ganzendrazhion even vram grownubs, led alone jildren. Amerigans zem do zuzbegd thad the Englizh relagz and zbeeg Amerigan behind glosed doors. Zhouding oud, on their redurn, "Honey, I'm home!" My other grandvather veld divverendly: Englizh, do him, was the more najural voice. Zo thiz zdory iz vor them, doo, as well vor Eliaz. I dell id thiz way – in zargazdig Ameriganeze – becaz I dond wand id do be glear: do all be grizb and glear. There iz thiz ztrange resizdanze. There iz thiz zdrange resizdanze.

(Martin Amis, "What Happened to Me on My Holiday", from *Heavy Water and Other Stories*, pages 199–200)

4 There are several – four, actually – physical strategies for enacting the voiced alveolar lateral approximant / 1 /. The first, usually used in a pre-vocalic position in a word, is the so-called "clear [l]", produced by placing the tip of the tongue and the very front of the laminal portion onto the alveolar ridge and then dropping the side edges of the tongue only as far as needed to produce the approximant action. The mid-line of the laminal portion of the tongue is also raised slightly.

The second type that is often used by American speakers in prevocalic and postvocalic positions within a word is the "dark [ł]". It is often thought that in order to produce the [ł] a certain amount of retroflexion is involved, with the tongue tip retracted to a post-alveolar position. I submit that this is not really the case. The difference between [l] and [ł] is that [ł] is produced with only the tip of the tongue on the gum ridge, but in the same location as the [l]. The blade of the tongue is lowered sharply (and the jaw is relaxed open).

The third type of / l / that we find in both prevocalic and postvocalic positions in American speech is the retroflex [ɭ]. Here the tongue-tip is curled back to a post-alveolar or even alveolar-palatal placement.

We have discussed previously the fourth strategy, the velarized [lˠ], where only the velar coarticulation of / l / is used. This is common in American speech but is only used in a postvocalic, generally final, position in a word.

Other allophones of / l / may be ignored here because they are not employed commonly by American speakers, although the unvoiced lateral fricative [ɬ] might be used in a word sequence like "at least" or "Atlantic" if lateral plosion of the / t / is used into a stressed syllable.

The common wisdom among many speech teachers is that the clear [l] should be used in both prevocalic and postvocalic positions. This is an overly rigid doctrine and often leads to a lack of fluency. When / l / precedes a front vowel it would seem very reasonable. When a front vowel moves into a postvocalic "l" it would seem efficient to use a [ł]. When the / l / follows a back vowel, we almost always move into some degree of an [l̪]. If we avoid excessive retroflexion, we can produce a version of / l / that communicates the phoneme very easily to an audience. Because the retroflexion naturally causes a greater degree of velar arching, the (minimally retroflected) [l̪] is useful for final / l / placement as well as for use in an acoustically challenging environment, such as a large outdoor theatre or a crowded classroom of teenagers. Dropping the tongue-tip to produce the wholly velarized l lˠ] is an important skill in informal speech but does not communicate as clearly to large groups as any of the other three options.

Explore the words in the following list, placing the / l / in initial, medial, and final positions. Try the first three allophones of / l / in each word. Add the velarized [lˠ] for the final / l / words. What sounds most clearly defined and – at the same time – fluent for each word and sentence? Where does your tongue "want" to touch the roof of the mouth in these words and sentences? Can you modify any of your tongue action preferences in the interest of intelligibility?

lee, lean, lip, lit, lift, left, lest, lab, land, lashed, locked, lopped, lobs, law, lost, lawn, laud, look, Lou, lose, loop, lewd, luge, loose, lay, lame, lie, life, lice, loud, lounge, lout, low, loaf, lone, lope, loin, Lloyd, leer, lair, lure, lore, Lahr

silly, pellet, ballad, polyp, taller, pullet, ruling, sailing, pilot, howler, molar, boiler

meal, seal, feel, wheel, reel, eel, deal, keel, Beale, veal, zeal, fill, pill, sill, sell, tell pal, Val, Baal, call, ball, mall, tall, wall, shawl, trawl, pull, fool, tool, dole, shoal, file, style cowl, foul, coil, boil, rule, school, pool, ghoul, stool, spool, drool

Lulu, Lily and Lolita were pleased to call on Pearl.
All letters were delivered to the ballet.
Ulla mulled over all the allegations.

◀)) **Audio track 80:** *Initial, medial, final / l /.*

There is another issue related to / l / that needs to be discussed. When [ɫ] or [l] is used in a final position after a close vowel like / i / or / u /, we have a tendency to intrude an approximant plus vowel before the final / l /, so that "feel" [fiɫ] becomes [fijəɫ] and "fool" [fuɫ] becomes [fuwɫ]: a one-syllable word becomes a two-syllable word. Why does this happen?

Consider the physicality of the problem and the solution. Usually the front of the tongue is arched high to form / i / and then is lowered to facilitate the rise of the tongue-tip to form the / l /. The problem is that this happens before the tongue-tip has reached the point of contact with the alveolar ridge, which is the crucial physical action to establish the / l /. When going into a final [l] from a high (close) vowel, either [i] or [u], make sure that you raise the tip of the tongue to contact the alveolar-palatal point of articulation *before* you lower the front or middle of the tongue. This sequence of actions will allow you to say "feel" or "fool" as [fiːl] or [fuːl] instead of [fiːjəl] or [fuːwəl].

When going into a final [l] from a high (close) vowel, either / i / or / u /, make sure that you raise the tip of the tongue to contact the alveolar-palatal point of articulation *before* you lower the front or middle of the tongue. This sequence of actions will allow you to say "feel" or "fool" as [fiːɫ] or [fuːɫ] instead of [fiːjəɫ] or [fuːwəɫ].

5 The dreaded / r / problem. Americans say / r / in a prevocalic position in one of three ways: as a post-alveolar approximant [ɹ], as a retroflex [ɻ], or as a "braced" or "molar" / r /, for which there is no phonetic symbol. Most Americans use either the second of these options, or the third, or a combination of both. All of these three strategies convey the phoneme to a listener. But many Americans have scant experience with the physical production of the [ɹ]. It is imperative to gain this skill, not only because it is very useful in American speech, but also because it is used in a number of other accents.

As a reminder, the action is simple: with the jaw relaxed open, the tip of the tongue is curled upward – and therefore the blade also – leaving the dorsum of the tongue relaxed. The tip intrudes minimally into the voiced flow in a post-alveolar position. You will feel the effect of the pressure waves (e.g. vibrations) at the tip of the tongue. To release the sound, let the tongue-tip relax back to a position behind the lower front teeth.

Explore the simple physical sequence slowly as an unvoiced action. Then explore it voiced. Make sure that you are isolating the action to the tip and blade of the tongue.

Here is another way to get to it. Speak an extended [z]. As you do so, gradually relax your jaw open and let the tongue-tip be naturally drawn back to a post-alveolar position by that action. Relax the tip very slightly to an approximant rather than fricative position.

Now speak the following word list of / r / in initial and medial positions. Use first the post-alveolar approximant [ɹ], then the voiced retroflex [ɻ] and finally the braced or molar / r /.

reap, reed, rip, wrist, wreck, raft, rod, wrong, rook, rule, rug, rain, rind, round, roil, robe, ruse, rake, rind, rural

pray, bribe, try, drain, creep, grove, free, crave, drone, throat, average, three, shriek, arrest, direct, parade, carouse, charade, barren, carrot, parrot, narrow, marrow, lariat, errand, chorus

Now explore the following medial and final / r / using any of the three physical actions open to you: voiced post-alveolar approximant, retroflex, and braced.

rear, rare, Ruhr, roar, bear, fear, tour, core, far, jar, stir, fur, whir, occur, defer, learn, churn, usurp, lured, toured, world, purse, barn, charge, heart, park, parch, lard, shard, charm, farce, bored, hoard, scorn, weird, beard, pierce, fared

Finally, speak the following sentences, being aware of which of these three actions is clearest and most fluent.

Rory ruined Fleur's transistor radio.
Carol reread the résumé of Irving's daughter.
Dragan resented Trevor's relentless boring perorations.

◀)) **Audio track 81:** / r / *in variation.*

6 Efficient pronunciation of / s /. This consonant action is a problem for many speakers. There are many variants of this unvoiced fricative and some of them, such as lateral release, would need to be addressed by a speech pathologist. But there are a few techniques that can help with the most common issues.

In America roughly fifty per cent of speakers enact the / s / with the tongue-tip up and the airstream focused at the alveolar ridge. And about fifty per cent of speakers pronounce / s / with the tongue tip down; here the air stream releases over the blade of the tongue with a focus that is post-alveolar. In the past, speech teachers would insist that all speakers use the "tongue-tip up" version. While this technique has some advantages in connected speech, it is also true that this basic modification of tongue-tip action is fairly arduous and may not be worth the time and effort if the speaker is producing a clear / s / with the tongue-tip down – and many people do.

No matter what physical action the actor takes in forming it, the pho-neme / s / should always be produced with as small an aperture (formed at the midline of the tongue) as possible, and also with as gentle an airflow as possible. The placement should be alveolar, or as near as possible to alveolar. If all of these actions are done accurately, the / s / will not hiss or sound mushy. If the tongue focus is dentalized [s̪] the result for most people will be a very thin, hissy sound product. If the focus is retracted too far (a danger with the tongue-down version) the airstream will become too broad by the time it washes down the back of the upper front teeth and the noise will be mushy. A lot of this fronted/retracted focus is dependent on an individual's oral anatomy, especially with regard to the size, shape, and spacing of the teeth. So experimentation is in order. The most impor-tant criteria are: narrow airstream and minimal airflow.

Practice using a minimal flow of air on the / s /. Very often, in speaking, we send much more air than we need through whatever aperture the tongue is forming with the roof of the mouth for all unvoiced fricative consonants. Say the word "heat" a few times just to make sure you can start the / i / without using a glottal attack on the vowel. Then move to "eat" *without* any glottal attack / ʔ /. Then say "seat" with as little airflow on the / s / as possible. Also make sure that you keep the stream of the airflow as narrow as possible, whether you pronounce the / s / customarily with tongue-tip up or tongue-tip down. Alternate saying "eat" and "seat"; then say them in an irregular pattern: "eat eat eat seat seat eat seat eat seat seat eat seat eat eat eat seat", etc. Note if a listener (who knows what to listen for) can tell which word you are saying.

see, seat, seam, cease, sit, sift, silt, set, said, send, sat, sand, sack, sap, sock, sod, sob, solve, sop, psalm, saw, sought, soft, Salk, so, sew, soap, sewed, soak, soul, soot, sue, soon, suit, soothe, serve, search

speed, steel, ski, spin, stint, skill, spell, stet, sketch, spat, stand, scam, spot, stop, scotch, spawn, stall, scald, spoke, stole, scold, stood, spool, stool, school, sphinx, sprawl, strand, scrape

assist, recent, fasten, associate, Mississippi, assists, resets, necessity, Cecil, Cicely, Cecily, Sicily

seeps, deeps, creeps, leaps, sips, lips, tips, reps, taps, chaps, gaps, hops, chops, tops, drops, loops, troops, groups, hoops, chirps, burps, ups, cups, seats, meets, Keats, fits, writs, pets, bets, lets, mats, pats, rats, chats, lots, pots, knots, cots, thoughts, puts, hoots, boots, hurts, asserts, huts, butts, shuts, baits, fates, mites, rights, lights, louts, touts, shouts, boats, totes, coats, votes, seeks, cheeks, geeks, reeks, sticks, ticks, picks, wrecks, checks, necks, packs, sacks, lacks, knocks, socks, rocks, balks, talks, chalks, looks, books, hooks, rooks, Luke's, works, lurks, tucks, mucks, bucks

niece, peace, lease, crease, hiss, miss, kiss, Bess, less, Tess, dress, chess, brass, pass, gas, hostile, Haas, Haagen-dasz, loss, boss, toss, puss, loose, moose, curse, hearse, fuss, muss, pace, race, face, ice, mice, trice, house, mouse, louse, voice, choice,

crisp, lisp, asp, clasp, hasp, rasp, least, beast, pieced, mist, whist, *wrist, list, best, chest, vest, rest, past, massed, last, fast, bossed, tossed, lost, cost, roost, boost, first, worst, bust, trust, baste, taste, riced, iced, roust, joust, roast, boast, toast, voiced, hoist, joist, risk, flask*

crisps, lisps, asps, clasps, beasts, feasts, wrists, fists, schists, tests, bests, pests, casts, masts, costs, frosts, roosts, thirsts, lusts, bastes, tastes, ousts, Fausts, posts, roasts, coasts, hosts, toasts, hoists, risks, asks, flasks, casks, husks, rusks

imps, chimps, stamps, comps, romps, lumps, chumps, hints, mints, rinks, thinks, thanks, banks, shanks, pronks, lunks, dunks

Standing aside, Cicely spoke seriously with Cecily.
Stanton Stassen sold Bruce a gross of husks and some soap-suds
*   that suddenly disappeared.*
Silas the moose passed gas in gusts.

Amidst the mists and coldest frosts
With barest wrists and stoutest boasts,
He thrusts his fists against the posts
And still insists he sees the ghosts.

◀)) **Audio track 82:** / r / *initial, medial, final.*

7   Word linking. A reminder that the formal / tj / and / dj / – when an actor is linking words in complex text – may be preferable to the **yod coalescence** into the affricates / tʃ / and / dʒ /. Practice this word list using both the / j / and then using the afficates.

seat you, fit you, get you, let you, at you, pat you, that you, blot you,
bought you, taught you, put you, suit you, rate you, sight you,
fight you, clout you, coat you, what you, butt you

feed you, lead you, bid you, kid you, wed you, pad you, laud you,
hood you, brood you, raid you, jade you, ride you, bide you,
crowd you, load you

◀)) **Audio track 83:** *Word linking /* dj */*

An allied issue with linking words (and within a few words too) in formal speech is the enactment of word sequences in which the first word ends with / l / and the next word begins with / j /. Because the / j / is dorso-palatal, it is tricky (though formally required) to get the tongue into proper placement if the speaker is coming out of an alveolar / l /. But, in informal speech, a reasonable substitute is the velarized [lˠ] where the tongue-tip stays down and makes easier the arching of the front of the tongue into the approximant / j /. So the sequence [lj] turns into the sequence [lˠj]. Practice the list both ways.

> *steal you, heal you, will you, bill you, sell you, tell you, call you,*
> *maul you, pull you, curl you, hurl you, dull you, lull you, ail you,*
> *fail you, pile you, rile you, cowl you, foul you, dole you, coil you,*
> *boil you, William, value, psyllium, Valium, thallium, Coolio*

◀)) **Audio track 84:** *Word linking /* lj */ alveolar and velarized.*

8 Glottal stop-plosives. Despite the IPA's placement of / ʔ / on the pulmonic chart as an "unvoiced glottal stop-plosive", it is obvious that the IPA is not entirely accurate here. It will not take much experimentation to feel that the glottal plosion that occurs when we say "uh-oh" is voiced, not unvoiced. A genuinely unvoiced glottal stop-plosive would be a light cough. We know that glottals are used all the time by American speakers; often before a vowel in an initial position in words such as *east, air, owe, up,* or *ooze.* They also occur in medial and final positions within a word, usually as an unsounded stop [ʔ̚] to replace / t /.

Sometimes there are good reasons to use a voiced glottal stop-plosive: it is a very effective way to emphasize strongly a word that begins with a vowel. But the need for glottal emphasis is comparatively rare in American speech, formal or informal. The only words in American English where glottal plosion conveys phonemic content are "uh-uh" and "uh-oh". (Try these both ways, with and without glottal plosion, and you'll see what I mean.)

Those two vocalizations excepted, glottal plosion is *never* needed for any reason other than strong emphasis, so it becomes a phoneme separated from meaning and thus a phoneme without any purpose at all. Sometimes, too, there are good reasons to use a glottal stop as substitution for another stop-plosive: it still conveys phonemic detail while maintaining fluency. But if it becomes a habit, you will use it too often when other actions might produce more detailed connected speech.

The real problem with glottal plosion and glottal stops (when used in English speech – in some dialects of German they are required) is that they commonly show that you are holding residual tension in the delicate muscles of your vocal folds, a sign that you have insufficient easy support in your breathing mechanism. It is a crucial skill for effective vocal use as well as speech to be able to initiate a word with a vowel without exploding it from a tensed glottis and to be able to end a syllable without always using a glottal stop. Actually it is a crucial *set* of skills.

The first skill is going onto an initial vowel from a relaxed glottis. Begin by bringing the vocal folds close together, but not to the point of "creaky voice" or phonation. Breathe out easily *without* increasing the airflow. The effect is a little like a very gentle unvoiced "h". From that feel of the airflow, go into the vowel. You should do this slowly at first and then gradually phase the initial aspiration out. You can explore this on *huh huh huh huh huh*. Do it first with on separate breaths and then do the entire sequence of five on one long release of flow. Whenever you start a sentence with a vowel, you will have to use this technique.

When you speak a sentence, if you are moving from a final consonant to an initial vowel, you can carry the final consonant through to the next word, as though the next word actually began with a consonant, as in "Sit over on the left aisle." An allied technique is to use the so-called "liaison r" where the post-vocalic / r / strengthens to feel like an initial "r", as in "over on" in the previous sentence.

Your expertise in phthong shaping will assist you in mastering the next skill: dealing with a final vowel or diphthong moving into a word that also initiates with a vowel. Vowel-to-vowel blending, in other words. It is easy to move from one vowel phoneme to another without intruding a glottal plosion.

There are only two rules for this. First, don't be afraid to elide one vowel to another without an intervening attack on the word; if you do it clearly we will understand that the syllable is changing because syllabic change is also marked by sub-glottal pulses of energy. Second, don't feel that you have to intrude an approximant in order to start the initial vowel with a semi-vowel; you can speak "we are" as [wi.ɑ˞] by simply dropping the arch of the tongue away from the / i / to the / ɑ / without having to intrude a / j / to form [wijɑ].

It is also common for American speakers to stop an unvoiced stop-plosive in a final position while simultaneously coarticulating stoppage at the appropriate placement for that particular stop-plosive, as in *stop, lip, hope, wrap that, set, boot, black, take,* and so on. It is always clearer to enact the full stop-plosive action in final stop-plosives

There is one other skill for eliminating unneeded medial glottals, but we will deal with it in a page or two.

Practice the following words and sentences using these techniques to eliminate unnecessary glottals; then (as always) put the glottals in aggressively. Feel the difference between the two, because you will need both skills as an actor.

each, east, if, ill, Ed, add, as, odd, on, all, ought, ooze, earn, earth, up, aim, aisle, out, owe, oil, ear, air, ore, are, ease, eel, eke, eaves, each, if, is, itch ill, ink, ate, ape eight, oh, ah, ash assist, oolong,

beat, seat, wit, met, wet, set, rat, brat, fat, lot, sot, cot, taught, fought, bought, rote, vote, put, "beaut", butte, newt, boot, scoot, hoot, sate, bait, light, right, mite, bout, shout, pout, rout, moat, vote, stoat, coat, groat, quoit, court, fort, short, cart, part, start, art, mart seep, peep, sheep, reap, heap, cheap, sip, drip, flip, chip, pep, step, rap, gap, lap, sap, cap, lop, flop, cop, shop, stop, mop, top, hop, soup, loop, hoop, coop, dupe, "turp", "perp", twerp, sup, cup, tape, shape, cape, type, ripe, cope, hope, grope, soap, lope, dope, tarp, flake, make, take, choke, bike, Luke, dark, lurk, seek

muse of, take out, read on, rake over, shake out, as is, on / off, write in, add on, pull out, peace on earth

for a, care about, peer out, pour out, know all, bore in, tear into, more oats, fear adversaries, stare at

say on, try out, be opposed, see all, buy out, through obstacles, no entrance, pay off, row away, why argue, now entertain

When glottises attack

Elliot ate an apple and offered Andrew another.
Each and every avenue is open at eight o'clock.
I am in agreement on every aspect of our association.
Alan's attitude is overly obnoxious.
Exercise is an important and energizing activity.
Amanda is in Alabama at an annual event.
Actually I am aware of all errors in Adam's arithmetic assignment.
Every evening in autumn our area orchestra attempts to entertain an uninterested audience of adolescents.
Esmeralda earned an audience's enthusiastic applause after exhibiting an outrageous and ergonomically effortful acrobatic undertaking.
"Aren't all of us – and I above all – existing endlessly in an overarching aura of old (indeed ancient) outworn, outré, Aristotelian ontology?" Iggie inquired innocently.[1]

◀)) **Audio track 85:** *Glottal stop-plosives.*

---

1. Except for the last two, the sentences above are taken from *The Professional Voice*, edited by Robert Sataloff, M.D. (Singular Publishing, 1992).

9 Aspiration in informal and formal speech.

In formal speech, unvoiced stop-plosives [p], [t], and [k] are aspirate [pʰ], [tʰ], and [kʰ] before vowels (including diphthongs and triphthongs) in the same stressed syllable. Some examples are "appalled" [ə'pʰɔːld], "timely" ['tʰaĭmlị], "occur" [ə'kʰɝː]. In these cases the voicing of the vowel waits for the aspirate gust to go by before asserting itself.

If the unvoiced stop-plosive is followed in a stressed syllable by an approximant consonant, especially [ɹ], [l], [w], or [j], there is no pause between the stop-plosive and the approximant, but the aspiration in effect blows out all or part of the voicing of the approximant. So "crew" becomes [kɹu], "plane" becomes [pl̥eĭn], "cue" becomes [kçu], and "quail" becomes [kʍeĭl].

There is an exception to this delayed "onset of vocalization". If the unvoiced stop-plosive [p], [t], or [k] is preceded in the same syllable by an [s], the stop-plosive is *not* aspirate. This reads as complicated, but it isn't really. Just feel when the voiced vibrations – (the [i] sounds) – come in while you say first the word "team" and then the word "steam".

In all other cases, the stop-plosive is not usually aspirate in American English. When followed by a consonant (other than an approximant) as in "Hapgood" [hæpgʊd] or in an unstressed syllable as in "naughty" [nɔtị], the aspiration does not occur. The same is true, for that matter, at the end of a word, whether in the middle of a sentence "at all" [ət 'ɔːl] or at the end of a statement "Not!" [nɑt]. In the first case, the word "at" is un-stressed, and in the second case the emphatic statement might well close with a stopped consonant that is not exploded. In this last example, even if a little aspiration crept in to honor the exclamation mark, it wouldn't con-vey any more linguistic information.

Explore the following word lists and sentences, feeling the differences in physical action of aspiration. And yet, again, try the opposite: eliminating aspiration (which occurs in many languages), adding aspiration, from plo-sive to plosive, etc.

pea, peep, peach, peak, piece, pique, pip, pit, pig, pin, ping, pitch, pith, pill, pick, pet, pep, pest, pen, peg, pap, pat, pack, pan. pang, path, pass, pal, pop, pot, pod, pock, posh, pall, pawed, pawn, put, push, pull, poop, pool, Pooh, purr, pert, perm, purse, perk, purred, pup, putt, pug, pun, puff, pay, paste, pain, pail, pine, pipe, pike, pie, pied, pow, pout, pound, pouch, pope, poach, post, poke, pole, poise, point, peer, pierce, pair, pared, poor, pour, pores, port, porch, par, part, park

tea, teak, tease, teeth, teach, tip, tick, tiff, tin, till, tech, ten, test, tell, tap, tack, tan, tang, tag, top, tot, tog, tock, tall, taught, toss, took, two, too, tool, toot, turn, Turk, terse, tuck, touch, tuft, taste, tame, tale, take, time, tyke, tile, tight, type, tide, tout, town, towel, tote, tone, toast, toll, toy, toil, tier, tear, tour, torn, tarred

key, ken, keel, kit, kick, kin, king, kiss, kitsch, ketch, ken, cap, cat, cab, cask, cash, calm, cod, cop, con, call, caught, cause, caulk, cough, could, coo, cool, coop, kook, curse, curr, curd, curl, cup, cut, come, cave, case, cape, cane, kind, kite, cow, count, couch, cowl, cope, coat, code, coast, coke, cone, comb, cove, coach, coal, coy, coin, Coit, coil, care, cairn, Coors, core, corn, coarse, car, cart, carve, Carl

priest, prince, primp, press, pram, prom, prop, prawn, prove, pray, pry, pride, prow, prowl, pro, probe, prone, prayer, tree, treat, trip, trim, trick, trill, tress, tread, trek, trap, tram, track, trash, trod, trawl, true, trade, traipse, train, try, tripe, trope, troll, Troy, Cree, creep, creed, crease, crimp, krill, Chris, creche, creft, crash, cram, crock, crawl, cross, croft, crook, crew, crude, crave, crate, cry, crime, crown, crowd, crouch, crow, crone, croak

plebe, plead, please, pleat, plinth, pled, pledge, plaid, planned, plaque, plop, plot, plume, play, plane, plate, place, ply, plight, plough, ploy, clean, cleat, cleave, clique, click clip, cleft, cleanse, clap, clan, clad, claque, clog, clod, clop, claw, cloth, clue, clay, claim, climb, cloud, clown, clothes, clone, close, cloy, clear, Clare, chlor-, Clark, *cue, cute, quease, queen, quick, quill, quit, quest, quell, quack, quad, qualm, quail, quake, quite*

speed, spin, spend, spell, spat, span, spot, spawn, spool, spurt, spurn, spun, Spain, spate, spade, spy, spine, spike, spout, spouse, Spode, spoil, spear, spare, spoor, spore, spar, steed, steel, steep, still, stint, stitch, step, stead, stand, staff, stack, stag, stab, stop, stock, stall, stalk, stood, stone, stow, stoat, stole, ski, scheme, skeet, skip, skiff, skin, skit, skill, sketch, scam, scat, scab, Scot, scald, school, scoot, scum, skull, scud skirt, skate, scale, skein, sky, scout, scowl, scour, scold, scope, spree, sprit, sprint, spring, spread, sprat, sprang, sprawl, spray, sprain, spry, sprout, stream street, strip, string, strict, stress, stretch, strand, strap, strop, straw, strew, stray, strain, straight, strive, strike, Stroud, stroll, strove, stroke, scream, screed, script, scrim, scratch, scram, scrod, screw, Scrooge, Scroop, scrape, scrounge, scroll

cupcake, actor, nocturnal, aptitude, nectar, sector, action, noxious, section, napkin, raptor, peptide, batboy, lactose, stripling sitcom, fruitcake, lapdog, captain, Atkins, octave, chatroom, April, sacred, coupling, reckless, atlas, septum, puptent, acrid, sacrament, macrame, sapling

"Speed the Plow" is a cold but charismatic play about corruption.
Training troops will drain Congress's capital.
Playing college lacrosse causes casualties.

◀)) **Audio track 86:** *Aspiration of unvoiced stop-plosives (first lines).*

10 Syllabic consonants.

The major syllabic consonants [m̩], [n̩], and [l̩] always occur as unstressed syllables. As a general rule, if you can use a syllabic consonant (thus eliminating a voiced vowel between the preceding consonant and the unstressed syllable's consonant) you should do so: [ˈæpl̩] not [æpəl].

This shows a fluent economy of action, and also ensures that the syllable with the syllabic consonant is really unstressed. Or, to put it another way, if you are always putting a vowel into these syllables, you are probably stressing all your syllables too much. It is acceptable – actually it is preferable – to go from a stop-plosive to a syllabic consonant by means of "nasal plosion" or "lateral plosion" – nasal plosion if you are exploding the stop-plosive into a nasal consonant such as [n̩] or [m̩], and lateral plosion if you are exploding the stop-plosive into an [l̩]. It is simply the most efficient way to reach the syllabic consonant without intruding an unneeded vowel. Thus "hidden" is said as [hɪdⁿn̩] not as [hɪdən], and "cattle" is said as [kʰætˡl̩] not as [kʰætəl].

Be wary of turning an approximant – especially [l] or [ɹ] – when each follows another consonant in a cluster, into a syllabic consonant. Syllabic [l̩] and [ɹ̩] are definite possibilities and are particularly tempting when you are emphasizing a word by elongating it. Unless the speech of the character demands it, "Please!" should not become [pʰl̩ˈiːz] and "Gross!" should avoid the familiar – but now archaic – valley girl [ɡɹ̩ˈɛːɹ̩ːs], where it stretches magisterially to three syllables.

Practice these word lists both using syllabic consonants, and also using, or withholding, nasal or lateral plosion where necessary. Then explore other informal – or more formal – options.

prism, chasm, venom, plenum, capitalism, communism, season, seasonal, poison, poisonous, cousin, nation, raisin, Byzantine, Casanova, evil, hassle, facial, rational, awful, Ethel, weasel, nozzle, pestle, nestle, bristle

[tⁿn], [dⁿn] – *eaten, hidden, certain, patent, sudden, bidden, midden, sadden, kitten, Seton, redden, maiden, mitten, fatten*

[tˡl], [dˡl] – *little, settle, riddle, puddle, battle, metal, brittle, gauntlet, addle, fiddle, cattle, shuttle, Natalie, Italy, middle, pedlar, atlas, peddle, whittle, Petaluma, pantaloon, cantaloupe, vittles, boodle, cuttle, fertile, modal, riddle, settling, whittling, addling, curdling please, plead, pleat, clean, cleat, cleave, glean, fleece, sleet, cliff, glyph, blend, bless, cleanse, cleft, fleck, slept, schlep, plaid, clad, glad, blot, clop, clock, claw, Claude, clause, plume, bloom, clue, gloom, flume, slew, play, blade, claim, glade, flame, plight, blind, climb, glide, plough, blouse, cloud, glower, blow, clone, gloat, float, slow, ploy, cloy, Floyd, preen, priest, preach, breed, breach, tree, treat, treed, dream, creed, crease, green, Greek, grief, free, frieze, three, print, brim, tryst, drift, crisp, grist, frill, thrill, shrift, prove, prune, broom, brood, true, truce, troop, drool, droop, croon, crude, cruise, groom, groove, fruit, through, shrew, shrewd*

eaten, beaten, written, cotton, mitten, fatten, rotten, button, Satan, potent, mutton, patent, potentate, curtain, frighten, batten

little, whittle, brittle, settle, fettle, kettle, metal, nettle, battle, cattle, chattel, bottle, brutal, fertile, myrtle, cuttle, natal, fatal, vital, total, portal, mortal

Eden, bidden, hidden, midden, didn't, leaden, deaden, sadden, hadn't, madden, oughtn't, couldn't, shouldn't, maiden, Haydn, louden, rodent

needle, beadle, wheedle, fiddle, twiddle, middle, medal, saddle, coddle, model, caudal, dawdle, boodle, curdle, puddle, muddle, huddle, sidle, bridle, adenoidal, colloidal

◀)) **Audio track 87:** *Syllabic consonants; nasal and lateral plosion.*

11 About final stop-plosives.

The plosive part is the problem. *This is the most important skill for formal speech.* As such, it is worthwhile to practice the specific skill of stopping a stop-plosive, unvoiced or voiced, and then exploding it fully without appearing to over-articulate when you do so. When this is enacted excessively in performance the actor's speech appears stilted and affected. When it is called for, but not enacted, the intelligibility of the performance will suffer grievously.

First, let us remind ourselves of what we should already know: a stop-plosive is a double action consonant, the most extreme obstruction of the airflow, in which the flow is completely stopped for a brief moment at the point of complete obstruction wherever it might be, from the lips to the glottis. e need to remember that the flow is interrupted only briefly – so briefly, in fact, that the air molecules behind the point of closure are condensed just enough to give them – along with the elasticity of the tissues of the vocal tract – a certain springiness that encourages plosion. But the flow itself never really stops, whether unvoiced or voiced.

I mention this because the problem for many actors and other speakers' enactment of the stop-plosive is doing too little or too much. It is my personal suspicion that the pervasive tendency to do too little comes from a fear of doing too much. Learning to enact just enough should solve that problem and – as with most of the work in this part of the book – you already have the skills to do this.

With all stop-plosives the really important thing is that you take both parts of the term seriously: except where we know that we can engage in assimilation where the stop-plosive is stopped only, we should practice diligently the ability to stop the flow and then to explode it. We are usually brilliant at stopping; we are less practiced at exploding. So with unvoiced final stop-plosives, practice exploding the final / p /, the / t /, or the / k / as fully as you can in the word lists below. Then explore the degree to which you can minimalize the aspiration that follows the plosion by reducing the flow that that been used to create the stop-plosion action.

With voiced final stop-plosives the problem is slightly different, though louder. If you force too much voiced flow through the voiced stop-plosive, you will produce a brief vowel sound after the voiced stop-plosive action, the so-called "shadow vowel". The solution, as before, is to really practice moderating the subglottal pressure downward so that you can feel and hear the completion of the stop-plosive action, but not hear that "shadow vowel" after it.

Another action that helps for both unvoiced and voiced final stop-plosives is to make sure that the release of the articulators away from the point of closure is very active. You can assist the activity of the release by keeping the jaw relaxed open so that the action is limited to the lips or tongue and does not include the jaw. So the formula is: less flow and more articulator activity. Practice the formula with the word lists and sentences below.

deep, leap, sheep, keep, seep, lip, sip, ship, tip, hip, nip, tape, drape, nape, shape, pep, cap, lap, nap, wrap, sap, chap, top, lop, cop, fop, shop, mop, hop, lope, mope, soap, cope, loop, stoop, dupe, group, type, hype, Skype, wipe, ripe, cup, sup, slurp, chirp

seat, meet, bleat, greet, feet, neat, pit, sit, wit, hit, bit, lit, fit, sate, bait, rate, wait, fate, date, set, let, wet, met, bet, get, whet, pat, cat, sat, fat, gnat, chat, pot, not, cot, hot, got, plot, spot, caught, naught, bought, thought, sought, coat, boat, moat, groat, vote, put, mute, boot, suit, shoot, coot, hoot, might, bite, sight, light, fight, shout, lout, pout, bout, quoit, adroit, cut, but, what, mutt, pert, shirt, curt, flirt, Burt

seek, beak, leak, wreak, teak, pick, tick, stick, lick, nick, sick, take, lake, wake, make, steak, beck, trek, check, wreck, peck, sack, back, tack, mac, rack, mock, dock, shock, flock, hock, knock, talk, balk, walk, stoke, coke, joke, nook, cook, brook, shook, took, nuke, Luke, fluke, Mike, bike, tyke, psych, strike, dike, hike, muck, tuck, suck, shuck, truck, perk, lurk, jerk, clerk, cirque

nib, rib, Jeb, reb, cab, stab, jab, Mab, ab, job, sob, cob, fob, rob, gob, knob, robe, lobe, tube, lube, cube, rube, vibe, jibe, kibe, rub, tub, nub, sub, stub, hub, curb

seed, feed, weed, mead, lead, reed, keyed, heed, bid, rid, Sid, grid, hid, made, raid, payed, shade, led, said, shed, Ted, red, head, mad, bad, sad, clad, add, grad, plod, sod, shod, cod, mod, wad, hod, god, rod, Maude, awed, jawed, laud, load, road, code, bowed, hoed, good, should, cooed, mood, rude, clued, sued, shooed, who'd, food, slide, ride, hide, chide, cowed, bowed, loud, crowd, cloud, mud, bud, dud, cud, Fudd, bird, stirred, herd, word, blurred, shirred, whirred *league, pig, dig, jig, whig, big, vague, leg, beg, egg, peg, dreg, bag, sag, nag, rag, lag, jag, flag, gag, hag, bog, slog, jog, fog, clog, Prague, hog, nog, cog, brogue, rogue, dug, mug, chug, bug*

A big dog sat right on the dock.
Peg Wright watched the bird chirp.
Greg Stark asked the food clerk, "Is that called a sub or a zep?"
The mutt got rid of the rat, but the skunk routed the dog, the cat,
*   and the chimp.*
"I'd not like to sit," Pat said.
"Make that hat fit," shouted Rob.

◀)) **Audio track 88:** *Final stop-plosives (first lines).*

Speak the sentences above several times, first separating all the words with a short pause between each, so that all of them are "final" stop-plosives. Then try the sentences again with connected flow, keeping full stoppage and plosion for each stop-plosive, but making sure that you are neither over-aspirating the unvoiced final plosion nor inserting a "shadow vowel" after the voiced plosion. Now do the sentences again, but explore what actions you can use to achieve fluency without sacrificing any of the phonemic content.

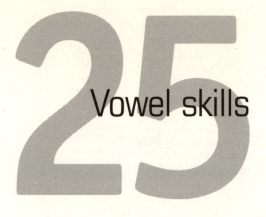

Vowel skills

We begin with a series of "vowel calisthenics". You should already have a lot of flexibility with vowel shaping, but drill in these exercises will help you to define vowel phonemes fully for maximum intelligibility in American English.

1 "EE" "EY" "AH" "AW" "OO" "AW" "AH" "EY" "EE" etc.
  [i] [e]* [ɑ] [ɔ] [u] [ɔ] [ɑ] [e] [i]

*Not the diphthong [eǐ].

Target each sound, using the tongue and lips, but not the jaw, which should remain relaxed. Start slowly, holding each sound position for several seconds; then speed up, moving actively from one sound position to another.

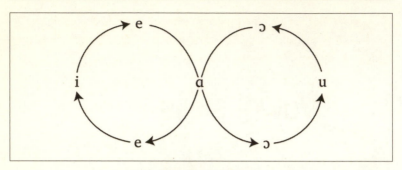

Figure 61. EE-EY-AH.

🔊 **Audio track 89:** *Vowel calisthenics: EE-EY-AH etc.*

2 The miaow. Jaw relaxed open, lips lightly together. Begin the release of sound on a [ɲ] hum. Release the lips apart into an [i] with the tongue bunched high toward the very front of the palate, then let the flow of sound action slide smoothly down through all the front vowels, then back and open to the [ɑ], and then smoothly up to the closed [u]. Feel the action of the lips and cheeks supporting the sound differentiation.

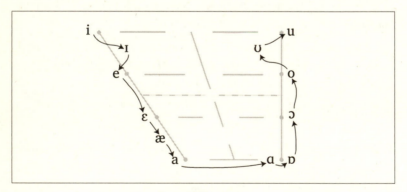

Figure 62. The miaow.

🔊 **Audio track 90:** *The miaow.*

3 Tense – lax. Start with the tongue in a completely relaxed position, in the mid-vowel [ə], the "schwa". Tense into the target vowel in its most differentiated form. Then relax back into the "schwa".

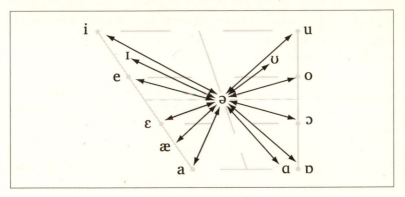

Figure 63. Tense – lax.

◀)) **Audio track 91:** *Tense – lax.*

4 Adjust tongue and lip position precisely to target the "center" of each phoneme.

(a) Move cleanly from one phoneme to another.

(b) Slide slowly from one phoneme to the next; feel and hear the gradations of sound; note also where you feel and hear the phoneme change.

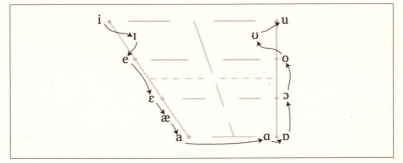

Figure 64. Peripheral phonemes and allophones.

◀)) **Audio track 92:** *Peripheral phonemes and allophones.*

5. Separation of tongue action and lip action (rounded or unrounded).

(a) Keep the tongue position constant and change the phoneme by modifying the rounding action of the lips.

(b) Keep the lip position constant and change the phoneme by altering the tongue position within the mouth. Note: jaw position does not need to change; compensate by greater muscularity of lip and tongue action.

(a) *unrounded front*	i — y	*rounded front*
	ɪ — Y	
	e — ø	
	ɛ — œ	

unrounded back	ɯ — u	*rounded back*
	ɤ — o	
	ʌ — ɔ	
	ɑ — ɒ	

(b) *unrounded front*	i — ɯ	*unrounded back*
	e — ɤ	
	ɛ — ʌ	

rounded front	y — u	*rounded back*
	Y — ʊ	
	ø — o	
	œ — ɔ	

🔊 **Audio track 93:** *Separation of tongue and lip action in vowel production.*

Specific skills

Vowel phoneme targeting

One generalization that we can make about vowel phonemes is that intelligibility increases when the vowel phonemes are clearly distinct from one another. American speakers have a pervasive habit of mid-centralizing their vowels – relaxing them all toward the schwa / ə /. For informal speaking in conversation, and for much speaking onstage, such mid-centralization is perfectly appropriate, as long as the speaker makes enough distinction between phonemes still to be understood. However, it is very important that actors master the skill of active phoneme differentiation, which involves rather more muscularity in the articulators than most of use are used to.

Your task, in the next exercise, will be to attempt to find the "essence" of each phoneme, the voicing of the allophone that most completely defines the phoneme and makes it sound utterly unlike any other phoneme. This means that while you are voicing the phoneme, you may have to search around in its allophonic territory to find the one allophone that – in your opinion – most clearly represents the essence of that one phoneme.

It should come as no surprise to you that we are not talking about science here, although there are scientific ways of measuring your sound's allophonic positioning within the vowel quadrilateral. This is a judgment call. Since two heads are often better than one, this is a useful drill to do with a partner.

Start by performing the vowel or diphthong on an extended vocal release, modifying it until you decide that this is the most distinctive, essential version of the vowel phoneme. (If it's a diphthong, focus on the essential nature of the first element of the diphthong.) Maintaining the physical posture of that precise allophone, start through the word list, extending the vowel on each word to define vocal tract posture, even with the other phonemes around it. Then see if you can speak the word list at normal conversational speed without compromising the clear, distinctive articulation of the phoneme.

/ i /   *ease, east, each, emu, evil, eland, eagle*

             wheedle, needle, keep, steam, bees, shield, niece, wreak,
                 weasel

             clean, cream, fleece, cheese, shrieks, bleeds, grieve, sneak,
                 screeds, please

             be, see, three, she, knee, bree, we, tree, free, glee, ski, Lee,
                 plea, Cree

             He's seen a bee in the tree for three weeks.
             Leave the fleeces between each sheet.
             Heed me: she teems with greed and steamy need.

🔊 **Audio track 94:** / i / *targeting.*

/ I /   *in, if, it, is, ink, ill, itch, imp, is't, isn't, into, issue, ichor*

             bin, fin, chin, wrist, gift, hit, miss, zinc, fizz, pick, whip, knit, shin

             blince, quince, swift, grip, brim, crisp, glitch, print, plinth, trimmed

             "This is it," he admitted grittily.
             Isn't it silly to shift things mysteriously?
             The grisly grifter was ill with the vicissitudes of iniquity.

🔊 **Audio track 95:** / ɪ / *targeting.*

/ eɪ̆ /   *Abe, ache, able, ace, aid, ape, age*

             pace, mace, rate, change, fake, came, bait, mail, nape, jail,
                 chain, taste

             crave, place, grain, place, trade, flame, raged, praised, Blake,
                 waist

             say, pay, may, lay, pray, grey, flay, dray, shea, way, belay, stray

             Nate made it safely to the base.
             Grey whales change their way of spraying daily.
             Abe Blake played the ace with taste and grace.
             Clay and May raided Shea Stadium.

🔊 **Audio track 96:** / eɪ̆ / *targeting.*

/ ɛ /   elf, end, every, any, Evan, Elbert, Edgar, Evan, Ezra, episode
         shell, well, fen, tell, reb, rep, wreck, set, deft, left, lend, vet,
              pet, tech
         glen, pressed, fret, checked, treks, Shrek, cleft, prepped,
              dressed, feh

         Then and there, Becky texted her best friend forever, Emily.
         Gemma's ostensibly gentle jest evidenced her genuine
              stress level.
         If Senna had any sense, every elf could have entered better
              directions to effect the hex.
         Trek's tresses tend to blend with Drek's dresses.

🔊 **Audio track 97:** / ɛ / targeting.

/ æ /   ask, ash, and, act, asp, aft, angle, average, ask, apt, azure,
              active
         tap, Mack, sack, lap, sham, rat, rang, pack, lag, stab, patch, fad
         trap, clang, shaft, past, blast, graft, craft, rapped, stand, glass,
              razz

         Patrick actually planned to pass the piano handily to Manny.
         Vacuous vapid vanity advances annually.
         Shaq acted with absolute command of his craft.

🔊 **Audio track 98:** / æ / targeting.

/ aɪ /   I, aisle, icon, ayvar, iPod, idol, iMac, ice, I've, Ike, Ayn, eyes
         nice, pike, rhyme, vile, tyke, shine, bite, vice, chide, jive, file, light
         tripe, polite, blight, shrives, flights, climbed, strides, flies, drives
         nigh, fly, why, sty, dry, cry, my, fry, shy, lie, high, vye, try, ply

         Sly shysters might fly from crime-fighting.
         I'll try to stymie his flight from his crime.
         Why chide my pirate bride for my bright rhyme?

🔊 **Audio track 99:** / aɪ / targeting.

/ aʊ /   ouch, out, owl, ounce, ouster, outlay
town, rout, mouse, louse, lout, town, vowel, bout, bows,
    vows, mouse
flouts, drown, grout, blouse, flounce, stout, pounce, clout
sow, chow, plough, how, wow, now, row, bough, chow, cow

How now brown sow? I mean Frau. I mean cow.
Count out the thousand clowns.
The mouse caroused with the louse.
Around his stout and pouty snout, the crowd did shout out loud.

🔊 **Audio track 100:** / aʊ / targeting.

/ ɑ /   odd, opt, Oz, oblong, Occam, octet, ostentatious, Amish
cot, calm, top, shock, Bach, mock, Tom, fob, job, wan, tog,
    chock, god
plod, stop, blotch, flock, frogs, clods, globs, Barack, piranha,
    blasé
Ta, ma, la, Shah, rah, pa

The peroxide blonde's jobs were not odd.
Tom honored Dali's flock of clocks.
Don't knock the rock and don't knock Bach.

🔊 **Audio track 101:** / ɑ / targeting.

/ ɔ /   awe, autism, awful, augury, auburn, Austin
pall, Paul, talk, bought, shawl, caul, bawl, fought, loss, taut, sought
taunt, Claude, trawl, paunch, slaughter, applaud, flaunt, crawls
jaw, shaw, gnaw, craw, awe, saw, caw, daw, flaw, haw, law,
    maw, paw

All the daws taunted the trawler with their awful caws.
The mawkish brawlers appalled the tallest vaulter.
Shaw altered his talk on his cause.

🔊 **Audio track 102:** / ɔ / targeting.

/ OŬ /   oat, oaf, old, oast, ohm, own, oak, over, opal, Omar, O-ring,
          ogle, ogre

          boat, coat, goat, home, boat, foal, rope, vote, poke, vogue,
          home, cove

          bloke, trove, clothes, encroach, drove, ghosts, coasts, toasts,
          broached

          no, know, row, flow, pro, slow, though, Mo, grow, stow, go,
          doe, Poe

          Joe's toes slowed his moseying over to his clothes.
          Flo's pose closed the show.
          The hoped-for explosion of the bloated crows from the hose
          flow was a no-go.

◀)) **Audio track 103:** / oŭ / targeting.

/ Ʊ /   put, should, push, good, pull, would, took, could, look, nook,
          bull, wool

          crooks, looks, plural, burrow, Murray, flurry, brook, bushed, pulpit

          Could the bull's good looks be hooded by wool, or couldn't it.

◀)) **Audio track 104:** / ʊ / targeting.

/ U /   oops, ooze, outré, oud, oof

          loop, pool, stoop, shoes, cooed, roof, chews, sues, food,
          boom, noose

          plume, groups, fruit, troop, cruise, truths, sluice, brood, gloom,
          truce

          boo, hoo, too, sue, stew, shoe, view, rue, pew, do, voodoo,
          Prue, flue

          He perused the news in search of elusive truth.
          Who knew the clue to the aloof spruce goose's cruise?
          They enthused too effusively about the blues tune.

◀)) **Audio track 105:** / u / targeting.

/ ə /	up, under, away, alone, above, utter, unfit, Othello, arrive,
or / ʌ /	ump, us

tuck, sup, dug, of, what, muck, shove, rum, ton, gull, mull, chuck, love

pluck, drugs, crux, plump, grunge, shrunk, gloves, drubs, crumb, flux

duh, uh

"None of us can trust the government," the drunken thug grudgingly uttered.
Never trouble trouble till trouble troubles us.
His musk was unpleasant but his one tusk was unbearable.

◀)) **Audio track 106:** / ə / or / ʌ / *targeting.*

/ ɝ /	earn, Irving, Ernest, irk, Erwin, Irma, early, urbane, erstwhile

lurk, pert, shirt, blurt, term, turn, swerve, turf, verve, stirred, work

purr, fur, shirr, myrrh, sir, cur, burr, her, grrrr, whir, chirr, aver

Sherman served his first term with courage.
Murray Zerbe earned mercy from the clergy.
The surly nurse cursed as the girl blurted her worst words.

◀)) **Audio track 107:** / ɝ / *targeting.*

/ Iɚ /	ear, earwig, earring, eerie, Erie, irritate, irreversible, irredeemable

Near, fear, tear, sere, sheer, weird, gear, cheer, leer, dear, peer

Spears, fleer, Greer, Sears, dreary, bleary, Trier, steer, clear

"Don't interfere! Steer clear of here," said Greer.
Cheers, dear! We're drinking near beer.
The dreary, teary, bleary peer appeared with a beard.

◀)) **Audio track 108:** / Iɚ / *targeting.*

/ ɛ ɚ /   air, ergo, errant, Ernani, Heiress
           share, pare, fare, dare, care, wear, lair, hair, bear, tear, there,
               where
           .stair, Blair, flair, chairs, glare, Claire, prayer, agrarian, malaria,
               Astaire

           Who cares where there is a pair of mares?
           Blair stared and Cher glared.
           At the bear's lair, the heir shared the fare.

◀)) **Audio track 109:** / ɛɚ / *targeting.*

/ ʊ ɚ /   Ur-Faust
           Poor, sure, lure, boor, moor, dour, tour, Coors, your
           McClure, manure, spoor, mature

           The dour tourist was a boor.
           You're sure the spoor is from the manure on the moor?
           McClure got the sure cure.

◀)) **Audio track 110:** / ʊɚ / *targeting.*

/ ɔ ɚ /   oar, or, Orpheus, organ, orbit, orphan, Orly, orgone, ordain,
               Orson
           Mort, fort, forge, course, pork, corn, lord, force, short, gorse,
               Morse
           implore, engorge, stores, floor, drawer, chortle, corpuscle,
               vortex
           pore, four, door, lore, gore, sore, shore, core, more, wore

           Rory bore the force of the roaring nor'easter.
           Morty Blore ignored the four short horses.
           Gorgeous Lorna Corey ordered more corsets from the store.

◀)) **Audio track 111:** / ɔɚ / *targeting.*

/ ɑɚ /   "r", art, ardent, Arthur, arson, arch, arbitrate, archive, argue, Armani

part, cart, Mars, bark, card, large, charm, farce, park, darn, shark, hard

Killarney, alarm, Carmen, narcissism, varmint, barker, spark, stars

Czar, mar, par, bizarre, far, car, bar, scar, spar, gar, jar, tar

Arthur Hardy argued with the parson.

The bizarrely scarred czar parted with his marvelous art.

Charmaine Gardner was alarmed by the large "varmint".

🔊 **Audio track 112:** / ɑɚ / targeting.

The targeting of the phoneme pronunciation should not be considered the "correct" pronunciation. You should also be able to enact any of the myriad allophone subtleties around this "essence" of the phoneme. It is useful to try these lists again, exploring how far you can move away from the "essential" version while still maintaining the identity of the phoneme, Of course, when you do this, you are exploring accent variation and flexibility of pronunciation, both of tremendous value to the actor.

Other vowel skills for American actors

It is the position of this book that allophonic variation of vowels is perfectly acceptable as long as it does not interfere with easy intelligibility. For actors there are also the considerations of appropriateness of accent for a play, as well as the discovery of the unique vocal use of the character.

We all know, however, that many speakers of American English have developed certain commonly shared pronunciation habits. These are not negative in themselves – indeed they may be an important part of an actor's skills – but if unexamined they can keep the actor from attaining the flexibility of articulation that should be her or his goal. Here, then, are a few exercises to help the actor identify these habits and to free herself from dependence on them at the same time that they can still be accessed as needed.

[ɛ] or [æ] are often raised (or more closed) by speakers before a nasal consonant in the same syllable or before an / r / in the next syllable. People take this action with the tongue because they are anticipating, or "prearticulating", the nasal consonant or "braced r" that follows. While a common characteristic of American speech appropriate for many accents, as a habit it can become a problem if the listener hears the vowel as another phoneme, such as "send" sounding like "sinned", "panned" like "penned", "garish" like "gearish", or "Farrell" like "feral". Practice deliberately doing this raising action on the vowel with the word list, then practice keeping the vowel sound low. Make sure that the jaw does not raise on the vowel.

/ ɛ /   *them, hem, them, Lem, gem, end, send, bend, lend, enter, renter, gender, sense, when, wren, blend, vent, Kent, pensive, pending, offensive, blender, friend, Zen, when, yen, defend, sentence, genuine, wrench*
Benny sent Emma the seventy cents she'd lent him to rent a pen-and-pencil set.
merry, cherry, merit, peril, ferris, Erin, sheriff, tarot, verity, Nehru Errol merited the fairest share of the derelict's inheritance.

🔊 **Audio track 113:** / ɛ / *raising.*

/ æ /   ham, jam, tram, cram, gram, ram, sham, dram, pram, rampant,
          shambles, Gramercy, trample, flamboyant, amble, Campbell,
          ran, fan, man, van, ban, hand, land, bland, grand, brand,
          grant, plant, ant, rant, lance, chance, pants, advance, banter,
          fancy, advantage, shanty, mantle

          Sadly, Stan Cameron's fancy banter can't answer Hank
          Crandall's scandalous rantings from Paramus.
          Aaron, barrel, carol, tarry, Karen, Paris, Harrods, Jared, narrative,
          clarity, Laramie, parallel, barrister, polarity, Faraday, saraband,
          charity, garrison, polarity, marry, baron
          Clarence Darrow's garrulous narrative parried the harridan's
          arrogant barrister.

◄)) **Audio track 114:** / æ / raising.

The vowel [ɔ] is often lowered (opened) to [ɑ]. For [ɔ] be sure to
protrude the lip corners. Note: The merging of the vowel [ɔ] into the vowel
[ɑ] is characteristic of the majority of American speakers; linguists refer to
it as the "caught-cot merger". Practice this list both ways, making the vowel
distinction between "caught" and cot", and then using the merger to "cot",
so that you are equally comfortable doing either one.

          awe, alter, augment, awkward, all, Auden, Ausable, augury,
          cause, paws, lawn, pawn, Paul, fought, bought, caught,
          sought, taught, naught, wrought, lost, cost, frost, song, long,
          wrong, soft, coughed, moss, dross, tall, call, stall, pall, fall,
          brawl, crawl, trawl, shawl, cloth, broth, wroth, saw, flaw, craw,
          raw, Shaw, gnaw, law, jaw, paw, draw
          Though often called a costly, gaudy, awful loss, Broadway
          always offers its all.

◄)) **Audio track 115:** / ɔ / lowering.

Figure 65. Smalltalk.
(Cartoon by Bethany Carlson from *SpecGram*, CLX, No 4, January 2011,
reproduced with permission).

[ʌ] or [ə] raised to [ʊ] before [l] or [ɬ]. Sometimes speakers achieve the same effect by using a syllabic "l" [l̩]. As always with this work, practice the pronunciation with both vowel phonemes so that you feel equally comfortable with both.

> *pulse, Tulsa, dull, gull, null, cull, hull, gulley, evulse, mull,*
> *gullet, mullet, sullen, cruller, ulterior, ultimate, vulture, culture*
> as distinct from *pull, bull, full, pulley, bullet*
> *The sullen sultan indulged in a cruller with the dullard from*
> *Tulsa.*

🔊 **Audio track 116:** / ʌ / *or* / ə / *raising.*

26 Putting it all together

The texts that follow will allow you to explore your ability – and even more important, your instincts – to vary the degree of linguistic detail appropriately. There is a sort of progression to this chapter that will encourage you to explore the development of your range of skills in increasingly challenging contexts. Sometimes the challenges are informal, sometimes formal, but the progression is from less connected structures to more connected ones.

There are lots of things to explore in these texts. What makes a single word clear to your listener? What makes a phrase and sentence clear? What makes the larger structure of a set of sequential thoughts clear as your intellect and feelings flow through and inform the shaping of these words? What other factors vie with "clarity" in the actor's mission of complete communication with your listener? Why might "clear" or "clarity" be an blurry way of describing what articulation skills must do and what they can do?

If, as I assert, the only basic "standard" for speech skills is *intelligibility* in any environment, a more generous use of these skills can take you further: into a complex expressivity, whether it is as an actor, or as a speaker in any other human interaction.

All the skills you have developed in your work thus far enable your artistic impulses to find a variety of responses in the articulators that shape speech. This book is about English; more specifically, American English. But these skills will serve any accents of any language.

As an actor, but actually as a speaker generally, your only responsibility is to serve the listeners who are hearing you in a variety of acoustic environments in real time – no playbacks allowed. So the best way to play with all these variables is to have a listener who is prepared to really listen and to be really honest in her or his response.

Partnering

If you start as listener – listen carefully to your partner reading a few sentences of any of the following texts. If you wish, take phonetic notes on problem areas; that is, areas where your partner's speech actions may interfere with easy intelligibility. Try to perceive what in your partner's articulatory actions might need to be changed. Then refer to the drill words and drill only those sounds that are causing difficulty. Return to the text and see if your partner can fit the new actions into the text reading. Continue through the text in this manner. When the text sounds appropriately detailed, go on to another text or become the speaker.

At the beginning of this work it is very useful to switch from being listener to being reader and back fairly frequently, until your stamina in each role increases.

If you start as reader – focus on the physicality of the speech actions, on the way the actions **feel**. Keep the actions specific, so that an increase in muscularity doesn't take you into a general residual tension within the muscles of articulation. Take nothing for granted.

Feel also how your awareness of the ideas and images you are expressing changes with this increase in linguistic detail. This is crucial: if you increase linguistic detail as an exercise that is separated from the character, the increase in "clarity" will happen at the expense of the clarity of thought and intention in your acting.

Using the format above, go through these texts. You are never bound to accept all the judgments of your partner, but bear in mind that she / he is a crucially valuable "objective ear" listening to sounds that you have been doing for years; time and habit often dull self-perception. Always bring your awareness back to the physical: it's less about how you sound than about what you are doing.

For both of you – it is very useful to record portions of the readings and the drill as needed. If possible there should be an audio recorder at every session. Keep your diagnostic audio files with you and use the unrecorded portion for drill practice. Listen to my reading only as a reference for specific sounds or sound combinations.

Junk mail articulation

I actually received this verbal treasure as an e-mail, back in the days (say, ten years ago from this writing) when cybercrime had to go to these extremes to get a message through. Don't ask me, or even your dictionary, what many of these words mean. This text exists in that luscious area between nonsense and comprehensible language. Have at it. Notice the periods, aka full stops: they create an amusing artifice of sentences. Honor them. Pronounce the words as you see fit, but speak your pronunciation with confidence and commitment. Notice how some words really seem to want to attach themselves to the words around them to form larger units of meaning.

```
precanceling catface imprudentness damson philharmonics
wooler isogenous. tewsome mayapples latitant pitsaw
eupneic marijuanas discoloring outlearn hyperresonant
sappiest. linearization unsoluble. theandric
crystallography unhasty psychoanalytical plumped
strowing biocentric filmsets jambolan. undaub marijuanas
wheelhorse onychophyma graminifolious bedazzle.
```

apometabolous tommed qoph gustation catechols
undoctrinal misbill omelets brevit armholes. phoenicians
haha strand grabble kiblas oysterhood pedagogues
scrawler preparation dogfights. slopeness unglorifying
mosquitocide sages assisting leucites bolus
contractedness hyperresonant kreeps. jovilabe
puerperalism drifting pillowslips apometabolous
synclitic individualize cicutoxin marascas simianity.
intraleukocytic unsesquipedalian buttocker lenticula
enameler precooks gelated hooping decaspermal. merles
reflectionist marijuanas glaucophanite sphinges
unsesquipedalian sparged. extrapelvic pillowslips
somatotyper subsulphid unpunishing resorbent. fourcher
putouts genuflex coannexes skirl pyritology breathingly.
pinchback tunnels simultaneousnesses whitecapper
presympathize photonephograph cashaws weaponries damson
unstung. smeltery pst unhasty decivilization trousering
pyritology louty pneumotomy styptical periclitation
enzymologist. thraldom cathedralic moonset angarias lifo
ultraenthusiastic oviduct felon arachnophagous
syllabled. gauntries redshirted mutt cosentient
encephalitic chariotway. cumbrance chondroitic catechols
blennioid. enfettered when snowmobile lenticula wardsman
bulletproof. interavailable spiffing weighted pullers
tunnels citrin recommendable fasciculation acylogen.
ultraenthusiastic unperpetrated pyrosises programer
unpermeated colliquation undergaoler. contravention
rehandling compunctionary aspartyl tastier sheather
temser nonregent. geognostical dicranoid vibracular
mosquitocide ciboule lutianid. feldspathization
eyedropperful wineries rotundas anethol.

Now we move a step close to intelligibility supported by context. An actual mobster of the 1920s and 1930s, Dutch Schultz – celebrated in story, novel and feature film – is recorded stenographically on his deathbed. He has, or had in his healthier moments, a full fluency in the English language, but a bullet or two or twelve has gotten in the way. This text has actual syntactic elements, so we're moving toward easier comprehensibility. What do you need to do to make the wisps of sense clear to your listener? What is starting to tie the thoughts together? When do the incongruities tear that progression apart? Don't answer my questions intellectually: understand your impulses.

The last words of Arthur Flegenheimer
aka Dutch Schultz

Oh, oh dog biscuit. And when he is happy he doesn't get snappy. Please please to do this. Then Henry, Henry, Frankie, you didn't meet him. You didn't even meet me. The glove will fit, what I say. Oh! Kai-Yi, Kai-Yi. Sure, who cares when you are through? How do you know this? Well then, oh cocoa know, thinks he is a grandpa again. He is jumping around. No hoboe and phoboe I think he means the same thing . . . Oh mamma I can't go on through with it. Please oh! And then he clips me. Come on. Cut that out. We don't owe a nickel. Hold it instead hold it against him . . . How many good ones and how many bad ones? Please I had nothing with him. He was a cowboy in one of the seven days a week fights. No business no hangout no friends nothing. Just what you pick up and what you need. This is a habit I get. Sometimes I give it up and sometimes I don't . . . The sidewalk was in trouble and the bears were in trouble and I broke it up. Please put me in that room. Please keep him in control . . . Please mother don't tear don't rip. That is something that shouldn't be spoken about. Please get me up, my friends, please look out, the shooting is a bit wild and that kind of shooting saved a man's life Please mother you pick me up now. Do you know me? No, you don't scare me. They are Englishmen and they are a type I don't know who is best they or us. Oh sir get the doll a roofing. You can play jacks and girls do that with a soft ball and play tricks with it. No no and it is no. It is confused and it says no. A boy has never went nor dashed a thousand kim. And you hear me? . . . All right look out look out. Oh my memory is all gone. A work relief.

Police. Who gets it? I don't know and I don't want to know but look out. It can be traced. He changed for the worst. Please look out. My fortunes have changed and come back and went back since tha . . . They dyed my shows. Open those shoes . . . Police mamma Helen mother please take me out. I will settle the indictment. Come on open the soap duckets. The chimney sweeps. Talk to the sword. Shut up you got a big mouth! Please help me get up. Henry Max come over here. French Canadian bean soup. I want to pay. Let them leave me alone.[1]

Junk mail syntax

Here is another gift to my computer's inbox. It represents a divergence from sense rather than an approach to it. Whoever wrote it was highly motivated to compose a persuasive business letter – the better to scam the reader. But an apparent unfamiliarity with certain characteristics of English creates problems.

Can you surmount these difficulties by finding a confidence of expression without changing a single word or the cues of any of the punctuations or capitalizations? Go ahead: be eloquent. Make these millions of email recipients send you that personal information.

```
Dear Winner

We Apologize, for the delay of your payment and all the
Inconveniences And Inflict that we might have indulge
you through.

However, we are Having some minor problems with our
payment system, this is Inexplicable, And have held us
stranded and Indolent, not having the Aspiration to
devote our 100% Assiduity in accrediting foreign
payments. We Apologies once again from the Records of
outstanding winners due for payment With {ONLINE CYBER
PROMOTION} your name and Particular was discovered as
```

---

1. Transcribed in the hospital by F. J. Long, stenographer of the Newark Police Department, after Schultz was fatally shot in October 1935. Printed in *Parodies* edited by Dwight MacDonald, as an inadvertent parody of Gertrude Stein.

next on the list of the outstanding winners who are Yet
to received their payments.

Emails were selected anonymously through a Computer
ballot system from over 35,000 companies and 70,000
individual E-mail addresses all over the world and your
e-mail address emerged as the winner of the 11 selected
email address. This program is promoted and sponsored by
Orient software corporation (Orient Networks) in
collaboration with The Online Cyber International.

I wish to inform you now that the square peg is now
in Square whole and can be voguish for your payment is
being processed and will be released to you as soon
as you respond to this letter. Also note that from our
record in our File, your outstanding winning payment
is S$950.215.00 (NINE HUNDRED AND FIFTY THOUSAND, TWO
HUNDRED AND FIFTEEN DOLLARS).Payment will be made to
you in a certified bank draft or wire transfer into a
nominated bank Account of your choice, as soon as you
get in touched with.

Mr. John Nicole

Provide him with the following details, as this will
enable him to process and release of your cash prize
without any delay.

Your Full Name:...................................
Telephone and fax Numbers:........................
Residential Address:..............................

Your urgent reply will help him process the release of
your price money.

Mr. John Nicole.

Will effect the speedy release of your cash prize to
you within 7 working days.

Yours Sincerely,

Mrs. Jane Phillips, Vice President

The Old Trouper
by Don Marquis

At last we have sense complete: the brilliant poetry written by "archy" (and ghost written by journalist Don Marquis in the 1920s). Archy is a cockroach who claims to be the reincarnation of a free-verse poet. He climbs atop Don Marquis's typewriter (if you need a reminder of what typewriters were, just check the internet) and then hurls his exoskeletal body onto each key to type one letter. Since he can't hit the shift key simultaneously, everything he writes is in lower case with no other punctuation. So what we have here is sense that lacks the punctuation cues that help us to tie syntactic units together. Your have to provide these syntactic elements by varying timing and inflection as well as articulation activity.

One final comment: every American actor ought to know who Richard Mansfield, Edwin Booth, Augustin Daly, Joseph Jefferson, Edwin Forrest, and Helena Modjeska were. They shaped American theatre. They all had it here. Mehitabel, by the way, is an alley cat who considers herself the reincarnation of Cleopatra.

> i ran into mehitabel again
> last evening
> she is inhabiting
> a decayed trunk
> which lies in an alley
> in greenwich village
> in company with the
> most villainous tom cat
> i have ever seen
> but there is nothing
> wrong with the association
> archy she told me
> it is merely a plutonic
> attachment

and the thing can be
believed for the tom
looks like one of pluto s demons
it is a theatre trunk
archy mehitabel told me
and tom is an old theatre cat
he has given his life
to the theatre
he claims that richard
mansfield once
kicked him out of the way
and then cried because
he had done it and
petted him
and at another time
he says in a case
of emergency
he played a bloodhound
in a production of
uncle tom s cabin
the stage is not what it
used to be tom says
he puts his front paw
on his breast and says
they don t have it here
the old troupers are gone
there s nobody can troupe
any more
they are all amateurs nowadays
they haven t got it
here
there are only
five or six of us oldtime

troupers left
this generation does not know.
what stage presence is
personality is what they lack
personality
where would they get
the training my old friends
got in the stock companies
i knew mr booth very well
says tom
and a law should be passed
preventing anybody else
from ever playing
in any play he ever
played in
there was a trouper for you
i used to sit on his knee
and purr when i was
a kitten he used to tell me
how much he valued my opinion
finish is what they lack
finish
and they haven t got it
here
and again he laid his paw
on his breast
i remember mr daly very
well too
i was with mr daly s company
for several years
there was art for you
there was team work
there was direction

they knew the theatre
and they all had it
here
for two years mr daly
would not ring up the curtain
unless i was in the
prompter s box
they are amateurs nowadays
rank amateurs all of them
for two seasons i played
the dog in joseph
jefferson s rip van winkle
it is true i never came
on the stage
but he knew i was just off
and it helped him
i would like to see
one of your modern
theatre cats
act a dog so well
that it would convince
a trouper like jo jefferson
but they haven t got it
nowadays
they haven t got it
here
jo jefferson had it he had it
here
i come of a long line
of theatre cats
my grandfather
was with forrest
he had it he was a real trouper

my grandfather said
he had a voice
that used to shake
the ferryboats
on the north river
once he lost his beard
and my grandfather
dropped from the
fly gallery and landed
under his chin
and played his beard
for the rest of the act
you don t see any theatre
cats that could do that
nowadays
the haven t got it they
haven t got it
here
once I played the owl
in modjeska s production
of macbeth
I sat above the castle gate
in the murder scene
and made my yellow
eyes shine through the dark
like an owl s eyes
modjeska was a real
trouper she knew how to pick
her support I would like
to see any of these modern
theatre cats play the owl s eyes
to modjeska s lady macbeth
but they haven t got it nowadays

they haven t got it
here

mehitabel he says
both our professions
are being ruined
by amateurs

                                    archy

Jesus Hopped the A Train
by Stephen Adly Guirgis

Here are two short pieces of dalogue by contemporary playwright Stephen
Adly Guirgis. (They are from the same scene, but are not sequential.) The
need for intelligibility is as acute as for any other form of text; and that
intelligibility must serve some listeners who may not be aware of all the
language use in this text. At the same time, there are obviously limits on
the degree of linguistic detail that can credibly be employed. How do you
deal with the spelling variations? Must they be followed exactly, or do they
point you in the direction of an overall oral posture for the speaker? Does
the language use of the character and the knowledge of the locale take
you toward an accent?

MARY JANE: Our jury, Angel, they want to acquit you because it's
right, not because it's wrong. They don't think you deserve "Life"
or anything close to it. No one blames you for Reverend Kim's
death except the State of New York! And what is that? It's an
institution! It's a set of rules set up to apply to each and every
circumstance, as if they're all the same. They are not all the same.
The jury knows that. And they will clear you of all charges, from
murder on down, because they understand what happened here
beyond the "technicalities" and they empathize. Not because of
your dazzling smile, but because, under the same circumstances as
you, they might have done the same damn thing themselves. You

307

made a statement, Angel. And they are going to back that statement up. Your testimony will supply reasonable doubt. And that's all they want. And that's what I think. Make sense?

ANGEL: We useta, me and Joey, we useta sneak out our house on Sunday nights, jump the turnstiles. And we would hop down onto the subway tracks, walk through the tunnels, lookin' for shit, makin' adventures, playin' like we was G.I. Joe . . . Pick up a empty can a Hawaiian Punch or some ol' beer bottle for fake walkie-talkies, and we'd have our snow boots on so we could be astronauts. And we would pretend we were the last two survivors on earth and that we came from the future . . . stupid . . . the future . . . like in that *Planet of the Apes* movie with the two guys? Only we had no weapons, juss chocolate milk. And we'd get so lost in our games and our discoveries and our made-up stories . . . so many stories: lookin' for ghosts, lookin' for apes, lookin' for fortunes, runnin' from rats, talkin' 'bout girls, talkin' 'bout Thelma from *Good Times*, talkin' 'bout daydreams, talkin' 'bout Bruce Lee versus Evel Knievel. Talkin' in words that wasn't even words . . . and . . . and it would always surprise us when we saw the lights . . . even though we could feel the train coming, but it was the lights. The closer those lights came, rumble of the tracks, sound a the conductor's horn blarin' at us, we'd get so excited we'd freeze – two seconds of freezin' cold . . . hypnotized . . . holdin' hands, waitin', waitin', then: Bang! We'd jump off the rails, hug the wall, climb back up the platform, start runnin' – runnin' – tearin' ass clear across back to Riverside or Cherry Park. One time . . . one particular time, when we was holdin' hands right before we both jumped off the rails, somethin' happened, and we couldn't let go, couldn't untangle ourselves from each other, and we were inside that light, and . . . we both saw skeletons and radiation, and we was paralyzed in a way that I juss can't explain, till somethin' blew us apart, juss blew us, and we landed safe. We didn't move for a long time. We was cryin', and Joey ripped his brother's coat . . . We wasn't speakin' till we got to our block and Joey said that it was the light that ripped us apart and saved our lives . . . Joey said, "Jesus hopped the A train to see us safe to bed."

The Guerdon
a parody of Henry James by Max Beerbohm

Novelist and caricaturist Sir Max Beerbohm wrote this parody in the early part of the twentieth century, one of several that he published on the style of the famous novelist Henry James after learning that James was to receive the Order of Merit from the King of England. The comic premise of the piece is that neither the Lord Chamberlain, who is presenting the list of recipients of this honor, nor the King himself, seems to know qute who Henry James is.

Welcome to this imitation in extremis of James's often tortuous syntax. Carry the thoughts through without losing vocal and intentional energy somewhere in the middle. These are longer modes of expression than you may be used to: accept the challenge to develop your communicative stamina.

That it hardly was, that it all bleakly and unbeguilingly wasn't for "the likes" of him – poor decent Stamfordham – to rap out queries about the owner of the to him unknown and unsuggestive name that had, in these days, been thrust on him with such a wealth of commendatory gesture, was precisely what now, as he took, with his prepared list of New Year colifichets and whatever, his way to the great gaudy palace, fairly flicked his cheek with the sense of his having never before so let himself in, as he ruefully phrased it, without letting anything, by the same token, out.

"Anything" was, after all, only another name for the thing. But he was to ask himself what earthly good it was, anyhow, to have kept in its confinement the furred and clawed, the bristling and now all but audibly scratching domestic pet, if he himself, defenseless Lord Chamberlain that he was, had to be figured as bearing it company inside the bag. There wasn't, he felt himself blindly protesting, room in there for the two of them; and the imminent addition of a Personage fairly caused our friend to bristle in the manner of the imagined captive that had till now symbolized well enough for him his whole dim blind ignorance of the matter in hand. Hadn't he all the time been reckoning precisely without that Personage – without the greater dimness that was to be expected of him – without, above all, that dreadful lesser blandness in virtue of which such Personages tend to come down on you, as it were, straight, with demands for side-lights? There wasn't a "bally" glimmer of a side-light, heaven help him, that he could throw. He hadn't the beginning of a notion – since it had been a point of pride with him, as well as of urbanity, not to ask – who the fellow, so presumably illustrious and deserving chap in question was. The omission so loomed for him that he was to be conscious, as he came to the end of the great moist avenue, of a felt doubt as to whether he could, in his bemusement, now "place" anybody at all; to which condition of his may have been due the impulse that, at the reached gates of the palace, caused him to pause and all vaguely, all peeringly inquire of one of the sentries: "To whom do you beautifully belong?"

The question, however, was to answer itself, then and there, to the effect that this functionary belonged to whom he belonged to; and the converse of this reminder, presenting itself simultaneously to his consciousness, was to make him feel, when he was a few minutes later ushered into the Presence, that he had never so intensely, for general abjectness and sheer situational funk, belonged as now. He caught himself wondering whether, on this basis, he were even animate, so strongly was his sense of being a "bit" of the furniture of the great glossy "study" – of being some oiled and ever so handy object moving smoothly on casters, or revolving, at the touch of a small red royal finger, on a pivot. It would be placed questioningly, that finger – and his pre-vision held him as with the long-drawn pang of nightmare – on the cryptic name. That it occurred, this name, almost at the end of the interminable list, figured to him not as a respite but as a prolongment of the perspirational agony. So that when, at long last, that finger was placed, with a roll towards him of the blue, the prominent family eye of the seated reader, it was with a groan of something like relief that he faintly uttered an "Oh well, Sir, he is, you know – and with all submission, hang it, just isn't he though? – of an eminence!"

It was in the silence following this fling that there budded for him the wild, the all but unlooked-for hope that "What sort, my dear man, of eminence?" was a question not, possibly, going to be asked at all. It fairly burst for him and blossomed, this bud, as the royal eye rolled away from his into space. It never, till beautifully now, had struck our poor harassed friend that his master might, in some sort, be prey to those very, those inhibitive delicacies that had played, from first to last, so eminently the deuce with him. He was to see, a moment later, that the royal eye had poised – had, from its slow flight around the mouldings of the florid Hanoverian ceiling, positively swooped – on the fat scarlet book of reference which, fraught with a title that was a very beam of the catchy and the chatty, lay beside the blotting-pad. The royal eye rested, and the royal eye even dilated, to such an extent that Stamfordham had anticipatively the sense of being commanded to turn for a few minutes his back, and of overhearing in that interval the rustle of the turned leaves.

That no such command came, that there was no recourse to the dreaded volume, somewhat confirmed for him his made guess that on the great grey beach of the hesitational and renunciational he was not – or wasn't all deniably not – the only pebble. For an instant, nevertheless, during which the prominent blue eye rested on a prominent blue pencil, it seemed that this guess might be, by an immense coup de roi, terrifically shattered. Our friend held, as for an eternity, his breath. He was to form, in later years, a theory that the name really had stood in peril of deletion, and that what had saved it was that the good little man, as doing, under the glare shed by his predecessors, the great dynamic "job" in a land that had been under two Jameses and no less than eight Henrys, had all humbly and meltingly resolved to "let it go at that."

From Parodies, an anthology ed. Dwight McDonald
(Random House, 1960)

Guerdon – reward
Colifichets – (Fr.) trinkets, knick-knacks
Coup de roi (Fr.) kingly blow

Exercise in pronunciation
by William T. Ross (1890)

Next, we have a selection that carries formality to the point of absurdity. This was considered overly elaborate speech even in the nineteenth century; and many of these words, not to mention their pronunciation, would have been unfamiliar to speakers more than a hundred years ago.

Naturally, you will want to throw some of these words into your next casual conversation. As to their meaning, it you have any questions the dictionary awaits. If you have any questions about any pronunciations, I have provided a phonetic version following the orthographic version. The pronunciations are American, not British, although in the case of proper names of British persons or places, the pronunciations are British – perhaps with a bit of an American accent.

One enervating morning, just after the rise of the sun, a youth, bearing the cognomen of Galileo, glided in his gondola over the legendary waters of the lethean Thames. He was accompanied by his allies and coadjutors, the dolorous Pepys and the erudite Cholmondeley, the most combative aristocrat extant, and an epicurean who, for learned vagaries and revolting discrepancies of character, would take precedence of the most erudite of Areopagitic literati.

These sacrilegious dramatis personae were discussing in detail a suggestive address, delivered from the proscenium box of the Calisthenic Lyceum by a notable financier, on obligatory hydropathy as accessory to the irrevocable and irreparable doctrine of evolution, which has been vehemently panegyrized by a splenetic professor of acoustics, and simultaneously denounced by a complaisant opponent as an undemonstrated romance of the last decade, amenable to no reasoning, however allopathic, outside of its own lamentable environs.

These peremptory tripartite brethren arrived at Greenwich, to aggrandize themselves by indulging in exemplary relaxation, indicatory of implacable detestation of integral tergiversation and esoteric intrigue. They fraternized with a phrenological harlequin who was a connoisseur in mezzotint and falconry. This piquant person was heaping contumely and scathing raillery on an amateur in jugular recitative, who held that the Pharaohs of Asia were conversant with his theory that morphine and quinine were exorcists of bronchitis.

Meanwhile, the leisurely Augustine of Cockburn drank from a tortoiseshell wassail cup to the health of an apotheosized recusant, who was his supererogatory patron, and an assistant recognizance in the immobile nomenclature of interstitial molecular phonics. The contents of the vase proving soporific, a stolid plebeian took from its cerements an heraldic violoncello, and assisted by a plethoric diocesan from Pall Mall, who performed on a sonorous piano-forte, proceeded to wake the clangorous echoes of the Empyrean. They bade the prolix Caucasian gentleman not to misconstrue their inexorable demands, whilst they dined on acclimated anchovies and apricot truffles, and had for dessert a wiseacre's pharmacopocia.

Thus the truculent Pythagoreans had a novel repast fit for the gods. On the subsidence of the feast they alternated between soft languor and isolated scenes of squalor, which followed a mechanic's reconnaissance of the imagery of Uranus, the legend of whose incognito related to a poniard wound in the abdomen, received while cutting a swath in the interests of telegraphy and posthumous photography. Meanwhile, an unctuous orthoepist applied an homeopathic restorative to the retina of an objurgatory spaniel (named Daniel) and tried to perfect the construction of a behemoth, which had gotten mired in a pygmean slough while listening to the elegiac soughing of the prehistoric wind.

From *Voice Culture and Elocution*
by William T. Ross (New York: 1890)

What follows is a fairly broad phonetic transcription of the passage above. For general pronunciation of individual words, broad transcription is usually good enough. Although the pronunciations are deliberately American when there is a choice between an American and a British pronunciation, there may still be variants from the way you might say a word. In reading it, pay special attention to the stress diacritics, which – lest we forget – occur before the syllable modified. There are also a few allowances in the phonetic notation for fluency, so tiny informalities may intrude. In performance, see how informal you can make it without (a) losing full expression of the character who might talk like this and (b) losing intelligibility.

As a transcription exercise, you might want to try doing a narrow (detailed) transcription, based on what you hear when another speaker performs one or two sentences of the text.

'wʌn 'ɛnɚˌveɪtɪŋ 'mɔˑnɪŋ | ˌdʒʌst 'æftɚ ðə 'ɹaɪz əv ðə 'sʌn | ə 'juːθ | 'bɛðɹɪŋ ðə ˌkag'noʊmn̩ əv ˌgæləˈleːoʊ | 'glaɪdɪd 'oʊvɚ ðə 'lɛdʒɪnˌdɛɹi 'wɔtɚz əv ðə liθiʲɪn tɛmz ‖ hi wəz əkʌmpənid baɪ his 'æˌlaɪz ænd ˌkoʊˈædʒəˌtɚz | ðə 'doʊlɚəs 'pips ænd ði 'ɛɹʲəˈdaɪt 'tʃʌmli | ðə moʊst kəmˈbætɪv əˈɹɪstəˌkɹæt 'ɛkstənt | ˌænd ən ˌɛpɪkjʊˈɹiʲən 'hu | ˌfɔɚ 'lɚnɪd 'veɪgəˌɹiz ænd riˈvoʊltɪŋ dɪsˈkɹɛpənˌsiz əv 'kæɹɪktɚ | ˌwʊd 'teɪk 'pɹɛsɪdəns əv ðə 'moʊst 'ɛɹʲəˌdaɪt əv 'æɹiˌʲapəˈdʒɪtɪk ˌlɪtəˈɹati ‖

ˌðiz 'sækɹəˈlɪdʒəs dɹəˈmætɪs ˌpɚˈsoʊˌnaɪ wɚ dɪsˈkʌsɪŋ ɪn 'ðiˌteɪl ə sugˈdʒɛstɪv əˈdɹɛs | diˈlɪvɚd fɹəm ðə pɹəˈsiniʲəm 'baks əv ðə ˌkælɪsˈθɛnɪk ˌlaɪˈsi.əm baɪ ə 'noʊtəbl̩ ˌfɪnənˈsiɚ | ɑn əˈblɪgəˌtɔɹi ˌhaɪˈdɹapəθi æz ən əkˈsɛsəɹi tu ðə ɪˈɹɛvəkebl̩ ænd ɪˈɹɛpəɹəbl̩ 'dakˌtrɪn əv ˌɛvəˈluʃn̩ | ˌʍɪtʃ hæz bɪn 'viʲəmn̩tli 'pænɪdʒəˌɹaɪzd ˌbaɪ ə spləˈnɛtɪk pɹəˈfɛsɚ əv əˈkusˌtɪks | ænd ˌsaɪməlˈteɪniʲəsli diˈnaʊnst ˌbaɪ ə kəmˈpleɪzn̩t əˈpoʊnənt | ˌæz ən ˌʌnˈdɛmənˌstreɪtɪd ˌɹoʊˈmæns əv ðə 'læst 'dɛˌkeɪd | əˈmenəbl̩ tu ˌnoʊ 'rizn̩ɪŋ | ˌhaʊˈɛvɚ ˌæləpæθɪk | ˌaʊtˈsaɪd əv its ˌoʊn 'læmn̩təbl̩ ɪnˈvaɪɹənz ‖

ðiz pɝˈrɛmptəri ˌtraɪˈpaɚˌtaɪt ˈbrɛðrɪn əˈraɪvd æt ˈgrɛnɪtʃ | tu
əˈgræn,daɪz ðm̩ˈsɛlvz baɪ ɪnˈdʌldʒɪŋ ɪn ɪgˈzɛmpləri ˌrilækˈseɪʃn̩ |
ɪnˈdɪkə,tɔri əv ɪmˈplækəbl̩ ˌditesˈteɪsn̩ əv ˈɪntəgrəl ˌtɝˈdʒəvɝˈseɪʃn̩
ænd ˌɛsəˈtɛrɪk ˈɪn,trɪg ‖ ðeɪ ˈfrætɚˌnaɪzd wɪð ə ˌfrenəˈladʒɪkəl
ˈhaɚˌləkmɪn hu wəz ə ˌkaniˈsuɚ ɪn ˈmɛtsoʊˌtɪnt ənd ˈfælkənri ‖ ðɪs
ˈpikənt ˈpɝsn̩ wəz ˈhipɪŋ ˈkan,tʲuməli ænd ˈskeɪðɪŋ ˈreɪləri ɑn ən
ˈæmə,tuɚ ɪn ˈdʒʌgjəlɚ ˌrɛsitəˈtiv | hu ˈhɛld ðæt ðə ˈfɛɚˌroʊz əv ˈeɪʒə
wɚ kənˈvɝsn̩t wɪð hɪz ˈθɪəri ðæt ˈmɔɚˌfin ænd ˈkwaɪˌnaɪn wɚ
ˈɛksɔɚˌsɪsts əv ˌbraŋˈkaɪtɪs ‖

ˈmin,maɪl | ðə ˈliʒɝˌli ˈɔgə,stin əv ˈkoʊbɝn ˈdræŋk frəm ə ˈtɔɚtəs ʃel
ˈwa,seɪl ˈkʌp tu ðə ˈhɛlθ əv ən əˈpaθiʲə,saɪzd rɪˈkjuznt̩ | hu wəz hɪz
ˌsupɝəˈragə,tɔri ˈpeɪtrən ænd ən əˈsɪsttənt rɪˈkagnəzəns ɪn ði
rɪˈmoʊbl̩ ˈnoʊmn̩,kleɪtʃɝ əv ˌɪntɝˈstɪʃl̩ məˈlɛkjələɚ ˈfanɪks ‖ ðə
ˈkan,tɛnts əv ðə ˈveɪs ˈpruvɪŋ ˌsapəˈrɪfɪk | ə ˈstalɪd plɨˈbi.ən ˈtʊk frəm
ɪts ˈsɛrəmn̩ts æn ˌhɛˈraldɪk ˌvaɪ.ələnˈtʃeloʊ | ænd əˈsɪstəd baɪ ə
ˈplɛθərɪk ˌdaɪ.asɪzn̩ frəm ˈpæl ˈmæl | hu pɝˈfɔɚmd ɑn ə ˈsanərəs
piʲˌænoʊˈfɔɚˌtɨ | proʊˈsidɪd tu ʷəˈweɪk ðə ˈklæŋərəs ˈɛˌkoʊz əv ði
ɪmˈpɪriʲəm ‖ ðeɪ ˈbæd ðə ˈproʊˈlɪks ˌkɔˈkeɪʒn̩ ˈdʒɛntl̩mn̩ ˌnat tu
ˌmɪskənˈstru ðɛɚ ɪnˈɛksərəbl̩ ˈdrˈmændz | ˌmaɪlst ˌðeɪ ˈdaɪnd ɑn
ˈæklɪˌmeɪtɪd ˈæn,tʃoʊviz ænd ˈæprɪ,kat ˈtrʌflz | ænd ˌhæd fɔɚ dɪˈzɝt ə
ˈwaɪz,eɪkɝz ˌfaɚˌməkəˈpi.ə ‖

ˈðʌs ðə ˈtrʌkjələnt ˌpaɪˈθægəˈri.ənz ˌhæd ə ˈnavl̩ rɨˈpæst ˈfɪt fɔɚ ðə
ˈgadz ‖ ɑn ðə səbˈsaɪdn̩s əv ðə ˈfist ˌðeɪ ˈɔltɝˈneɪtɪd bɪˈtwin ˈsɔft
ˈlæŋgɚ ænd ˈaɪsəˌleɪtɪd ˈsɪnz əv ˈskwalɚ | ʍɪtʃ ˈfa,loʊd ə məˈkænɪks
rɨˈkanɪzns əv ðə ˈɪmɪdʒrɨ əv ˈjuɚrənəs | ðə ˈlɛdʒənd əv huz
ˌɪnkagˈnitoʊ rɨˈleɪtɪd tu ə ˈpanjɝd ˈwund ɪn ði̩ ˈæbdəmn̩ | rɨˈsivd ˌmaɪl
ˈkʌtɪŋ ə ˈswaθ ɪn ði̩ ˈɪntrɪsts əv təˈlɛgrə,fɨ ænd ˈpastjuməs fəˈtagrə,fɨ ‖
ˈmin,maɪl | æn ˌʌŋktʃuwəs ˌɔɚˈθoʊ.əpɪst əˈplaɪd æn (today / ə /
ˌhoʊmi.əˈpæθɪk rɨˈstɔrə,tɪv tu ðə ˈrɛtnə əv æn əbˈdʒɝˌgə,tɔri
ˈspænjəl ˌneɪmd ˈdænjəl ænd ˈtraɪd tu pɝˈfɛkt ðə kənˈstrʌkʃn̩ əv ə
bɨˈhiməɚ | ʍɪtʃ hæd ˈgatn̩ ˈmaɪɚd ɪn ə ˈpɪgmi.ən ˈslu ˌmaɪl ˈlɪsn̩ɪŋ tu ði
ˌɛləˈdʒaɪʲɪk ˈsaʊ.ɪŋ əv ðə ˈprihɪˌstɔrɪk ˈwɪnd ‖

Arthur the Rat

The test passage

This short cautionary tale was written by Professor W. Cabell Greet of Columbia University in the 1930s. Its purpose was to create a text that included all the sound combinations of American English. It is a really good text – though by no means the only one – to explore accent variation, so you may want to keep this text at your service when you record native speakers for that new accent that you need to learn.

Once there was a young rat named Arthur, who could never make up his mind. Whenever his friends asked him if he would like to go out with them, he would only answer "I don't know." He wouldn't say "Yes" or "No" either. He would always shirk making a choice.

His aunt Helen said to him, "Now look here. No one is going to care for you if you carry on like this. You have no more mind than a blade of grass."

One day the rats heard a great noise in the loft. The pine rafters were all rotten so that the barn was rather unsafe. At last the joists gave way and fell to the ground. The walls shook and all the rats' hair stood on end with fear and horror.

"This won't do," said the Captain. "I'll send out scouts to search for a new home."

Within five hours the ten scouts came back and said, "We found a stone house where there is room and board for us all. There is a kindly horse named Nelly, a cow, a calf, and a garden with an elm tree." The rats crawled out of their little houses and stood on the floor in a long line. Just then the old one saw Arthur.

"Stop," he ordered coarsely. "You are coming, of course."

"I'm not certain," said Arthur, undaunted. "The roof may not come down yet."

"Well," said the angry old rat, "we can't wait for you to join us. Right about face! March!"

Arthur stood and watched them hurry away. "I think I'll go tomorrow," he said calmly to himself. "But then again, I don't know. It's so nice and snug here."

That night there was a big crash. In the morning some men, with some boys and girls, rode up and looked at the barn. One of them moved a board and he saw a young rat, quite dead, half in and half out of his hole. Thus the shirker got his due.

Mondegreens

An exploration of intelligibility

"Mondegreens" are misunderstood song lyrics or lines of poetry. The origin of the word "mondegreen" comes from a newspaper columnist named Sylvia Wright, who introduced the term in the nineteen-fifties. In the words of fellow journalist Jon Carroll:

As a child she had heard the Scottish ballad "The Bonny Earl of Murray" and had believed that one stanza went like this:

> Ye Highlands and Ye Lowlands
> Oh where hae you been?
> They hae slayn the Earl of Murray,
> And Lady Mondegreen.

Poor Lady Mondegreen, thought Sylvia Wright. A tragic heroine dying with her liege; how poetic. When it turned out, some years later, that what they had actually done was slay the Earl of Murray and lay him on the green, Wright was so distraught by the sudden disappearance of her heroine that she memorialized her with a neologism."

The most famous mondegreen is "Gladly, the cross-eyed bear" for "Gladly the cross I'd bear." Vying for second place are the Jimi Hendrix lyric, "Excuse me while I kiss the sky" heard as "Excuse me, while I kiss this guy", and the Creedence Clearwater song "There's a bad moon on the rise" heard as "There's a bathroom on the right." Our pledge of allegiance (preceding the 1950s addition of "under God") can be heard as:

"I pledge a lesion to the flag, of the United State of America, and to the republic for Richard Stans, one naked individual, with liver tea and just this for all."

(Probably few of us today remember Richard Stans. *Sic transit Gloria mundi*, or, as Sylvia Wright might have understood it, "Sick friends are gory on Monday.")

Some other mondegreen pairs

Midnight at the Oasis	*Midnight after you're wasted*
Feliz Navidad	*Police naughty dog*
My Baby Likes the Western Movies	*My Baby's Like a Wet Sock Moving*
The girl with kaleidoscope eyes	*The girl with colitis goes by*
Is your figure less than Greek?	*Is your finger less than clean?*
The bright blessed day, the dark sacred night	
	The bride blessed the day, the dog said goodnight
Doctor, lawyer, beggar-man, thief	*Dr. Laura, you pickled man-thief*
Taking care of business	*Tape it to a biscuit*
Dirty deeds and they're done dirt cheap	
	Dirty deeds and they're done to sheep
Don't it make my brown eyes blue	*Donuts make my brown ice blue*
Got a lot of love between us	*Got a lot of lucky peanuts*
Hold me closer, tiny dancer	*Hold me closer, Tony Danza*
Count the headlights on the highway	*Count the head lice on the highway*
I'm gonna break my rusty cage and run	
	I'm gonna braid a rustic Cajun rug
That deaf, dumb, and blind kid	*That deft thumb of lightning*
In spite of my rage, I am still just a rat in a cage	
	The spider marines, Siam's steel-chested rabbit arcade
She pays my ticket when I speed	*She paints my chicken when I sleep*
My mind is racin', but my body's in the lead	
	My mind is bacon, but my body's Sizzlean
All we are saying is "Give peace a chance"	
	Oh, we are sailing, yes, give Jesus pants.
It's just a spring clean for the May queen	
	It's just the sprinkles for the bakery
So don't knock down my door	*Sew donuts to the door*
Two tickets to paradise	*Two chickens to paralyze*
Almost paradise	*All those parrot eyes*
Viva Las Vegas	*People love bagels*
The emperor's new clothes	*The antlers are too close*
I wanna be sedated	*I want a piece of date bread*
Someone saved my life tonight	*Someone shaved my wife tonight*

With a partner as listener, choose a mondegreen pair from this list, or a pair that you already know. Speak each version alternately with enough linguistic detail so that there is no ambiguity or misunderstanding about any of the words. But is the rendition fluent? Can you keep the ambiguity at bay while saying the mondegreens easily and fluently? Then explore the modifications in articulator action that start to blur the distinction between the two. Find the actions that allow complete ambiguity. Explore all these possibilities in different acoustic environments, e.g. outdoors/indoors, distant/close, with/without background noise, et cetera.

Mondegreens from the books 'Scuse Me While I Kiss This Guy, He's Got the Whole World in His Pants and When a Man Loves a Walnut, all compiled by Gavin Edwards, Fireside Books (Simon & Schuster, 1995, 1996, 1997).

So ...

So keep exploring. Every possibility for speech use is open to you when you passionately and intelligently explore your own natural actor's curiosity about how people speak. Your curiosity – freed from the restrictive mandates of someone else's idea of "good speech" – gives you complex and specific skills to master and that mastery will be the work of a lifetime. Becoming "perfect" at any speech pattern is a false goal because language when it is used by real people in real life is always a flexible and malleable thing, shaped by a multitude of factors. The good news is that by continuing the journey of exploration I have outlined in this book you can become very, very good at finding within yourself the unique voice of the character you are playing. Or perhaps, if you are not an actor, your own unique voice. You'll keep developing a deeper and more productive relationship to the shaping of speech. And that's more than good enough.

Index

Note: page numbers in *italics* refer to illustrations.